Cultural and Language Diversity and the Deaf Experience

The perspective that deaf people should be primarily regarded as a cultural and language minority group rather than as individuals with an audiological disability is gathering support among educators, linguists, and researchers involved in the education of deaf people. Minority empowerment movements across America – and American society's increased awareness of its own diversity – have brought a supportive context to the efforts of deaf people to have American Sign Language recognized in planning educational policies and curricula. This book considers in depth the notion that deaf people are members of a bilingual-bicultural minority group, whose experiences often overlap with the experiences of hearing minority group members but at other times are unique.

The contributors to this book include prominent deaf and hearing researchers, educators, and deaf community members. Part I presents an overview of mainstream research on bilingualism and biculturalism. Part II provides conceptual analyses and research that examine the impact of cultural and language diversity on the educational and psychosocial experiences of deaf people. The third and final part offers rich experiential evidence from deaf community members that brings home the emotional impact of living in the Deaf and Hearing worlds.

Cultural and Language Diversity and the Deaf Experience

Editor

ILA PARASNIS

*National Technical Institute for the Deaf,
Rochester Institute of Technology*

CAMBRIDGE
UNIVERSITY PRESS

CAMBRIDGE UNIVERSITY PRESS
Cambridge, New York, Melbourne, Madrid, Cape Town, Singapore, São Paulo, Delhi

Cambridge University Press
32 Avenue of the Americas, New York, NY 10013-2473, USA

www.cambridge.org
Information on this title: www.cambridge.org/9780521645652

First published 1996
First paperback edition 1998
9th printing 2009

Printed in the United States of America

A catalog record for this publication is available from the British Library.

ISBN 978-0-521-45477-3 hardback
ISBN 978-0-521-64565-2 paperback

To my grandparents S. B. and Shalini Ranade,
who taught me to appreciate life's complexity

and to my parents, M. R. and Kunda Parasnis,
who taught me to see its underlying simplicity

Contents

Preface

The perspective that deaf people should be primarily regarded as a cultural and language minority group rather than as individuals with an audiological disability is gathering support among educators, linguists, and researchers involved in the education of deaf people. Minority empowerment movements across America – and American society's increased awareness of its own diversity – have brought a supportive context to the efforts of deaf people to have American Sign Language (ASL), the language of their community, recognized in planning educational policies and curricula. This book considers in depth the notion that deaf people are members of a bilingual-bicultural minority group in America, whose experiences often overlap with the experiences of hearing minority group members but at other times are unique. It is hoped that this information will be useful in the future development of sociocultural models for understanding the life experiences of deaf people and in designing policies and curricula for the education of deaf students that take into account the cultural and language diversity of their experience. It is also hoped that this analysis will lead hearing society to a better understanding of the experiences of deaf people.

This book contains chapters written by deaf and hearing educators and researchers in the fields of the education of deaf people, Deaf culture, ASL linguistics, interpreter education, bilingualism, bilingual education, cognition, and sociology. The authors offer several different ways of understanding the cultural and language diversity of deaf people through their conceptual analyses, research, and experiential evidence.

The book is organized into three parts. Part I consists of an introductory chapter detailing the book's rationale and framework, and three chapters which give an overview of contemporary theory and research in the fields of bilingualism and biculturalism. The primary purpose of this part is to provide the reader with a general framework within which issues specific to deaf people can be examined.

Part II consists of eight chapters that discuss the impact of bilingual-bicultural minority status on the specific experiences of deaf people. This part provides conceptual analyses as well as research reports on a variety of issues specific to the educational and life experiences of deaf people.

Part III consists of six chapters and presents experiential evidence from ASL-English bilingual individuals living in Deaf and Hearing worlds. This part provides personal opinions on and analyses of issues specific to the life experiences of many deaf community members. It is included to show-case the diversity of their experiences and to document expressions of feelings, perceptions, and beliefs that would not otherwise find representation within a strictly traditional academic framework. The authors in this section were encouraged to be candid about their opinions and feelings in their reflections. The primary purpose of this part is to offer rich information on personal perspectives and experiences that may lead to fresh insights into the bilingualism and biculturalism of deaf people.

Recently, the issue of the validity of the perspectives of hearing people in understanding the experiences of deaf people has generated much discussion among professionals in the education of deaf people and members of the deaf community. In psychological terms, can someone who does not have the same life experiences understand what another person feels or thinks? In sociocultural terms, can someone who is not raised in a particular culture fully understand its values and way of life? Or, in political terms, can a member of the dominant social group understand what a member of the minority group experiences? These questions are not specific to understanding deaf people. They have been raised often among those who study gender, race, or cultural differences.

Although life experiences definitely influence the choice of issues one studies or the way in which they are studied, ultimately, in any academic inquiry, the thought has to be evaluated on the basis of its intrinsic merit, not on the sociocultural status of the thinker. Taking this as my premise, I have invited both deaf and hearing educators and researchers to contribute to this book only on the basis of the perceived value of their work and their perspectives.

Throughout this book, when deaf people are referred to as a bilingual-bicultural minority group, it is assumed that the two relevant cultures are

Deaf and Hearing cultures and that the two relevant languages are ASL and English. The terms "Deaf culture" and "Hearing culture" are used to refer to the customs and values of the deaf community and the hearing majority in the United States, respectively, even though it is recognized that both are heterogeneous in their composition by ethnic subgroups and both consist of minority groups who use languages other than ASL and English. Recently, there has been much discussion about what the term "Deaf culture" means and the distinction between "culture" and "community" in referring to the group experience of deaf people. However, for the purpose of examining the analogy between deaf people and other minority groups in America, the terms "Deaf culture" and "deaf community" have often been used in this book as if they are interchangeable. Use of the forms "Deaf" and "deaf" varies in the literature as well as in this book, and individual chapter authors have used the uppercase D or lowercase d as they see fit in discussing the experiences of deaf people. Some chapter authors have provided a footnote on their usage while others have not. A convention followed by many chapter authors including myself is to use the form "Deaf" to refer to those deaf people who share a language (ASL in this case) and cultural values that are distinct from the hearing society and to use the form "deaf" to refer to the audiological condition of deafness. Another convention followed by many chapter authors including myself is to use the form "deaf" in referring to the community (see Padden, 1980). By "deaf community," we mean those deaf and hearing people who may share that group identity but not necessarily the language. It should be noted that the diverse experiences of deaf people who do not know ASL, deaf people who are members of an ethnic minority group in America and use that group's language, deaf people who are new immigrants to the United States, and those deaf people who only use speech and speechreading are not being considered in this book. How these groups are viewed by the American deaf community and how they themselves perceive their self-identity and group identity issues are matters worthy of another book.

Acknowledgments

This book would not have been possible without the help of many people and I extend my gratitude and appreciation to all who have helped me along the way to make it a reality. In particular, I thank the contributors for their insightful and inspiring chapters. I also thank the reviewers: John A. Albertini, Gerald P. Berent, Paula M. Brown, Carol De Filippo, Susan D.

Fischer, Ronald R. Kelly, William J. Newell, Vincent J. Samar, M. Virginia Swisher, and Jyotsna Vaid, who read earlier drafts of the chapter manuscripts and provided thorough and thoughtful feedback on content and style. Special thanks go to Dominique Lepoutre with whom I organized colloquia on the topic of cultural and language diversity in education at the National Technical Institute for the Deaf (NTID), which inspired me to plan this book. I appreciate the supportive academic environment NTID has provided to me. I thank Julia Hough, editor, psychology and cognitive science, Cambridge University Press, for her support of this undertaking. Many thanks to Christopher McAuliffe and Liz Powers for their invaluable help in preparing the final copy of the manuscript and proofreading it with me.

Finally, my deep appreciation and thanks go to my husband, Vincent J. Samar, for his loving support and for his intellectual and emotional companionship; to my daughters, Anjali and Shalini Parasnis-Samar, whose love is a source of great joy and pride in my life; and to my parents, Manohar and Kunda Parasnis, for their love and confidence in me. For me, an Indian-American trilingual, editing this book has been a personally meaningful and enlightening experience which has revealed to me how enriched my family life has been because of its cultural and language diversity.

Ila Parasnis

Reference

Padden, C. (1980). The deaf community and the culture of Deaf people. In C. Baker & R. Battison (Eds.), *Sign language and the deaf community: Essays in honor of William C. Stokoe* (pp. 89–103). Silver Spring, MD: National Association of the Deaf.

PART I

Bilingualism-Biculturalism and the Deaf Experience: An Overview

On Interpreting the Deaf Experience within the Context of Cultural and Language Diversity

ILA PARASNIS

The functional roles that Deaf culture and American Sign Language (ASL) can play in the psychosocial development of deaf children and their relevance to the education of deaf people are much-discussed issues among those who are involved professionally or socially with deaf people in the United States.[1] There is a tremendous interest in the notion of empowering the deaf community through recognition and respect for its language (ASL) and culture, strengthening the self-identity of deaf children through articulation of their membership in the deaf community, and generally considering deaf children as members of a bilingual-bicultural minority group.

A systematic analysis of how these concepts can be applied to the education of deaf people is far from complete. There is a need for comprehensive discussion of the issues engendered by the terms "deaf com-

Ila Parasnis (Ph.D., Psychology, University of Rochester), Associate Professor, National Technical Institute for the Deaf, conducts and publishes research on visual cognition and bilingualism in deaf and hearing people. She has been involved in the field of deaf education for the past 15 years. Her address is: Department of Applied Language and Cognition Research, National Technical Institute for the Deaf, Rochester Institute of Technology, 52 Lomb Memorial Drive, Rochester, NY 14623.

[1] In this chapter the capitalized form "Deaf" is used to refer to those deaf people who share a language (ASL in this case) and cultural values that are distinct from the hearing society, and the lowercase form "deaf" is used to refer to the audiological condition of deafness. The form "deaf" is also used to refer to the community (see Padden, 1980). Furthermore, like the term "deaf community," the term "deaf people" is used with a lowercase d in referring to deaf people to include Deaf members as well as those members of the deaf community who may not use ASL fluently but may still have culturally and linguistically diverse experiences.

munity" and "Deaf identity" that avoids stereotypes and overgeneralizations of these terms. In the history of the education of deaf people, one
finds educational philosophies and practices dominated by a stereotypical
concept of the deaf child, or of that child's communication needs. It is time
now to acknowledge the heterogeneity of the deaf community and the
diversity of the educational and social experiences that influence the
development of identity in deaf people.

The primary goal of this book is to provide scholarly perspectives and
insights on the Deaf identity and experience, i.e., the individual or group
identity issues and experiences of deaf people who are members of the
deaf community, within the context of cultural and language diversity. A
discussion that considers the deaf community as a bilingual-bicultural
community and examines the influences of cultural and language
differences and of minority status on the experiences of deaf people can
help parents, educators, and professionals involved with deaf people to
develop sensitivity to these issues. Such information can also help deaf
people understand their own experience and develop their own identities.

' I will present in this chapter my perspective on interpreting the experiences of deaf people within the framework of cultural and language diversity. I will provide a historical and sociocultural context in which to examine the idea that deaf people are a bilingual-bicultural group. I will also
discuss issues related to the development of self-identity and group identity in deaf people and suggest comparisons of deaf people with other
minority groups in American society. Finally, I will present the specific
goals of this book and a brief description of each chapter.

Deaf People as Bilingual-Bicultural People

As Grosjean (1982) has pointed out, there does not exist a universally
accepted definition of bilingualism; he defines bilingualism as "the regular
use of two or more languages" (p. 1). Thus, bilingualism can be viewed as
a continuum that includes people who may vary considerably in their
linguistic knowledge, fluency, and age at which they acquired each
language.

Bilingualism in deaf people is aptly described by using Grosjean's
definition. Deaf people who use ASL and English may vary considerably
in their linguistic knowledge of ASL or English, their fluency in each of
those languages, and the age at which they acquired those languages.
Furthermore, in their daily life, regardless of their fluency in ASL or English, they tend to use English when communicating with hearing people

and ASL when communicating with members of the deaf community. I have followed Grosjean's definition in this chapter in referring to deaf people as bilingual people.

Grosjean (1982) defines biculturalism as "coexistence and/or combination of two distinct cultures" (p. 157) and states that it has been studied by very few researchers. The definition of culture is a complex issue and the discussion regarding the definition of Deaf culture is far from complete. In this chapter, I have used the term "culture" to refer to a way of life and have assumed that Deaf culture is transmitted through social interactions and the language of the deaf community.

As noted in the Preface, when deaf people are referred to as bilingual-bicultural people I have assumed that the two relevant cultures are the Deaf culture and the Hearing culture and that the two relevant languages are ASL and English. The terms "Deaf culture" and "Hearing culture" are used to refer to the customs and values of the deaf community and the hearing majority in the United States, respectively. I realize that both are heterogeneous in their composition by ethnic subgroups and both contain minority groups who use languages other than ASL and English. However, for the purpose of examining the global analogy between deaf people and other minority groups in America, I have used the terms "Deaf culture" and "deaf community" without further articulation of subcultural differences.

These terminological heuristics ignore the culturally and linguistically diverse experiences of deaf people who do not know ASL. Deaf people who are members of an ethnic minority group in the United States and use that group's language, deaf people who are new immigrants, and those deaf people who only use speech and speechreading are not being considered when the terms are used in this way. How these groups are viewed by the American deaf community and how they themselves perceive their self-identity and group identity are matters worthy of analysis and of another book, as I have noted in the Preface.

Historical Context

The realization that deaf people have their own language and community is not new. Although deafness has been viewed as a disability, educators of deaf people since the early part of the last century have acknowledged that deaf people, unlike blind people, often belong to a socially distinct, cohesive group with its own language and social norms. In fact, until 1880, the use of sign language in school was encouraged in the United States, and it is estimated that around that time about 50% of the teachers of deaf people in the United States were themselves deaf (see Lane, 1984, p. 371; Sacks, 1990, p. 27). However, in 1880, at the International Congress of Educators of the Deaf in Milan, Italy, it was decided to proscribe the use of sign language in schools. The pendulum thus swung to the use of speech as the primary means of communication in the classroom, and the number of deaf teachers steadily decreased to about 12% by the 1960s (see Lane, 1984, p. 371; Sacks, 1990, p. 27). Since then the use of sign and speech in the education of deaf people has been a topic of controversy and debate and has motivated numerous studies on the success of different communication methods including speech, cued speech, simultaneous communication, total communication, invented sign systems, etc. In this flurry of activity, ASL and Deaf culture were given little attention by comparison, although they continued to exist and grow. In the 1960s and 1970s, linguists discovered that ASL had its own grammar and met the universal criteria for a human language (e.g., Stokoe, Casterline, & Croneberg, 1965; Klima & Bellugi, 1979), and slowly the pendulum started to swing back. The deaf community and its language once again started to receive attention from educators and researchers, and momentum has built considerably since then. Several books have been published on the sociocultural context in which deaf people live (e.g., Baker & Battison, 1980; Cohen, 1994; Higgins, 1980; Lane, 1992; Padden & Humphries, 1988; Wilcox, 1989), on the history of the deaf community (Gannon, 1981; Van Cleve, 1987), and on ASL and communication (e.g., Garretson, 1990; Lucas & Valli, 1992; Siple, 1978; Strong, 1988). With the success of the " Deaf President Now" movement in 1988, which resulted in I. King Jordan's becoming the first deaf president of Gallaudet University in Washington, D.C., the rights of deaf people as a cultural and linguistic community in this society have attracted significant media attention. Recent articles in *Atlantic Monthly Review* (Dolnick, 1993) and *The New York Times* (Solomon, 1994), for example, have brought the deaf community to the attention of the general public. The passage of the Americans with Disabilities Act (ADA) by the U.S. Congress in 1990 has also brought public attention to issues surrounding the accommodation of deaf people in the work place.

There has been a small revolutionary shift in the field of education of deaf people away from a medical model of deaf people as disabled to a sociocultural model of deaf people as a minority group with its own language and culture (e.g., Cummins & Danesi, 1990; Johnson, Liddell, & Erting, 1989; Strong, 1988; Woodward, 1989). In addition, Lane (1992) has offered an extensive political analysis of deaf people as an oppressed minority. A recent survey of residential schools for the deaf (Walter, 1992) shows that the percentage of teachers in the residential school system who are deaf is now on the rise (18% compared to 12% reported in the 1960s).

General Sociopolitical Context

It is interesting to examine how this course of events fits in with sociopolitical movements in the larger society. The historical decision to proscribe sign language in school came at a time when there was "a trend to Victorian oppressiveness and conformism, intolerance of minorities, and minority usages, of every kind – religious, linguistic, ethnic" (Sacks, 1990, p. 24). Note further that research on sign language gathered momentum in the 1960s when the counterculture movement was arguing for the cultural relativity of values and social norms. In the 1980s, the notions of plurality and multiculturalism and their place in education started to receive greater attention because of the changing demographics of American students who came from increasingly diverse backgrounds. The old "melting pot" metaphor was now being challenged by the "salad bowl" metaphor of American society, and the rights of minority groups and women were much-debated causes in the larger society. In education, sociocultural and linguistic issues related to the development of the self-identity and cognitive abilities of minority group members received extensive attention (see Baron, 1990; Belenky, Clinchy, Goldberger, & Tarule, 1986; Gilligan, 1982; Grosjean, 1982; Hakuta, 1986; Hamers & Blanc, 1983; Skutnabb-Kangas & Cummins, 1988; Steele, 1990). There has certainly been a great interest in studying Deaf culture and the deaf community since the 1980s.

It is not my intention to argue that general sociopolitical movements have necessarily dictated the chronology of important milestones in the history of the education of deaf people. However, I do wish to draw attention to possible connections between the two and to point out that considering the general cultural framework within which social and educational decisions regarding deaf people are made might help to illuminate general trends in the education of deaf people.

One obvious benefit of such a consideration is that it enables us to anticipate major shifts in perspective within the field of the education of deaf people based on general sociopolitical trends. For example, if the current focus on the rights of minority groups were to shift back to the notion of "majority rules," or if the "English Only" movement were to gather support from the general society, then the issue of the role of ASL in the education of deaf people might become much more political in nature. If the ADA and the inclusion theme were not to be enforced effectively in the larger society, the educational and employment opportunities available to deaf people might become more restricted. Generally, if minority group concerns were not to be addressed and validated by the society and if the socioeconomic status of minority groups were to decline, then the deaf community might not benefit from a sociolinguistic minority group status. How the larger American society and the deaf community deal with the issue of the rights of the deaf community is thus intertwined with how the rights of other minority groups are viewed and dealt with. It is important for the deaf community to conceptualize its efforts and position its agenda within the larger sociopolitical context of American society.

Medical Model versus Sociocultural Model

Shifting the focus from deaf people as a disabled group to deaf people as a minority group with its own culture and language has led to the discussion of whether deafness should be viewed as a disability or a natural variation. The debate centers on whether medical science should seek a cure for deafness on the view that it is a disability, or whether hearing status should be perceived as an innate physical characteristic exhibiting variation, such as race or skin color, and therefore be left alone.

Such a debate seems misguided and tends to polarize the community involved in the education of deaf people according to an artificial "either-or" dichotomy. Issues of medical management and cure are orthogonal to issues of minority status and minority rights. For example, unlike other minority hearing children, deaf children may indeed need audiological services and may need other forms of support to overcome barriers to spoken communication used by the majority of the society. Availability of hearing aids, FM systems, the ADA, the use of ASL, etc., may all be crucial forms of support a deaf person may require to succeed in school or at work. However, this does not mean that deaf people do not have a legitimate right to be considered a minority group. Alternative means to overcome communication barriers are often used with other minority groups (e.g., non-native speakers of English) without their sociocultural group identity being questioned.

Furthermore, society needs to recognize that concepts of normality and disability are stereotypes which have limited value in describing individual variation. With the advent of technology it has become easier to accommodate individual differences. Generally, the focus of social and educational planning should be on creating an environment that facilitates acceptance of diversity and individual differences. This is the hallmark of a civilized culture. Accordingly, our focus on a deaf child should not be solely on his or her "disability" but needs to be on identifying the psychosocial and language-related needs of that child as a minority child which are not adequately accommodated by the present educational system.

The Use of Sociocultural Models in Research

Viewing the deaf child as a bilingual-bicultural minority child shifts the focus of research away from documenting deficiencies to documenting differences. Traditionally, the language behavior and social behavior of deaf people have been documented under the medical model, i.e., what deficiencies deaf people have because of their disability. Although the factual data from many studies may remain informative, methods of data collection and interpretations based on the assumption of disability from many studies are of questionable value (see Lane, 1989). There is a need to develop sociocultural models to articulate how deaf bilingual-bicultural people function linguistically, cognitively, and socially in the Hearing world. This effort will depend crucially on research in the fields of bilingualism and biculturalism.

Historically, language learning in bilinguals was measured against the yardstick of language learning in monolinguals. However, there is a growing recognition among experts in the fields of bilingualism and bilingual education that language choice and language usage in bilingual-bicultural people are complex phenomena governed by many factors that do not influence monolinguals. For example, a bilingual's choice of which language to use or when to switch to another language seems to be influenced by specific situational and psychological variables. Monolinguals are generally unaware of these variables since the choice itself is not available to them. Another example is the daily communication behavior of a bilingual-bicultural person. A bilingual-bicultural person often deals with two different sets of rules and expectations in moving between two cultures and abides by them selectively in using two languages. A monolingual-monocultural person may never experience these challenges.

It can be argued easily that deaf people who use ASL and English may have similar experiences as other, hearing bilingual-bicultural people. It seems reasonable to assume that their choice and use of languages with respect to ASL and English are governed by the same situational and psychological variables as those influencing other bilinguals and that their social behavior follows similar bicultural principles as they move between the Deaf and Hearing worlds. These experiences and behaviors have gone largely unnoticed in educational and work environments predominantly composed of monolingual-monocultural hearing people.

Studying deaf people within the framework of bilingual-bicultural research can yield rich information for designing educational programs for deaf people and for increasing our understanding of the Deaf experience. It is clear that much research is needed on understanding such important issues as language development and language learning in ASL and English, code switching between ASL and English, the influence of knowledge of ASL on cognitive development and on cognitive skills, the influence of Deaf role models on development of self-identity, and so on.

Hyphenated Identity

Considering the deaf child as a minority child raises the issue of "hyphenated" identity. People use a hyphenated term of identity, such as "African-American" or "Hispanic-American," to show that just one description does not fit their life experiences or their perception of who they are. The issue of a hyphenated identity is often debated these days, as America becomes more diverse and minority groups become more empowered. This issue may produce anxiety because historically the United States has promoted only English as the language of our nation and European immigrants as the de facto model for the national identity. What will happen to patriotism and our unity as a nation if we allow American society to fragment itself into ethnic subgroups? How can we communicate among ourselves if we officially allow languages other than English to be used in the United States? These questions raise many fundamental issues regarding what defines patriotism and national identity, and how to decide which language should be the "official language" of the nation. But in fact, a significant number of Americans have an ethnic identity in addition to an American identity and many know a language other than English. These people are going through an educational system which does not officially recognize the psychosocial experiences that form their identity.

Having a hyphenated identity is not necessarily equivalent to having a fragmented identity or divided sociopolitical loyalties. Just as a bilingual person is not two monolinguals rolled into one, a bicultural or multicultural person is not a committee of natives of different cultures housed in one person. Bicultural and multicultural people integrate the values, behaviors, and language of each culture into their own psychological makeup, as Grosjean (1982) has noted. Very little work has been done on how bicultural and multicultural people navigate through life while maintaining their affiliation to their different primary groups. The concept of marginality is often used in referring to people who belong to more than one primary group. This term, when used colloquially, also evokes the image of someone who might be psychologically burdened with negative feelings about being on the outskirts of both groups, fully belonging to neither. Although some bicultural people may, indeed, feel that way, many bicultural people also report being able to blend into both cultures and feel comfortable with their identity (see Grosjean, 1982, pp. 157–166, for discussion).

Deaf people also share a hyphenated identity as Deaf-Americans (see Padden & Humphries, 1988). Furthermore, those deaf people who belong to the various ethnic minority groups in America or are first generation immigrants may have even more hyphenated identities (for discussion see Delgado, 1984; Christensen & Delgado, 1993). Arguably, how deaf people develop and regard their identity is similar in many ways to how hearing American minority people develop and regard their own identities. However, the analogy of a deaf person as a minority group member is not perfect. There are environmental barriers that exist for a deaf person that do not generally exist for members of other ethnic minority groups. Most ethnic minority groups in the United States have a reference culture that they can trace back to another country where their group is in the majority, even though that culture often varies significantly from the one developed in their new country. Nevertheless, the everyday life experience of an American deaf person is similar in many ways to that of an American hearing minority person. Both may experience attitudinal barriers in their professional and social lives. Both experience conflicts in holding their group identity while developing a general American identity. And both may perceive being mainstreamed into American culture as a threat to their language and culture.

Self-Identity and Group Identity

Development of self-identity and group identity as a Deaf person is often a long process of discovery since in most cases there is no transmission of Deaf culture and ASL from parents to children. It is estimated that only

10% of deaf children are born to deaf parents (Schein & Delk, 1974) and it is well known that many deaf people acquire ASL and knowledge of their cultural norms and values from their peers when they attend residential schools for the deaf. Thus, generally there is a lateral transmission of culture (peer to peer) rather than vertical (parent to child), and deaf people tend to develop a strong peer network. The deaf community in this regard is similar to the gay community, as Solomon (1994) has pointed out.

One interesting comparison that can be made is between an adoptive child from a different race and culture and a deaf child born to hearing parents. Transracial families in which white parents, typically with a Judeo-Christian background, adopt nonwhite children from other cultures are becoming frequent in the United States. These parents often face issues similar to those facing hearing parents of deaf children. They have to accept that their children will be treated differently by the society and that their children may be automatically identified with other cultural-linguistic groups whether they are practicing members of those groups or not. How should American white parents raise their adopted Korean child, for example? Many experts suggest that the child should be given a dual identity and introduced to the Korean culture and language. But how? The practical dilemma facing these parents is quite similar to that facing hearing parents of deaf children. They most likely cannot become experts in a culture and a language that is foreign to them even though they may try hard and have the best intentions. For the child also it is a difficult matter. The immediate and extended family is generally not Korean and hence Korean role models are not readily available, nor is there any pressing social need to acquire the Korean culture. The child, as he or she becomes adolescent and starts to deal with issues of self-identity and group identity, may acquire and come to terms with a hyphenated identity. But the process is not smooth, as it would be in a family where parents and children share the same racial and cultural identity.

Although this analogy, in many ways, is instructive in considering a deaf child's experiences from a sociocultural perspective, it has an important drawback. A Korean child who is hearing can acquire the adoptive parents' language naturally. Typically, this choice is not available to a deaf child of hearing parents, who grows up in a restricted language environment because the parents' spoken language is not fully accessible.

Another major comparison that can be drawn is between the development of group identity of women and that of deaf people. It took many years for American society to realize and accept that women as a group have a minority status in this society, although in terms of their number they are not a minority. Women are dispersed throughout all strata of society. They belong to different racial, ethnic, cultural, and language groups and their socioeconomic status and family and educational backgrounds vary tremendously. However, women, regardless of their heterogeneous origins, share a common group identity tied to their gender. Since most deaf people are born to hearing parents (Schein & Delk, 1974), they are similarly dispersed throughout the societal strata. Like women, they share a common group identity. In many ways the women's movement can inform the efforts of the deaf community as it establishes its minority group status. Like women's studies programs, establishment of academic programs of Deaf studies on university campuses may benefit the effort and bring it visibility. The strategy of establishing consciousness-raising groups, as feminists did early in their movement, might also be effective for the deaf community in reaching out to deaf people across America. Like feminists, deaf people already have their own newsletters, magazines, presses, national organizations, and conferences which promote issues of concern to the deaf community and allow networking among community members.

An important parallel between women and deaf people is their common historical experience of social discrimination based partly on the presumption of lower intellectual and cognitive skills. Although the issue of general intelligence differences between men and women and between deaf and hearing people has now essentially been settled in favor of equality, there is currently a vigorous scientific interest in the issue of how gender or hearing status influences specific domains of cognitive and linguistic functions. It is far from settled whether fundamental sex or hearing status differences exist and whether they might be due to neural and genetic factors or due to selective socialization. However, regardless of the outcome of this line of psychological research, it seems clear that any such differences in cognitive profile cannot justify the general discriminatory practices toward women and deaf people that have evolved in traditional society.

Summary

The issues that face deaf people during development of their identity seem to overlap with those of hearing minority groups in the United States but in some cases are unique. An analysis that treats deaf people as a bilingual-bicultural minority group within a general framework of cultural and language diversity can freshly motivate and inform the efforts of deaf people to define their self-identity and group identity.

The Goals and Scope of the Book

The ultimate goal of this book is to facilitate an understanding among deaf and hearing people which supports a mutual respect for their human diversity. As the noted Indian philosopher S. Radhakrishnan (1956) has remarked:

> The unity of civilization is not to be sought in uniformity but in har-
> mony. . . . Today the circle of those who participate in the cultural synthesis
> has become wider and includes practically the whole world. The faith of the
> future is in cooperation and not identification, in accommodation to fellow-
> men and not imitation of them, in toleration and not absolutism. (p. 9)

This book is divided into three parts. A brief description of the goals of each part and of each chapter in the parts follows.

I. Bilingualism-Biculturalism and the Deaf Experience: An Overview

The goal of Part I is to present current information from the fields of bilingualism and bilingual education that provides a framework to understand the Deaf experience as a bilingual-bicultural minority experience.

This part contains four chapters including this one. François Grosjean presents in Chapter 2 a psychological overview of how a bilingual-bicultural person functions within two languages and two cultures. He also discusses his perspective of deaf people as bilingual-bicultural people and the implications of such a perspective for the education of deaf people. Chapter 3, by Kenji Hakuta and Elizabeth Feldman Mostafapour, presents an overview of the politics of bilingualism and bilingual education in America. In particular, the authors discuss the sociopolitical factors that have influenced research and policies in bilingual education programs and that have implications for linguistic minority groups such as the deaf community. Chapter 4, by Josiane F. Hamers, provides an overview of the cognitive and language development of bilingual children that includes a discussion of major theoretical models of bilingual development. The author also discusses the sociocultural variables that influence second-language learning of minority groups and considers the implications of this research for studying the bilingual development of a deaf child as an ethnolinguistic minority child.

II. Psychosocial, Cognitive, and Language Experiences of Deaf People

The goal of Part II is to present diverse perspectives and research on the psychosocial, cognitive, and language experiences of deaf people as a bilingual-bicultural minority group. The relationships of these experiences to the development of Deaf identity are also addressed.

This part begins with two consecutive chapters by Carol A. Padden. In Chapter 5 the author offers an analysis of the rhetoric of portraying the deaf community as a cultural and bicultural group and discusses how this rhetoric has influenced how the modern deaf community views itself and is viewed by others. The author also provides evidence on how the educational process can incorporate and nurture the bilingual-bicultural identity of deaf children. The focus of Carol Padden's second chapter, Chapter 6, is on the bilingual development of deaf children: Here she discusses issues related to studying bilingualism in deaf people and presents her research on the acquisition of fingerspelling in ASL and written spelling in English by ASL-English bilingual deaf children.

In Chapter 7, Susan B. Foster gives an ethnographic account of the communication experiences of deaf people. In particular, she draws on her research to discuss the impact of language barriers on deaf people and the social isolation they often experience in predominantly hearing educational and employment communities. In Chapter 8, R. Greg Emerton presents a sociological perspective on the concept of marginality and discusses its relationship to biculturalism. He also considers the marginality of the deaf community in the hearing society and its effect on the development of social identity in deaf people. In Chapter 9, Gerald C. Bateman discusses his ethnographic study of the deaf community leaders in the Rochester, New York, area. In particular, he discusses the attitudinal barriers deaf people experience and the various attitudes they hold toward political activism and the political process. He also compares the deaf community with the Hispanic-American community and notes the parallels between these two minority groups.

In Chapter 10, Bonnie Meath-Lang presents a phenomenological perspective on representing cultural and language diversity in the curriculum. The author reviews some of the historical trends and their influence on current beliefs and practices in the education of deaf people. Meath-

Lang also discusses the use of journals and writing for introspective reflection and its pertinence to understanding the Deaf experience. The subject of Chapter 11, by Joan B. Stone, is minority empowerment and the education of deaf people. The author discusses Paulo Freire's approach to education and the notion of minority empowerment. She also discusses how she incorporates the ideology of Freire in her math curriculum for deaf college students. Chapter 12, by Thomas K. Holcomb, discusses the role of the school environment in the social assimilation of deaf people. In particular, Holcomb presents a qualitative analysis of the high school social experience for deaf students from residential schools for the deaf, mainstreamed deaf students, and hearing students, and suggests that the mainstreamed deaf students often have impoverished social experiences because of communication barriers. He also discusses the implications of his findings for the education of deaf people.

III. The Deaf Experience: Personal Reflections

The primary goal of Part III is to improve our understanding of the issue of Deaf identity within the larger context of cultural diversity and language differences. This part, a unique feature of the book, offers rich first-hand accounts of the life experiences of deaf and hearing fluent signers. It is included to showcase the diversity of the experiences of the deaf community members and to document expressions of feelings, perceptions, and beliefs that would not otherwise find representation within a strictly traditional academic framework. There are many complex issues that bilingual-bicultural people must deal with, and the language choices and cultural affiliation choices they make have a strong influence on how they function and how they view themselves. The narratives offer a window into the heart of those deaf and hearing people who live in the Deaf and Hearing worlds and are profoundly affected by their bilingual-bicultural experience. It is hoped that these personal perspectives and experiences will lead to fresh insights into the bilingualism and biculturalism of deaf people.

Part III begins with Chapter 13 by Susan C. Searls and David R. Johnston, which is based on a videotaped conversation in ASL between the two authors, translated into English by Susan D. Fischer. The authors then edited this English draft to arrive at the final draft of the manuscript. The conversational format and ASL were used to facilitate free expression of personal reflections. The authors discuss their experiences of growing up with Deaf parents and ASL, but going through different kinds of educational experiences. For example, one went to an "oral" school, the other to a school where sign language was used. They also discuss their family experiences, the language choices they have made in raising their children, and their views on some of the issues facing the deaf community.

In Chapter 14, Patrick A. Graybill reflects on his life experiences as a Deaf native signer and shares his insights into how the recognition of Deaf culture and ASL leads to empowerment of deaf people. In Chapter 15, Gary E. Mowl discusses the experience of raising Deaf children in a hearing society, particularly when dealing with hearing people and the public education system. He also discusses the significant differences in perspectives between culturally Deaf native ASL signers and hearing people. In Chapter 16, Dianne K. Brooks reflects on her experiences as a deaf African-American who lost her hearing at age twelve. She describes some of the social, interactive, and psychological issues surrounding her sudden hearing loss and discusses how she came to accept her deafness. She also discusses how she resolved her feelings of marginality within the deaf community and within the hearing society.

Lynn Finton discusses in Chapter 17 the bilingual-bicultural experiences of her family as she, a hearing fluent ASL signer, and her husband, a Deaf ASL-English bilingual, raise their hearing children in both Deaf and Hearing cultures. In the final chapter of this part and of the book, Chapter 18, Patricia Mudgett-DeCaro reflects on her bicultural identity as a Hearing-Deaf person and her bilingual identity as an English-ASL user. She describes her experiences growing up as a hearing child of deaf parents who were ASL-English bilinguals. She also offers introspective and anecdotal evidence regarding a bilingual's language choices and usage and the effect of the internalization of both cultures on the self-perception and social interactions of a bicultural person.

References

Baker, C., & Battison, R. (Eds.). (1980). *Sign language and the deaf community: Essays in honor of William C. Stokoe*. Silver Spring, MD: National Association of the Deaf.

Baron, D. (1990). *The English-only question: An official language for Americans?* New Haven, CT: Yale University Press.

Belenky, M. F., Clinchy, B. M., Goldberger, N. R., & Tarule, J. M. (1986). *Women's ways of knowing: The development of self, voice, and mind*. New York: Basic Books.

Christensen, K. M., & Delgado, G. L. (Eds.). (1993). *Multicultural issues in deafness*. White Plains, NY: Longman.

Cohen, L. H. (1994). *Train go sorry: Inside a deaf world*. New York: Houghton Mifflin.

Cummins, J., & Danesi, M. (1990). Denial of voice. In *Heritage languages: The development and denial of Canada's linguistic resources* (pp. 81–98). Montreal, Quebec: Our Schools/Our Selves Education Foundation.

Delgado, G. L. (Ed.). (1984). *The Hispanic deaf: Issues and challenges for bilingual special education.* Washington, DC: Gallaudet University Press.

Dolnick, E. (1993, September). Deafness as a culture. *Atlantic Monthly Review, 272 (3),* 37–51.

Fischgrund, J., & Akamatsu, T. (1993). Rethinking the education of ethnic/multicultural deaf people: Stretching the boundaries. In K. M. Christensen & G. L. Delgado (Eds.), *Multicultural issues in deafness* (pp. 169–178). White Plains, NY: Longman.

Gannon, J. R. (Ed.). (1981). *Deaf heritage: A narrative history of deaf America.* Silver Spring, MD: National Association of the Deaf.

Garretson, M. D. (Ed.). (1990). *Communication issues among deaf people: A Deaf American Monograph. 40, 1–4.* Silver Spring, MD: National Association of the Deaf.

Gilligan, C. (1982). *In a different voice: Psychological theory and women's development.* Cambridge, MA: Harvard University Press.

Grosjean, F. (1982). *Life with two languages: An introduction to bilingualism.* Cambridge, MA: Harvard University Press.

Hakuta, K. (1986). *Mirror of language: The debate on bilingualism.* New York: Basic Books.

Hamers, J. F., & Blanc, M. H. (1983). *Bilinguality & bilingualism.* New York: Cambridge University Press.

Higgins, P. C. (1980). *Outsiders in a hearing world: A sociology of deafness.* Beverly Hills, CA: Sage Publications.

Johnson, R. E., Liddell, S. K., & Erting, C. J. (1989). *Unlocking the curriculum: Principles for achieving access in deaf education.* Gallaudet Research Institute Working Paper 89-3.

Klima, E., & Bellugi, U. (1979). *The signs of language.* Cambridge, MA: Harvard University Press.

Lane, H. (1984). *When the mind hears: A history of the deaf.* New York: Random House.

   (1989). Is there a "psychology of the deaf"? *Exceptional Children, 55,* 7–19.

   (1992). *The mask of benevolence: Disabling the deaf community.* New York: Alfred A. Knopf.

Lucas, C., & Valli, C. (1992). *Language contact in the American Deaf community.* San Diego: Academic Press.

Padden, C. (1980). The deaf community and the culture of deaf people. In C. Baker & R. Battison (Eds.), *Sign language and the deaf community: Essays in honor of William C. Stokoe* (pp. 89–103). Silver Spring, MD: National Association of the Deaf.

Padden, C., & Humphries, T. (1988). *Deaf in America: Voices from a culture.* Cambridge, MA: Harvard University Press.

Radhakrishnan, S. (1956). *Kalki or the future of civilization.* Bombay, India: Hind Kitabs Limited.

Sacks, O. (1990). *Seeing Voices: A journey into the world of the deaf.* New York: Harper Perennial.

Schein, J., & Delk, M. (1974). *The deaf population of the United States*. Silver Spring, MD: National Association of the Deaf.

Siple, P. (Ed.) (1978). *Understanding language through sign language research*. New York: Academic Press.

Skutnabb-Kangas, T., & Cummins, J. (Eds.). (1988). *Minority education: From shame to struggle*. Philadelphia: Multilingual Matters.

Solomon, A. (1994, August 28). Defiantly deaf. *The New York Times Sunday Magazine*, 40–45, 62, 65–68.

Steele, S. (1990). *The content of our character: A new vision of race in America*. New York: St. Martin's Press.

Stokoe, W. C., Casterline, D., & Croneberg, C. (1965). *A dictionary of American Sign Language on linguistic principles*. Silver Spring, MD: Linstok Press.

Strong, M. (1988). *Language learning and deafness*. New York: Cambridge University Press.

Van Cleve, J. V. (Ed.). (1987). *Gallaudet encyclopedia of deaf people and deafness*. New York: McGraw-Hill.

Walter, G. (Ed.). (1992, April). *Diversity in the schools for the deaf: A report to the membership of the CEASD from the research committee*. Report presented at the Annual Conference of the Convention of the Educators and Administrators Serving the Deaf (CEASD). Charleston, SC.

Wilcox, S. (Ed.). (1989). *American Deaf culture: An anthology*. Burtonsville, MD: Linstok Press.

Woodward, J. (1989). How you gonna get to heaven if you can't talk with Jesus?: The educational establishment vs. the deaf community. In S. Wilcox (Ed.), *American Deaf culture: An anthology* (pp. 163–172). Burtonsville, MD: Linstok Press.

CHAPTER TWO

Living with Two Languages and Two Cultures

FRANÇOIS GROSJEAN

This chapter contains three main sections. In the first, we describe the bilingual person and address such issues as bilingual language behavior, the psycholinguistics and neurolinguistics of bilingualism, as well as the psychology of the bilingual individual. In the second section, we introduce the bicultural person and discuss topics such as bicultural identity and bicultural behavior. Finally, in the last section, we describe the Deaf bilingual and bicultural.

The Bilingual Person

Few areas of linguistics are surrounded by as many misconceptions as is bilingualism. Most people think that bilingualism is a rare phenomenon found only in such countries as Canada, Switzerland, and Belgium and that bilinguals have equal speaking and writing fluency in their languages, have accentless speech, and can interpret and translate without any prior training. The reality is in fact quite different; bilingualism is present in practically every country of the world, in all classes of society and in all age groups; in fact, it has been estimated that half the world's

François Grosjean (Ph.D., Psycholinguistics, University of Paris), Professor of Psycholinguistics and Language Processing at the University of Neuchâtel, Switzerland, is an experimental psycholinguist who conducts and publishes research on the perception, comprehension, and production of language in monolinguals and bilinguals. He is the author of the well-known *Life with Two Languages: An Introduction to Bilingualism* (1982, Harvard University Press) and has also coedited *Recent Perspectives on American Sign Language* (1980, Harvard University Press) with Harlan Lane. His address is: Laboratoire de Traitement du Langage, Université de Neuchâtel, Avenue du Premier-Mars 26, 2000 Neuchâtel, Switzerland.

population is bilingual. As for bilinguals themselves, the majority acquired their languages at various points during their lives and are rarely equally fluent in them. Furthermore, few bilinguals are proficient interpreters and translators. (See the following for general overviews of bilingualism: Appel & Muysken, 1987; Baetens-Beardsmore, 1986; Clyne, 1972; Grosjean, 1982; Hakuta, 1986; Haugen, 1969; Romaine, 1989; Weinreich, 1968.)

In this first section, which is based to a large extent on Grosjean (1982, 1985, 1994), Baetens-Beardsmore (1986), and Haugen (1969), we will describe the many facets of the bilingual person. We will concentrate on the adult and focus on the stable bilingual, that is, the person who is no longer in the process of acquiring a second or third language.

Describing the Bilingual

We will call bilingual those people who use two (or more) languages (or dialects) in their everyday lives. Thus, our definition includes people ranging from the migrant worker who speaks with some difficulty the host country's language (and who cannot read and write it) all the way to the professional interpreter who is totally fluent in two languages. In between we find the foreign spouse who interacts with friends in his first language, the scientist who reads and writes articles in a second language (but who rarely speaks it), the member of a linguistic minority who uses the minority language at home only and the majority language in all other domains of life, the Deaf person who uses sign language with her friends but a signed form of the spoken language with a hearing person, and so forth. Despite the great diversity that exists among these people, all share a common feature: they lead their lives with two (or more) languages.

The causes that bring languages into contact and hence foster bilingualism are many: migrations of various kinds (economic, educational, political, religious), nationalism and federalism, education and culture, trade and commerce, intermarriage, and others. These factors create various linguistic needs in people who are in contact with two or more languages and who develop competencies in their languages to the extent required by these needs. In contact situations it is rare that all facets of life require the same language (people would not be bilingual if that were so) or that they always demand two languages (language A *and* B at work, at home, with friends, etc.). In fact, bilinguals acquire and use their languages for different purposes, in different domains of life, with different people. It is precisely because the needs and uses of the languages are usually quite different that bilinguals rarely develop equal fluency in their languages. The level of fluency attained in a language (more precisely, in a language skill) will depend on the need for that language and will be domain-specific. It is thus perfectly normal to find bilinguals who can only read and write one of their languages, who have reduced speaking fluency in a language they only use with a limited number of people, or who can only speak about a particular subject in one of their languages.

The failure to understand that bilinguals normally use their languages for different purposes, with different people, and in different domains of life has been a major obstacle to obtaining a clear picture of bilinguals and has had many negative consequences: bilinguals have been described and evaluated in terms of the fluency and balance they have in their two languages; language skills in bilinguals have almost always been appraised in terms of monolingual standards; research on bilingualism has in large part been conducted in terms of the bilingual's individual and separate languages; and, finally, many bilinguals evaluate their language competencies as inadequate. Some criticize their mastery of language skills, others strive their hardest to reach monolingual norms, others hide their knowledge of their "weaker" language, and most simply do not perceive themselves as being bilingual even though they use two (or more) languages in their everyday lives.

Bilinguals are now starting to be viewed not so much as the sum of two (or more) complete or incomplete monolinguals but rather as specific and fully competent speaker-hearers who have developed a communicative competence that is equal to, but different in nature from that of monolinguals. They make use of one language, of the other, or of the two together depending on the situation, the topic, the interlocutor, and so on. This in turn has led to a redefinition of the procedure used to evaluate the bilingual's competencies. Bilinguals are starting to be studied in terms of their total language repertoire, and the domains of use and the functions of the bilingual's various languages are now being taken into account.

We should note finally that as the environment changes and the needs for particular language skills also change, so will the bilingual's competence in his or her various language skills. New situations, new interlocutors, new language functions will involve new linguistic needs and will therefore change the language configuration of the person involved. Extreme cases of restructuring are language forgetting and a return to functional monolingualism, be it in the person's first, second, or third language.

The Bilingual's Language Modes

In their everyday lives, bilinguals find themselves at various points along a situational continuum which induce different language modes. At one end, bilinguals are in a totally monolingual mode in that they are speaking (or signing or writing) to monolinguals of one – or the other – of the languages that they know. At the other end, bilinguals are in a bilingual language mode in that they are communicating with bilinguals who share their two languages and with whom they normally mix languages (i.e., code-switch and borrow; see below). We will refer to the two end points of the continuum when speaking of the monolingual or bilingual language modes, but we should keep in mind that these are end points and that intermediary modes do exist.

In the monolingual language mode, bilinguals choose the language of the monolingual interlocutor(s) and deactivate as best they can their other language(s). In fact, deactivation of the other language is rarely total, as is clearly seen in the interferences bilinguals produce (these are also known as between-language deviations). An interference is a speaker-specific deviation from the language being spoken due to the influence of the other "deactivated" language. Interferences can occur at all levels of language (phonological, lexical, syntactic, semantic, pragmatic) and in all modalities (spoken, written, or sign). They are of two kinds: static interferences, which reflect permanent traces of one language on the other (such as a permanent accent, the meaning extensions of particular words, specific syntactic structures, etc.); and dynamic interferences, which are the ephemeral intrusions of the other language (as in the case of the accidental slip on the stress pattern of a word due to the stress rules of the other language, the momentary use of a syntactic structure taken from the language not being spoken, etc.). Examples of interferences produced by a French person speaking English are as follows. At the phonetic level, pronouncing "Sank evven for dees" instead of "Thank heaven for this"; at the lexical level, using "corns" (from French *cornes*) instead of "horns" in "Look at the corns on that animal!"; at the syntactic level, saying "I saw this on the page five" (instead of "on page five"); and in writing, using the misspellings "adress" or "appartment" (based on the French *adresse* and *appartement*). In addition, if one of the bilingual's languages is mastered only to a certain level of proficiency, deviations due to the person's interlanguage (known as within-language deviations) will also occur. These include overgeneralizations (for example, taking irregular verbs and treating them as if they were regular), simplifications (dropping pluralization and tense markers, omitting function words, simplifying the syntax, etc.) as well as hypercorrections and the avoidance of certain words and expressions. It should be noted that both types of deviations, although sometimes quite apparent (such as a foreign accent), usually do not interfere with communication. This is because bilinguals develop their languages to the level of fluency required by the environment. Deviations in bilingual speech are thus of the same nature as slips of the tongue and hesitation phenomena. They are present but do not usually affect communication.

In the bilingual language mode, bilinguals first adopt a language to use together, what is known as the "base language" (also the "host" or "matrix" language). Language choice is a well-learned behavior (a bilingual rarely asks the conscious question, Which language should I be using with this person?) but it is also a very complex phenomenon which only becomes apparent when it breaks down. Usually, bilinguals go through their daily interactions with other bilinguals quite unaware of the many psychological and sociolinguistic factors that interact to help them choose one language over another. Once a base language has been chosen, bilinguals can bring in the other language (the "guest" or "embedded" language) in various ways. One of these ways is to code-switch, that is, to shift completely to the other language for a word, a phrase, a sentence. (For example, "Va chercher Marc AND BRIBE HIM avec un chocolat chaud WITH CREAM ON TOP" – Go get Marc and bribe him with a hot chocolate with cream on top.) Code-switching has long been stigmatized, and has been given a number of pejorative names such as Franglais (the switching between French and English) and Tex-Mex (the switching between English and Spanish in the southwestern United States). The consequence of this has been that some bilinguals never switch while others only switch in situations in which they will not be stigmatized for doing so. Recent research has shown that switching is not simply a haphazard behavior due to some form of "semilingualism" but that it is, instead, a well-governed process used as a communicative strategy to convey linguistic and social information (Heller, 1988; Myers-Scotton, 1993; Poplack, 1980).

The other, less activated, language can also be brought in by borrowing a word or short expression from that language and adapting it morphologically (and often phonologically) into the base language. Most often both the form and the content of a word are borrowed (to produce what has been called a loanword or more simply a borrowing), as in the following examples taken from French-English bilinguals: "Ça m'étonnerait qu'on ait CODE-SWITCHÉ autant que ça" (I can't believe we code-switched as often as that) and "Maman, tu peux me TIER [pronounced/taie/] mes chaussures" (Mummy, can you tie my shoes?). In these examples, the English words "code-switch" and "tie" have been brought in and integrated into the French sentence. It is important to distinguish idiosyncratic loans (also called "speech borrowings" or "nonce borrowings") from words which have become part of a language community's vocabulary and which monolinguals also use (called "language borrowings" or "established loans"). Thus, in the following text, every third or fourth word is an established loan from French which has now become part of the English language: "The POET lived in the DUKE'S MANOR. That day, he PAINTED, played MUSIC, and wrote POEMS with his COMPANIONS."

The Psycholinguistics and Neurolinguistics of Bilingualism

The psycholinguistics of bilingualism is aimed at studying the processes involved in the production, perception, comprehension, and memorization of the bilingual's languages (spoken, written, or signed) when used in a monolingual or a bilingual language mode. Until recently the emphasis has been put on the independence of the bilingual's languages (How does the bilingual keep the two languages separate? Does the bilingual have one or two lexicons?) to the detriment of issues such as the on-line processing of language, be it in a monolingual or in a bilingual language mode. Much research was conducted, for example, on the coordinate-compound-subordinate distinction (Weinreich, 1968; for a critical review, see Grosjean, 1982; Paradis, 1977). Another area of considerable investigation examined whether bilinguals possess one or two internal lexicons. A third issue of interest was the ability of bilinguals to keep their two languages separate in the monolingual mode. Researchers postulated the existence of a language switch which allows bilinguals to gate out the other language, and experimental studies were conducted, to no effect, to find evidence for this proposal.

Now that it is more generally accepted that the bilingual is not two monolinguals in one person, but a unique speaker-hearer using one language, the other language, or both together depending on the interlocutor, situation, topic, etc. (see above), current psycholinguistic research is trying to understand the processing of language in the bilingual's different language modes (Vaid, 1986; Harris, 1992). Researchers are studying how bilinguals in the monolingual mode differ from monolinguals in terms of perception and production processes, and they are investigating the actual interaction of the two languages during processing in the bilingual mode (see Grosjean, 1988, for an example of this).

As concerns the neurolinguistics of bilingualism, researchers have long been interested in describing how language is organized in the "bilingual brain" and how this organization differs from that of the monolingual. One approach has been to observe and test bilingual aphasics in order to better understand which languages have been affected by brain injury and which factors best account for the different patterns of recovery of the languages. Another approach has been to study normal bilinguals to ascertain whether language processing occurs mainly in the left hemisphere of the brain (as it appears to do in monolinguals) or in both hemispheres. Until a few years ago, and based on case studies of bilingual aphasics and on experimental results, some researchers proposed that bilinguals use the right hemisphere in language processing more than monolinguals. However, from further studies that were better controlled, there now appears to be clear evidence that monolinguals and bilinguals do not differ at all in hemispheric involvement during language processing (see Zatorre, 1989, for a review of the question). Finally, on the subject of language organization in the bilingual brain, most researchers agree that the bilingual's languages are not stored in completely different locations. In addition, it would appear that bilinguals have two subsets of neural connections, one for each language (each can be activated or inhibited independently), while at the same time possessing one larger set from which they are able to draw elements of either language at any time (Paradis, 1989). This said, the bilingual brain is still very much terra incognita, and only further experimental and clinical research will tell us how similar it is to the monolingual brain and in what ways it may be different.

The Psychology of Bilinguals

Several surveys (Grosjean, 1982; Kolers, 1978; Vildomec, 1971) have shown that either bilinguals have no strong feelings about their bilingualism (it is simply a fact of life!) or they see more advantages than inconveniences in having to live with two (or more) languages. Most appreciate being able to communicate with people from different linguistic and cultural backgrounds; others feel that bilingualism gives them a different perspective on life, that it fosters open-mindedness, allows one to read and often write in a different language, makes learning other languages easier, gives more job opportunities, etc. As for inconveniences, these are less numerous and involve such aspects as mixing languages involuntarily, having to adjust to different cultures, feeling one is losing one of the languages one possesses (usually a minority language), or having to act as a translator on various occasions. It is interesting to compare these reactions to the attitudes and feelings that monolinguals have toward bilingualism. These are extremely varied (Haugen, 1972), ranging from very positive attitudes (such as wonder at the fact that some bilinguals can speak and write two or more languages fluently) to very negative attitudes (such as surprise that many bilinguals do not master their two languages perfectly, that they cannot translate automatically from one language to another, etc.). It should be noted that most of the views that monolinguals have about bilinguals are usually based on socioeconomic and cultural considerations rather than on linguistic factors.

We know little about the languages used by bilinguals in their mental activities or how bilinguals react when under stress or in an emotional situation. It does seem to be the case that some mental operations are language-specific. Thus, bilinguals usually count and pray in the language in which they learned these behaviors. Thinking or dreaming can also be language-specific (although they can at times be alinguistic) and depend on the person, the situation, and the topic involved. When tired, angry, or excited, bilinguals will often revert to their mother tongue or to whatever language they usually express their emotions in. Stress may also cause more interference, problems in finding the appropriate words, and unintentional switching. In addition, it has been reported that bilinguals wish that the monolinguals closest to them (spouse, companion, friends) were also bilingual.

It has been reported by some bilinguals that when they change attitudes and behaviors they change language. This has been alluded to quite frequently in the literature: some bilinguals seem to hold slightly different views depending on the language they are speaking; some others are more authoritarian in one of their languages; others still are more reserved or gentle, and so on. Is it possible to conclude from this that there is some truth to the Czech proverb, "Learn a new language and get a new soul"? Some would answer in the affirmative and go as far as to say that the bilingual has a split personality. In fact, there appears to be no real evidence that bilinguals suffer any more from mental disorders than monolinguals. In fact, what is seen as a change in personality is simply a shift in attitudes and behaviors corresponding to a shift in situation or context, independent of language. As we saw above, bilinguals will choose a language according to the situation, the interlocutor, the topic, and the intent of the conversations. These factors trigger different attitudes, impressions, and behaviors (just as they do in monolinguals who modify the content and form of their discourse depending on the context), and thus what is seen as a personality change due to language shift may really be a shift in the situation and interlocutor. In a word, it is the environment as a whole that causes the bilingual to change languages, along with attitudes, feelings, and behaviors – and not language as such. The main difference between monolinguals and bilinguals in this respect is that bilinguals often shift languages (and hence appear to be different people) whereas monolinguals do not. In addition, bilinguals are often switching from one culture to another in their interactions (many are bicultural) whereas monolinguals usually remain within the same culture.

The Bicultural Person

Much less is known about biculturalism than bilingualism even though one sees the term "bicultural" almost as often as the word "bilingual." And yet many people are bicultural, although they are not as numerous as bilinguals, and many of the "advantages" or "disadvantages" of bilingualism are, in fact, tied to biculturalism and not to bilingualism. We should note at this point that bilingualism and biculturalism are not necessarily coextensive. Many people are bilingual without being bicultural (members of diglossic communities, inhabitants of countries that have lingua francas, etc.) and, similarly, some people are bicultural without being bilingual (members of a minority culture who no longer know the minority language but who retain other aspects of that culture, for example). In this section, which is based largely on Grosjean (1983, 1992), we will describe the bicultural person, discuss bicultural identity, and evoke bicultural behavior.

Describing the Bicultural

When we attempt to define the bicultural person, it is important to explain what we mean by culture. For our purpose here, culture reflects all the facets of life of a group of people: its organization, its rules, its behaviors, its beliefs, its values, its traditions, and so on. As humans, we belong to a number of cultures (or cultural networks): major cultures (national, linguistic, social, religious, etc.) and minor cultures (occupation, sport, hobby, etc.). What is interesting is that some cultures are complementary (it is permissible to belong to several or all of these at the same time) whereas others are mutually exclusive (belonging to one and the other is unacceptable and thereby raises problems; thus it was practically impossible during World War II to be both Japanese and American just as it is currently difficult to be both Croatian and Serb). In what follows, we will concentrate on people who belong to two major (often mutually exclusive) cultures.

Biculturals can be characterized by at least three traits: they live in two or more cultures, they adapt, at least in part, to these cultures (their attitudes, behaviors, values, etc.), and they blend aspects of these cultures. This latter point is important as it means that not all behaviors, beliefs, and attitudes can be modified according to the cultural situation the bicultural person is currently in. The French-German bicultural, for example, blends aspects of both the French and of the German culture and cannot, therefore, be 100% French in France and 100% German in Germany, however hard he or she tries. Other criteria have been put forward to define the bicultural, such as accepting one's bicultural status, having a good understanding of a second culture and being born bicultural, but these are probably not as important as the three we have put forward: living in two cultures, adapting to them, and blending aspects of each. Of course, the balanced bicultural who is as much part of one culture as of another is as rare as the balanced bilingual who is as fluent in all skills of one language as of another. Most biculturals have stronger ties with one culture than with another (at least in certain domains of life) but this in no way makes them less bicultural.

Bicultural Identity

An important aspect of biculturalism, especially for bicultural children and adolescents, concerns the acceptance of one's bicultural identity. To reach the point of saying, "I am bicultural, a member of both culture A and of culture B," a bicultural person often has to go through a long and often trying process. On the one hand, members of the two different cultures assess, indirectly of course, whether a person belongs to their culture or not by taking into account such factors as kinship, language, physical appearance, nationality, education, and attitudes. This double categorization, by each of the two cultural groups, can produce similar results (X is judged to belong solely to culture A or to culture B) or contradictory results (X is categorized as a member of culture A by members of culture B and as a member of culture B by members of culture A). Not only is this latter categorization contradictory but it is often absolute in the sense that cultures do not readily accept that a person can be part of their culture and also part of another culture. The attitude is either "You are A" or "You are B," but rarely "You are A and B."

Faced with this dual categorization, which is quite often contradictory, biculturals have to reach a decision as to their own cultural identity. To do this they take into account the perception that the two cultures have of them and bring in other factors such as their personal history, their identity needs, and their knowledge of the languages and cultures involved. The outcome of this long process is a decision to belong solely to culture A, to belong solely to culture B, to belong to neither culture A nor culture B, or to belong to both culture A and culture B. Of course, the optimal solution for biculturals is to opt for the fourth solution, that is, to accept their biculturalism, but unfortunately many biculturals, influenced as they are by the categorization of the cultural groups they belong to, choose one of the first three alternatives (A, B, neither A nor B). These solutions are not usually satisfactory as they do not truly reflect the bicultural person and they may have negative consequences later on. Those who choose either culture A or culture B (that is, turn away from their other culture) are often dissatisfied with their decision, and those who reject both cultures feel uprooted, marginal, or ambivalent. In the end, after a long and sometimes arduous process, most biculturals come to terms with their biculturalism. The lucky ones can belong to a new cultural group (see the many hyphenated groups in North America) and most others, who are isolated biculturals, will ultimately navigate with a certain degree of ease between and within their cultures.

Bicultural Behavior

One knows very little about the bicultural's cultural behavior: which aspects of a culture are adaptable to a specific cultural situation and which are not; how biculturals interact with the two (or more) cultures they belong to; how they switch from one culture to another, and so on. What is sure is that, like bilinguals, they often find themselves at various points along a situational continuum which require different types of behavior. At one end, they are in a monocultural mode and must deactivate as best they can their other culture. (The blending component in biculturals makes this very difficult, hence the frequent presence of cultural interferences). At the other end, they are with other biculturals like themselves with whom they use a cultural base to interact with (the behaviors, attitudes, beliefs, etc., of one culture) and into which they bring the other culture in the form of cultural switches and borrowings when they choose to.

The Deaf Bilingual and Bicultural Person

In this final section, which is based largely on Grosjean (1992), we will describe the Deaf bilingual and the Deaf bicultural, and we will end with implications for the bilingual and bicultural education of Deaf children.

The Deaf Bilingual

Bilingualism in the Deaf community remains a poorly understood topic despite the fact that most Deaf people are indeed bilingual. (On this topic, see, among others, Battison, 1978; Bernstein, Maxwell, & Matthews, 1985; Davis, 1989; Frishberg, 1984; Grosjean, 1986, 1992; Kannapell, 1974; Kettrick & Hatfield, 1986; Lee, 1983; Lucas, 1989; Lucas & Valli, 1992; Stokoe, 1969; Volterra & Erting, 1990.) The bilingualism present is a form of minority language bilingualism in which the members of the Deaf community acquire and use both the minority language (sign language) and the majority language in its written form and sometimes in its spoken or even signed form. (We will use the labels "sign language" and "majority language" throughout our text as we do not want to restrict ourselves to the case of one language pair, e.g. ASL and English or FSL [LSF] and French.) Sign language bilingualism can, of course, also involve the knowledge and use of two or more different sign languages, but this form of bilingualism is less common in the Deaf community and has been the object of fewer studies. Thus, given the definition of bilingualism presented above, most Deaf people who sign and who use the majority language in their everyday lives (in its written form, for example) are indeed bilingual.

Deaf bilinguals share many similarities with hearing bilinguals. First, they are very diverse. Depending on their degree of hearing loss, the language(s) used in childhood, their education, their occupation, their social networks, and so on, they have developed competencies in their languages (sign language and the majority language) to varying degrees. This, of course, is no different from hearing bilinguals who are also very diverse in their knowledge and use of their languages. Second, most Deaf bilinguals do not judge themselves to be bilingual. In some countries, some Deaf people may not be aware that sign language is different from the majority language, and in general many Deaf do not think they are bilingual because they do not fully master all the skills that accompany the majority language (or, at times, the sign language). This is a well-known phenomenon found among many bilinguals, be they hearing or Deaf, who have a tendency to evaluate their language competencies as inadequate. Some criticize their mastery of language skills, others strive their hardest to reach monolingual norms, others hide their knowledge of their "weaker" language, and most simply do not perceive themselves as being bilingual even though they use two (or more) languages regularly. Third, like hearing bilinguals, Deaf bilinguals find themselves in their everyday lives at various points along the language mode continuum. When they are communicating with monolinguals they restrict themselves to just one language and are therefore in a monolingual mode. They deactivate the other language and remain, as best they can, within the confines of the language being used (for example, a written form of the majority language). At other times, Deaf bilinguals find themselves in a bilingual mode, that is, with other bilinguals who share to some extent their two languages – sign language and the majority language – and with whom they can mix their languages. Here, depending on such factors as their knowledge of the two languages, the person(s) being addressed, the situation, the topic, and the function of the interaction, they choose a base language – usually a form of sign language (the natural sign language of the community or a signed version of the spoken language). Then, according to various momentary needs, and by means of signing, fingerspelling, mouthing, and so on, they bring in the other language in the form of code-switches or borrowings. The result has recently been called contact signing (Lucas & Valli, 1992).

Although the bilingualism of the Deaf shares many characteristics with that of hearing people, a number of aspects are specific to the Deaf group. First, until recently there has been little recognition of Deaf people's bilingual status. They are still seen by many as monolingual in the majority language, whereas in fact many are bilingual in that language and in sign. Second, Deaf bilinguals, because of their hearing loss, will remain bilingual throughout their lives and from generation to generation. This is not always the case with other minority groups who, over the years, can shift to a form of monolingualism (either in the majority language, in the minority language, or in some other form of language). Third, and again due to their hearing loss, certain language skills in the majority language (speaking, above all) may never be acquired fully by Deaf bilinguals. Fourth, although movement takes place along the language mode continuum, Deaf bilinguals rarely find themselves at the monolingual sign language end. Thus, unless they are communicating with a monolingual member of the majority language (via the written modality, for example), they will most often be with other bilinguals and will thus be in a bilingual language mode. Fifth, the patterns of language knowledge and use appear to be somewhat different, and probably more complex, than in spoken language bilingualism. When a sign language bilingual uses sign language with one interlocutor, a form of signed spoken language with another, a mixture of the two with a third, a form of simultaneous communication (sign and speech) with a fourth, and so on, the diverse behaviors are the result of a number of complex factors:

1. The bilingual's actual knowledge of the sign language and of the majority language. This competence, in terms of linguistic rules and lexical knowledge, can often be characterized in terms of how prototypical it is.
2. The modalities (or channels) of production: manual (sign, fingerspelling), oral (speech, mouthing with or without voice), written, and so forth. Some of these modalities are more appropriate for one of the two languages (speech or writing for the majority language), but others, such as the sign modality, can be used, to some extent at least, for one or the other language. How these modalities are combined during the interaction is of particular interest.
3. The presence of the other language in the bilingual communication mode. Here, either one language is chosen as the base language and the other language is called in at various points in time, or a third system emerges that combines the two languages (what Lucas & Valli, 1992, call contact signing). In both cases, the languages can interact in a sequential manner (as in code-switching) or in a simultaneous manner (signing and mouthing) and can involve various modalities (Frishberg, 1984).

The Deaf Bicultural

Two questions can be asked about biculturalism in the Deaf community. First, are Deaf people bicultural, and second, if some are, what is being done to help them come to terms with their bicultural identity? As to the first question, there is little doubt that many Deaf meet the three criteria that we put forward above: they live in two or more cultures (their family, friends, colleagues, etc., are members either of the Deaf community or of the hearing world); they adapt, at least in part, to these cultures; and they blend aspects of these cultures. Of course, such factors as deafness in the family, degree of hearing loss, or type of education may lead some Deaf people to have fewer contacts with the hearing world while others have more (their bicultural dominance can thus differ), but it is nevertheless true that most Deaf people are not only bilingual but also bicultural. (This is also the case for hearing children of Deaf parents and for some hearing people who have developed strong ties with the Deaf community.) Of

course, most Deaf people are Deaf-dominant biculturals in that they identify primarily with the Deaf community, but many of them also have ties
with the hearing world and interact with it and hence, in a sense, are also
members of it. This brings us to the second question: What is being done to
help Deaf people come to terms with their bicultural identity? Which in
turn raises a number of subsidiary questions: What identity signals are
being sent by the two cultures in question? Are they complementary or
contradictory? What is the outcome of the identity decision taken by each
Deaf person? Does the decision reflect that person's degree of biculturalism? Is the decision the right one for that person? As a hearing researcher
with few ties with the Deaf community, I am in no position to give answers
to these questions, but I do think that they should be addressed by all
concerned.

Implications

A number of implications emerge from what we are starting to know
about the bilingualism and biculturalism of Deaf people. As to their bilingualism, first it is necessary to continue studying its development and
its various facets, and to inform parents and educators about it. Too many
stereotypes still surround bilingualism, be it between two spoken languages or between a sign language and a spoken language. Second, it is
important that Deaf people realize that they are indeed bilingual, that they
accept this fact and that they take pride in it. They are not the sum of two
complete or incomplete monolinguals but are an integrated whole with a
unique communicative competence. Third, it is critical that Deaf children
be brought up bilingual – with sign language as their primary language
and with the majority language (especially in its written modality) as a
second language. How this is done is clearly a challenge for parents,
educators, and members of the linguistic communities involved.[1] Chil-

---

[1] The aim of this chapter is not to raise the issue of bilingual education, which is a topic in its
own right and the object of much discussion. Without wanting to enter the debate, but in
order to respond to a reviewer's questions, it is the author's personal belief that Deaf
children should be raised bilingually, that their first language should be sign language (if
they are diagnosed as having severe hearing loss), and that their second language should
be the majority language (especially in its written form). Sign language as a first language
is necessary in order to give children a natural language to communicate with as early as
possible and to allow full cognitive and social development. It is, in addition, the language
of the culture that will be dominant for many Deaf children when they reach adolescence
or adulthood, and it is a good base on which to acquire their second language. This second
language, the majority language, is also very important as it is the language of most

dren need to learn, among other things, that there are various languages and language modes and that they have to use them, as best they can, at different times and with different interlocutors. They should interact with various people (family, friends, teachers, etc.) with whom they need to use one or the other language and a variety of modes: the sign language monolingual mode with certain Deaf people, the majority language monolingual mode with most members of the hearing majority, and, finally, the sign language bilingual mode with other members of their community and with hearing signers. It is important that role models be offered to them for each language and each type of language mode and that they develop a need for each. As is well known, children only become bilingual (whatever the final level attained) if they have to, that is, if their life requires the use of two (or more) languages and language modes.

As for the biculturalism of Deaf people, it is especially important that Deaf children and adolescents be given every opportunity to learn about the Deaf and hearing cultures, that they be able to interact as best they can with these cultures, and that they be able to go through the process of choosing the cultures (or the culture) they wish to identify with. It is the task of parents, family members, educators, and members of the cultures involved to make sure this process takes place as early and as smoothly as possible.

Acknowledgments

This chapter is based on a talk given at NTID on September 30, 1991, and on preceding publications by the author. Its preparation was made possible by grants from the Swiss National Science Foundation (12-33582.92; 32-37276.93). The author wishes to thank Dr. Bill Stokoe for permission to reuse parts of a *Sign Language Studies* article (Grosjean, 1992). Special thanks go to the following people for their insightful comments at various stages during the preparation of this chapter: Robbin Battison, Penny Boyes-Braem, Christina Edenas-Battison, Nancy Frishberg, Lysiane Grosjean, Harlan Lane, Dominique Lepoutre, Ila Parasnis, and two anonymous reviewers.

children's parents and of the hearing culture. Because many Deaf children and adolescents have very real problems with the perception and production of speech, it is preferable to concentrate on written skills (reading and writing) so that their level of competence in them can be as high as possible. As for spoken skills, the debate remains open but their acquisition should not be achieved to the detriment of sign language or of written language or, for that matter, of the children's academic education.

References

Appel, R., & Muysken, P. (1987). *Language contact and bilingualism*. London: Edward Arnold.

Baetens-Beardsmore, H. (1986). *Bilingualism: Basic principles*. Clevedon, England: Multilingual Matters.

Battison, R. (1978). *Lexical borrowing in American Sign Language*. Silver Spring, MD: Linstok Press.

Bernstein, M., Maxwell, M., & Matthews, K. (1985). Bimodal or bilingual communication? *Sign Language Studies, 47*, 127–140.

Clyne, M. (1972). *Perspectives on language contact*. Melbourne, Australia: Hawthorne Press.

Davis, J. (1989). Distinguishing language contact phenomena in ASL interpretation. In C. Lucas (Ed.), *The Sociolinguistics of the Deaf Community* (pp. 85–102). New York: Academic Press.

Frishberg, N. (1984). *The sign language continuum as a dynamic construct. Evidence from simultaneous communication*. Unpublished manuscript.

Grosjean, F. (1982). *Life with two languages: An introduction to bilingualism*. Cambridge, MA: Harvard University Press.

(1983). Quelques réflexions sur le biculturalisme. *Pluriel, 36*, 81–91.

(1985). The bilingual as a competent but specific speaker hearer. *Journal of Multilingual and Multicultural Development, 6*, 467–477.

(1986). Bilingualism. *Gallaudet encyclopedia of deaf people and deafness*. Vol. 3 (pp. 179–182). New York: McGraw-Hill.

(1988). Exploring the recognition of guest words in bilingual speech. *Language and Cognitive Processes, 3*(3), 233–274.

(1992). The bilingual and the bicultural person in the hearing and in the deaf world. *Sign Language Studies, 77*, 307–320.

(1994.). Individual bilingualism. *The encyclopedia of language and linguistics* (pp. 1656–1660). Oxford: Pergamon Press.

Hakuta, K. (1986). *Mirror of language: The debate on bilingualism*. New York: Basic Books.

Harris, R. (Ed.). (1992). *Cognitive processing in bilinguals*. Amsterdam: North-Holland.

Haugen, E. (1969). *The Norwegian language in America: A study in bilingual behavior*. Bloomington: University of Indiana Press.

(1972). The stigmata of bilingualism. In A. Dil (Ed.), *The ecology of language* (pp. 307–324). Stanford: Stanford University Press.

Heller, M. (1988). *Code-switching*. Berlin: Mouton de Gruyter.

Kannapel, B. (1974, June). Bilingualism: A new direction in the education of the deaf. *Deaf American*, 9–15.

Kettrick, C., & Hatfield, N. (1986). Bilingualism in a visuo-gestural mode. In Vaid, J. (Ed.), *Language processing in bilinguals*. Hillsdale, NJ: Lawrence Erlbaum.

Kolers, P. (1978). On the representation of experience. In D. Gerver & H. Sinaiko (Eds.), *Language interpretation and communication* (pp. 1656–1660). New York: Plenum Press.

Lee, D. (1983). *Sources and aspects of code-switching in the signing of a deaf adult and her interlocutors.* Unpublished doctoral dissertation, University of Texas at Austin.

Lucas, C. (Ed.). (1989). *The sociolinguistics of the deaf community.* New York: Academic Press.

Lucas, C., & Valli, C. (1992). *Language contact in the American deaf community.* New York: Academic Press.

Myers-Scotton, C. (1993). *Social motivations for codeswitching.* New York: Oxford University Press.

Paradis, M. (1977). Bilingualism and aphasia. In H. Whitaker & H. Whitaker (Eds.), *Studies in neurolinguistics* (Vol. 3, pp. 65–121). New York: Academic Press.

(1989). Bilingual and polyglot aphasia. In F. Boller & J. Grafman (Eds.), *Handbook of Neuropsychology* (Vol. 2, pp. 117–140). Amsterdam: Elsevier.

Poplack, S. (1980). Sometimes I'll start a sentence in Spanish Y TERMINO EN ESPAÑOL: Toward a typology of codeswitching. *Linguistics, 18,* 581–618.

Romaine, S. (1989). *Bilingualism.* London: Blackwell.

Stokoe, W. (1969). Sign language diglossia. *Studies in Linguistics, 21,* 27–41.

Vaid, J. (Ed.). (1986). *Language processing in bilinguals.* Hillsdale, NJ: Lawrence Erlbaum.

Vildomec, V. (1971). *Multilingualism.* Leyden: A. W. Sythoff.

Volterra, V., & Erting, C. (Eds.). (1990). *From gesture to language in hearing and deaf children.* Berlin: Springer.

Weinreich, U. (1968). *Languages in contact.* The Hague: Mouton.

Zatorre, R. (1989). On the representation of multiple languages in the brain: Old problems and new directions. *Brain and Language, 36,* 127–147.

CHAPTER THREE

Perspectives from the History and Politics of Bilingualism and Bilingual Education in the United States

KENJI HAKUTA AND
ELIZABETH FELDMAN MOSTAFAPOUR

This chapter provides an overview of the current status of bilingual education in the United States, with a special focus on trends in research and policy in this area. In the context of the present volume, it is appropriate to acknowledge that bilingual education in this country refers almost exclusively to the education of "limited-English-proficient" (LEP) students who have an oral, non-English primary language. For example, the major federal instrument to support bilingual education, the Bilingual Education Act (also known as Title VII of the Elementary and Secondary Education Act), makes no mention of programs for deaf students. Despite many obvious parallels and similarities, there has been little contact between researchers, practitioners, and policy makers who work with LEP children and those whose concerns lie with another subpopulation of bilingual children, namely, the Deaf. This chapter is prepared from the perspective of researchers in bilingual education, rather than Deaf education, with the

Kenji Hakuta (Ph.D., Psychology, Harvard University), Professor of Education at Stanford University, is a developmental psycholinguist who conducts and publishes research on the phenomena of bilingualism and language acquisition and on bilingual education. He is the author of many books, including the well-known *Mirror of Language: The Debate on Bilingualism* (1986, Basic Books). His address is: Stanford University School of Education, Stanford, CA 94305.

Elizabeth Feldman Mostafapour (M.A., Education, Stanford University) is a doctoral student in the Language, Literacy, and Culture Program at the School of Education, Stanford University. Her research interests include foreign language education, language policy, and the education of linguistic minorities in the United States. Her address is: Stanford University School of Education, Stanford, CA 94305.

hope that the issues we raise may help to identify the parallels and differences that exist between these areas.

Definitions

A most pressing issue in the area of bilingual education has been to specify the definition of bilingualism. For a first-hand experience, the next time you have a captive group of people interested in bilingualism (as in a graduate seminar), try asking them to jot down spontaneously a definition of what it means to be bilingual. What you will likely find (based on a considerable number of replications of this "experiment" by the first author) is that most (roughly three in four) of the definitions will stress relative language *proficiency*, or the ability to perform particular functions in two languages. These are what we call "psycholinguistic" definitions of bilingualism. They may differ in detail, some focusing on vocabulary, others on grammar, others on functional skills, but they all refer, ultimately, to a psycholinguistic capability. On the other hand, a minority of definitions (the remaining one in four) will characterize bilingualism in terms of *social participation* in more than one speech community. For these people, the definition rests on degree of participation and group membership. We refer to this as a "sociolinguistic" definition. The importance of drawing a clear distinction between psycholinguistic and sociolinguistic definitions cannot be overemphasized. Confusion has resulted, both in research and in policy, because of a blurring of the boundaries.

In research, for example, some of the early studies on the relationship of bilingualism to intelligence were conducted on immigrant children in the 1920s and 1930s (see Hakuta, 1986, for a review of these studies). The definition employed in these studies was typically sociolinguistic, identifying children with foreign names who were from immigrant backgrounds as bilinguals. There were other studies published in reputable journals which compared bilingual and monolingual children in which the bilingual children were those who did not have Anglo last names, while monolingual children were those who did have Anglo last names. Yet another study "refined" this approach one step further by obtaining both the father's name and the mother's maiden name. If the father and the mother both had foreign last names, the children were considered true bilinguals. If one of the parents had an Anglo name, they were considered partial bilinguals, and so forth. These studies generally showed a negative correlation between bilingualism and IQ test scores.

On the other hand, a psycholinguistic definition has been used in more recent research on the same topic, beginning with Peal and Lambert's (1962) pathbreaking study that identified subjects on the basis of balanced language proficiency. These studies yielded very different results, showing a positive correlation between measures of intellectual performance and bilingualism. The point is that the apparent contradictions in the research in this area have to do with the varying definitions of bilingualism.

In education policy, the failure to draw a distinction between psycholinguistic and sociolinguistic definitions has also resulted in confusion. In American public schools, many LEP students are in bilingual education programs. While one might logically assume that a bilingual education program would consist of bilingual students, such is not the case. Bilingual programs generally do not contain bilingual students, in either sense of the word. In fact, if students are bilingual, meaning that they speak both languages proficiently, they would not be in bilingual education because such programs are defined in terms of low English proficiency. If students are labeled to possess a low level of English proficiency, then and only then are they qualified to be in a bilingual education program. Over the course of residence in this program the students will become bilingual, but once this occurs, they are "exited" from the program, usually a sign that they have "made it."

This dissonant situation results from the fact that the goal of bilingual education is a transitional one rather than one of maintenance. The primary argument for the use of the native language is related to psycholinguistic efficiency, i.e., that the native language serves as a foundation upon which English development can occur. Even in programs that maintain bilingualism, the primary interest is in the development of psycholinguistic bilingualism, rather than active participation in a multitude of speech communities. This general "avoidance" of issues sociolinguistic in nature is understandable in light of the highly political nature of language policy in the United States (Crawford, 1992).

Policy

Bilingual education in the United States is frequently discussed in terms of two time periods, pre–World War I and post-1968 (marked by Congressional passage of the Bilingual Education Act). Prior to World War I, bilingual education flourished in certain areas of the United States. During the eighteenth and nineteenth centuries bilingual education was especially prevalent in ethnic communities (particularly those of German heritage). The late nineteenth century and the movement for the Common School in which immigrant children were to be socialized and assimilated, however, resulted in linguistic xenophobia. Anti-immigrant sentiment was so strong, in fact, that by the early 1920s 34 states had English-only requirements in their schools (McFadden, 1983).

Thus, for a period of approximately 40 years following World War I, academic survival of linguistic minorities in the United States was largely determined by their ability to maneuver through the cruel waters of "sink or swim" programs (Malakoff & Hakuta, 1990). It would not be until the 1960s, with the advent of greater awareness for civil rights, that the predicament of non-English-speaking students would begin to receive political and legislative attention (McFadden, 1983).

The stage for bilingual education in federal policy was set primarily by two initiatives, the first of which was the Bilingual Education Act. In 1968 President Johnson signed Title VII of the Elementary and Secondary Education Act (ESEA). Title VII provided funds for staff and materials development as well as parental involvement for students with limited English skills. There was no requirement for schools to use a non-English language. From its inception, Title VII has been a clearly compensatory policy, specified for students who are both impoverished and "educationally disadvantaged because of their inability to speak English." In addition, the program is a competitive grants program, and as such, serves primarily as a symbolic statement of support by Congress, rather than a mandate.

Furthermore, despite Title VII's seminal role in highlighting the educational needs of language-minority students, its full potential as an engine to drive the development of the nation's linguistic resources has yet to be fulfilled. As noted in the Stanford Working Group's *A Blueprint for the Second Generation* (1993), federal policy is still enmeshed in a remedial philosophy that emphasizes English at the expense of the development of both academic content and the native language of the students.

Apart from Congressional action, civil rights enforcement through the courts has provided the important enforcement mechanism. In 1975, based on Title VI of the Civil Rights Act, the Supreme Court ruled in the *Lau* v. *Nichols* decision that the San Francisco school district was in violation of Title VI of the Civil Rights Act because of its failure to adequately serve the needs of its Chinese LEP (limited English-proficient) students. The Supreme Court's sole ruling on the rights of language-minority students stated that "there is no equality of treatment merely by providing students with the same facilities, textbooks, teachers, and curriculum; for students who do not understand English are effectively foreclosed from any meaningful education."

Lau, however, did not mandate bilingual education, and it failed to prescribe or even define any specific remedies. Interpretation of compliance with *Lau* was left up to the U.S. Department of Education for interpretation. During the Carter administration (1977–1981), remedies were issued that favored transitional bilingual education. However, this interpretation was not universally accepted, came under heavy attack during the Reagan administration (1981–1989), and to this day continues to be an open question (Baker & de Kanter, 1983).

Currently, the most common form of linguistic-minority education in the United States is transitional bilingual education (U. S. Department of Education). Because of a distinct tendency for English to supplant rather than supplement the native language in such programs, transitional bilingual education is usually defined as subtractive rather than additive. Subtractive bilingualism has been associated with lower levels of second language proficiency, scholastic underachievement, and psychosocial disorders, much to the detriment of the academic and psychological well-being of linguistic minorities in the country (Lambert, 1975).

As Spener (1988) explains, rapid mainstreaming of limited-English-proficient students into English-only programs often characterizes the principal goal of transitional programs. In fact, McLaughlin (1984) notes that in many transitional classrooms, "the first language is viewed as a necessary evil and is avoided to the extent that this is possible" (p. 7). This linguistic stance is perpetuated in the philosophy of transitional bilingual education, despite the fact that many knowledgeable researchers recommend native-language instruction of language-minority children. Such an assumption is supported by research demonstrating that lower levels of alienation and higher levels of English achievement are correlated with native-language use in instructional programs (Hernández-Chávez, 1984; McLaughlin, 1984; C. Snow, 1990).

As the *Stanford Working Group* reports:

> Two damaging assumptions remain implicit in Federal and State policies: (1) that language-minority students who are economically and educationally "disadvantaged" are incapable of learning to high standards, and (2) that instruction in the native language distracts these students from learning English. (1993, p. 8)

Sadly, there is an undeniable tendency among policymakers and educators to regard students' native languages and cultures as "obstacles to achievement – as academic deficits – rather than as potential strengths to build upon" (Stanford Working Group, 1993, p. 7). This "deficit" philosophy has permeated educational policy concerning linguistic minorities and jaded the reception of research favoring native-language instruction by bilingual education policymakers (Crawford, 1991; Hakuta, 1986).

Research

Contrary to the current policy direction, research informs us that the point of departure for policymakers should not be governed by deficit assumptions. If anything, research dictates an additive bilingual model, one which builds upon a student's linguistic foundation rather than replacing it with the second language. Bilingual education policy, however, has a long history of ignoring such research and continues to advocate the implementation of subtractive rather than additive programs.

Research in bilingual education can be divided into studies that emphasize program evaluation and those whose goal is the development of basic knowledge (Pease-Alvarez & Hakuta, 1992). Although these research activities can be complementary in nature, there has been a tendency in bilingual education research to focus on program effectiveness, usually defined in terms of which programs lead to the fastest development of English proficiency. This trend is particularly evident when one looks at funding patterns (see Meyer & Fienberg, 1992, p. 7).

Two of the more controversial and politically influential evaluation studies have been the "AIR" (Danoff et al., 1977) study and the Baker and de Kanter (1983) report. Both of these studies concurred in their findings that bilingual programs proved to be no more effective than alternative programs such as submersion or ESL (English as a Second Language). Comparing bilingual programs, however, is problematic in itself because of the tremendous variability which characterizes the methodologies of different bilingual programs. Furthermore, the concept of random assignment is nowhere to be found in most comparative studies (Willig, 1985). In some studies, the comparison group included students who had themselves formerly been in bilingual programs, thus biasing the results in the direction of the comparison group since students who exit from bilingual programs early tend to be the more academically gifted students.

One need not be a hardened cynic to question the political motives behind evaluation studies. Ramírez et al. (1991) conducted a study under contract from the U. S. Department of Education. It compared student performances in three different types of programs. These included two types of bilingual education programs: one early-exit program (which represents the majority of programs in this country where the goal is to exit the students as quickly as possible), and one late-exit program (which tend to be characterized by maintenance). The third type of program involved in the study was a variety of immersion in which the students received exclusively English instruction.

This study was commissioned at a time when the Department policy was interested in structured immersion programs as an alternative to bilingual education. The main problem was that immersion approaches did not exist in many sites, so a demonstration was needed to show that they could be effective. The results of the study were quite disappointing for advocates of structured immersion, for it failed to detect differences even in English acquisition between the groups. Indeed, it would be a strong piece of counterevidence for a "time-on-task" theory of second language acquisition, since the structured immersion students made no greater progress in English development, despite the fact that they were exposed to twice the amount of English as students in the bilingual programs (Cazden, 1992).

Hakuta and McLaughlin (in press) indicate that it may well be the case that these evaluation studies point to the limits of an approach – the so-called "horse-race studies" – that compares one program type with another. A National Academy of Sciences panel recently conducted a thorough review of the two major national longitudinal studies (Meyer & Fienberg, 1992). Aside from documenting the design flaws in the studies, the panel was critical of the general atheoretical orientation of the research program, essentially arguing that large studies cannot serve as theoretical prostheses. Rather, the panel recommended a model of knowledge development on a smaller scale, with targeted studies that test and refine the basic theoretical premises of bilingual education.

We contend that in politically controversial areas, basic research can serve a particularly useful function to ensure that policy remain grounded. In drawing up its recommendations for the reauthorization of the Bilingual Education Act, for example, the Stanford Working Group drew primarily on sources from basic research rather than from the generally flawed and politically charged evaluation studies.

Perhaps one of the more influential veins of basic research in bilingual education policy in the United States has been the work on the relationship between bilingualism and cognition. A substantial number of studies now supports the notion that the development of proficiency in two languages can influence cognitive development in positive rather than negative ways (see Diaz, 1983). In many respects, this literature is a product of the cognitive revolution of the 1960s, in which empiricist and associationist accounts of the development of language and mind (e.g., Skinner, 1957) were discredited in favor of approaches that recruited innate and often task-specific constraints (e.g., Chomsky, 1968).

A related concept, applied with great effectiveness to the field of bilingual education by Jim Cummins (1981), is the positive relationship between the first and second languages. This notion of *linguistic interdependence* suggests that academic skills can be developed in either language, and that knowledge and skills learned in one language transfer to the other.

Another line of research serving to highlight the positive aspects of bilingualism derives from the investigation of translation skills in young children. This skill is especially interesting because it requires high-level information processing and also has high social status. Systematic investigation of Puerto Rican and Mexican-American bilingual youngsters (Malakoff & Hakuta, 1990; Hakuta, 1990) showed virtually errorless performance on many translation tasks, despite the absence of any formal training. Furthermore, even though these students frequently engaged in code-switching behavior with other bilingual peers, they showed no signs of mixing or confusing their two languages. For example, when they ran across difficult words to translate, they stopped and asked the experimenter for the correct translation, rather than "importing" the word into the target translation. Undoubtedly, the continued reinforcement of the merits of bilingualism is an important function for basic research.

Research Directions

Recently, an electronic dialogue which specifically addressed educational research priorities was held between 700 participants and reported on in the journal *Educational Researcher* (Glass, 1993). One of the primary concerns raised in the dialogue was about the relationship between politics and education. Although it is admittedly impossible to separate education from politics, there is a definite need for educational research efforts to be "less subject to political pressure and ideology" (p. 17). Moreover, many of the participants advocated a halt to the practice of doling out federal research funding in exorbitant lump sums, and called for financial distribution of awards to cover a wider pool of investigator-initiated

projects. Furthermore, many participants argued for the inclusion of practitioners at some point in the research loop rather than relegating them to
outsider status.

Ideally, we believe that research should accept the role of fire brigade.
Research should attempt to bring a sense of objective knowledge to the
field and encourage further discourse, bringing theory and policy together. One important goal which research might take is to contribute to a
common world view regarding bilingualism and bilingual children – our
basic knowledge base about the field is still limited. Moreover, as Hakuta
and McLaughlin (in press) note, researchers must play the role of catalyst
in provoking practitioners and policymakers to expand their limited focus
on English acquisition (as in the case of Ramírez et al., 1991).

Research should further attempt to enrich the subject population from
which its samples are drawn. Conducting research with a diverse population can lead to the enrichment of basic theory. Traditional language research has studied middle-class children in monolingual settings, focusing
supposedly on the simplest, "purest" cases. The argument for this approach is that one should try to understand a process in its least contami-
nated form, i.e., monolingual acquisition, before more "complex" arrangements are addressed. That may be the case, or it may not. It is an empirical
question. To use a rough analogy from photography, black-and-white pictures are indeed "simpler" than color pictures, yet color pictures yield far
greater amounts of information. One way to gain a better understanding
of language and bilingualism may be to add different languages, different
social classes, and varying types of bilinguals (such as the Deaf) to the
picture in order to yield increasingly rich results. The more dimensions
that one adds to the research mix, in many ways, the more it might tell us
about both the invariants and variants of language. By enriching the subject base, one expands the opportunities to enrich the epistemological
underpinnings of the work.

Conclusions

When one steps back from this collage of research and policy in
bilingualism, one is struck by the continuity of the contrast between
"good" and "bad" forms of bilingualism. It appears that when under-
privileged, non-mainstream members of society are bilingual, sociolinguistic definitions of bilingualism are applied and negative connotations are invoked, such as separatist political agendas and inferior
intelligence. On the other hand, when privileged members of society be-

come bilingual, they are characterized in psycholinguistic terms and well respected for their bilingual capacities. Interestingly, when rigorous analysis of psycholinguistic proficiency is conducted among bilingual subjects who happen to be from less prestigious groups, they turn out to have many of the positive features of bilingualism that tend to be attributed to privileged groups (Hakuta & McLaughlin, in press).

There are undeniable differences which distinguish oral bilinguals and the Deaf. One of the most obvious differences at the psycholinguistic level is that sign language has no written counterpart. However, cases of bilingualism among populations whose native language does not have a literary tradition, such as the Hmong of Southeast Asia, would seem to share some potential similarities (Trueba, Jacobs, & Kirton, 1990). As another example, a large sociolinguistic difference lies in the definition of the speech community, since sign language is usually not shared between parents and offspring.

Despite such differences, oral bilinguals and the Deaf share many analogous problems. Biased studies (in the sense of how the questions are asked) have been a disservice to both groups, finding them to be cognitively inferior to monolinguals and the hearing. Both groups have had to respond to implications of a deficit philosophy that attempts to account for poor performances in a school system which ignores their intellectual talents and attempts to hold them to rigid standards of mainstream society. Interestingly, both oral bilinguals and the Deaf are often faced with a similar dilemma: integration into mainstream society or movement toward a distinct, separate identity.

The two linguistic minorities share practical dilemmas as well, such as the dire need for competent teachers who are deaf and for native speakers of minority languages to participate in bilingual education. Similarly, a lack of uniform interpretations of "total communication" for the deaf (Kannapell, 1989) and bilingual education for the hearing has plagued each group.

On a more optimistic note, an educational innovation that holds great promise for the future empowerment of *all* linguistic minorities is two-way bilingual education (also known as bilingual immersion education). In the traditional two-way bilingual program, English-dominant and non-English-dominant students are purposefully integrated *with the goal of developing bilingual skills and academic excellence for both groups* (M. A. Snow, 1986). As Crawford (1992) attests, language-minority students in two-way bilingual programs are no longer treated as language-disabled, but rather as language-empowered. As peer tutors, they enjoy a position of status rather than one of belittlement, and therefore stand to experience not only enhanced self-esteem, but improved scholastic attitudes and quite possibly academic performance as well. For example, Uyechi (1991) comments that "the explicit equal treatment of language in a two-way bilingual program is precisely the catalyst needed for disassociating deaf education from special education and associating it, instead, with bilingual education" (pp. 14–15).

It is our conviction that all sociolinguistic and psycholinguistic circumstances in which bilingualism can be found share overlapping features, and it is from this great variety that useful scientific, pedagogical, and policy knowledge can be gained. Ultimately, researchers, policymakers, and practitioners alike must not only recognize, but welcome the added richness of the dimension that bilingualism in deaf people can potentially contribute to language research and its educational applications.

References

Baker, K., & de Kanter, A. (Eds.). (1983). *Bilingual education: A reappraisal of federal policy*. Lexington, MA: Lexington Books.

Cazden, C. (1992). Language minority education in the United States: Implications of the Ramírez Report. *Educational Practice Report, 3*. Santa Cruz, CA: National Center for Research on Cultural Diversity and Second Language Learning.

Chomsky, N. (1968). *Language and mind*. New York: Hartcourt, Brace & World.

Crawford, J. (1991). *Bilingual education: History, politics, theory, and practice*. Trenton, NJ: Crane Publishing.

(1992). *Hold your tongue: Bilingualism and the politics of "English Only."* Reading, MA: Addison-Wesley.

Cummins, J. (1981). The role of primary language development in promoting educational success for language minority students. In *Schooling and language minority students: A theoretical framework* (pp. 3–49). Sacramento: California State Department of Education.

Danoff, M., Coles, G., McLaughlin, D., & Reynolds, D. (1977, 1978). *Evaluation of the impact of ESEA Title VII Spanish/English bilingual education programs* (Vols. 1–3). Palo Alto, CA: American Institutes for Research.

Diaz, R. M. (1983). Thought and two languages: The impact of bilingualism on cognitive development. *Review of Research in Education, 10*, 23–54.

Glass, G. (1993, August–September). A conversation about educational research priorities: A message to Riley. *Educational Researcher*, 17–21.

Hakuta, K. (1986). *Mirror of language: The debate on bilingualism*. New York: Basic Books.

(1990). Language and cognition in bilingual children. In A. Padilla, C. Valdez, & H. Fairchild (Eds.), *Bilingual education: Issues and strategies* (pp. 47–59). Newbury Park, CA: Sage Publications.

Hakuta, K., & McLaughlin, B. (in press). Seven tensions that define research in bilingualism and second language acquisition. In D. Berliner & R. Calfee (Eds.), *The handbook of educational psychology*. New York: Macmillan.

Hernández-Chávez, E. (1984). The inadequacy of English immersion education as an educational approach for language minority students in the United States. In *Studies on immersion education: A collection for United States educators* (pp. 144–183). Sacramento: California State Department of Education.

Kannapell, B. (1989). Student attitudes toward ASL and English. In C. Lucas (Ed.), *The sociolinguistics of the Deaf community* (pp. 191–210). San Diego: Academic Press.

Lambert, W. E. (1975). Culture and language as factors in learning and education. In A. Wolfgang (Ed.), *Education of immigrant students* (pp. 55–83). Toronto: Ontario Institute for Studies in Education.

Lau v. Nichols. 414 U.S. 563 (1974).

McFadden, B. J. (1983). Bilingual education and the law. *Journal of Law and Education, 12*, 1–27.

McLaughlin, B. (1984). *Second-language acquisition in childhood. Vol. 1: Preschool children*. Hillsdale, NJ: Lawrence Erlbaum.

Malakoff, M. E., & Hakuta, K. (1990). History of language minority education in the United States. In A. Padilla, H. Fairchild, & C. Valadez (Eds.), *Bilingual education: Issues and strategies* (pp. 27–43). Newbury Park, CA: Sage Publications.

(1991). Translation skill and metalinguistic awareness in bilinguals. In E. Bialystok (Ed.), *Language processing and language awareness in bilingual children* (pp. 141–166). Oxford: Oxford University Press.

Meyer, M., & Fienberg, S. (Eds.). (1992). *Assessing education studies: The case of bilingual education strategies*. Washington, DC: National Academy Press.

Peal, E., & Lambert, W. E. (1962). The relation of bilingualism to intelligence. *Psychological Monographs, 76* (27, Whole No. 546).

Pease-Alvarez, L., & Hakuta, K. (1992). Enriching our views of bilingualism and bilingual education. *Educational Researcher, 21*, 4–19, 24.

Ramirez, D. J., Yuen, S. D., Ramey, D. R., & Pasta, D. J. (1991). *Longitudinal study of structured-English immersion strategy, early-exit and late-exit transitional bilingual education programs for language-minority children* (Vols. 1–2). San Mateo, CA: Aguirre International.

Skinner, B. F. (1957). *Verbal behavior*. New York: Appleton-Century-Crofts.

Snow, C. (1990). Rationales for native language instruction: Evidence from research. In A. Padilla, H. Fairchild, & C. Valadez (Eds.), *Bilingual education: Issues and strategies* (pp. 60–74). Newbury Park, CA: Sage Publications.

Snow, M. A. (1986). Innovative second language education: Bilingual immersion programs. *Education Report No. 1*. Los Angeles: UCLA Center for Language Education and Research.

Spener, D. (1988). Transitional bilingual education and the socialization of immigrants. *Harvard Educational Review, 58*, 133–153.

Stanford Working Group. (1993). *Federal education programs for limited-English-proficient students: A blueprint for the second generation*. Stanford, CA: School of Education, Stanford University.

Trueba, H.T., Jacobs, L., & Kirton, E. (1990). *Cultural conflict and adaptation: The case of Hmong children in American society*. New York: Falmer Press.
Uyechi, L. (1991). *Bimodal bilingual Deaf education*. Unpublished paper, Department of Linguistics, Stanford University.
Willig, A. (1985). A meta-analysis of selected studies on the effectiveness of bilingual education. *Review of Educational Research, 55*, 269–317.

CHAPTER FOUR

Cognitive and Language Development of Bilingual Children

JOSIANE F. HAMERS

A recent trend in the research literature on deaf signers is to view them as a cultural and ethnolinguistic minority with its own specific characteristics as compared to hearing children (see, for example, Moores, 1990). For more than two decades researchers have been interested in drawing a parallel between signed and oral language; research has shown that American Sign Language (ASL) is a fully developed linguistic system (Siple, 1978; 1982), structured as a natural language although unlike English (Lidell, 1984). Signed languages have also been described as resembling pidgins (Woodward, 1973) or creoles (Fischer, 1978), sharing both sociolinguistic and grammatical features with these languages. Whereas there seems to be no difference in language processing when going from an oral-articulate mode to a visual-manual one (Grosjean, 1980), sign language is processed in different ways depending on whether it is acquired as a native or a non-native language (Mayberry & Fischer, 1989).

The scope of this chapter is not to draw a parallel between bilingual and deaf development. Rather, by reviewing extensively the present-day knowledge on bilingual development, we invite the reader to come to

Josiane F. Hamers (Ph.D., Psychology, McGill University), Professor of Psycholinguistics and Social Psychology of Language at Laval University in Quebec, Canada, conducts and publishes research on bilingual development, social psychological aspects of bilingualism and second-language acquisition, neuropsychology of bilingualism, multilingual behavior, and immigrant integration. She is an author of many books, including the well-known *Bilinguality and Bilingualism* (1983, Cambridge University Press) with Michel A. Blanc. Her address is: Department of Languages and Linguistics, Laval University, Cité Universitaire-Québec, G1K 7P4 Québec, Canada.

conclusions on how far this well-documented field can help us have a better understanding of the development of the deaf child. To what extent can a parallel be drawn between the signing deaf child and the hearing bilingual child? And to what degree does the signing deaf child have a unique developmental pattern distinct from his or her hearing bilingual counterpart?

In the first section we review the state of the art on bilingual development; then we describe the cognitive advantages linked to bilingual development. We then present three models of bilingual development; we further discuss the relevance of the sociocultural context for the development of bilinguality. Finally, we give examples of bilingual and second-language education for the Anglophone majority in Canada, for the Francophone majority in Quebec, and for ethnolinguistic minority children in North America. Although early bilingual experience influences all levels of the child's overall development, at the linguistic, neuropsychological, cognitive, and socio-affective levels, this chapter will focus on the bilingual child's cognitive development and its sociocultural correlates.

The Deaf Child: An Ethnolinguistic Minority Child?

The shift of focus from linguistic to sociolinguistic and psycholinguistic characteristics of signed languages is an important one as more attention is paid to social and developmental features of sign language acquisition. From the research on bilingual development, it appears that the social and psychological conditions in which language development occurs in the early years play a crucial role in the developmental outcome of a bilingual experience in early childhood (Hamers, 1991). Although no complete parallel can be drawn between speaking bilinguals and signing deaf children, both developments share some important features. Almost all deaf persons fit the definition of bilinguality, i.e., a psychological state of an individual who has access to more than one linguistic code as a means of social communication; the degree of access will vary along a number of dimensions which are psychological, cognitive, psycholinguistic, social psychological, social, sociological, sociolinguistic, sociocultural, and linguistic in nature (Hamers & Blanc, 1989).

Furthermore, bilingual children are more often than not members of an ethnolinguistic minority group, a social membership which has an important impact on their bilingual development. Research in bilingual children's cognitive and linguistic development has shifted from a description of their achievements to a process analysis (Bialystok, 1991). The child's linguistic development is viewed as a function of specific experiences. For the bilingual child this outcome results from the interaction between his social and cognitive experience with the two languages. The age of acquisition of bilingualism is relevant: Are both languages native for the child or is one of the languages acquired as a second language after the first language acquisition is completed? Relative social status and cognitive functions of both languages are important determinants of the bilingual child's cognitive growth (Hamers & Blanc, 1989).

What makes the bilingual deaf child's development a special case is not some obscure determinant feature of deafness which would attribute to him or her a number of unique characteristics – as Lane (1988) remarks, there is no psychology of the deaf, any more than there is a psychology unique to minority people, although there are deaf (or minority) people, deaf studies, and a deaf language – but rather the circumstances in which he or she acquires a first language. Because 92–97% of deaf children are born into normally hearing families which are not familiar with any sign language, most deaf signers learn sign language outside their home, frequently at an age beyond that at which language acquisition usually occurs (Mayberry & Fischer, 1989).

Cognitive Growth and Early Language Experience

Recent studies on bilingual development all point to the relevance of early language experience for cognitive growth. The harmonious development of the bilingual child and the potential cognitive advantages it can bring are rooted in the child's social interaction with significant others in his or her social network (Hamers & Blanc, 1989). In contrast to the additive bilingual child, who seems to develop a greater awareness of language functions (see, for example, Diaz & Klingler, 1991), it seems that the deaf child starts with severely impoverished communication at home; Moores (1982), for example, attributes the cause of the deaf child's poor cognitive development and maladjusted behavior to maladaptative responses produced first by parents and later teachers. It should be noted that not all children in contact with more than one language develop an additive form of binguality.

Although no complete parallel can be drawn between the deaf and the hearing bilingual child, identifying the specific features of bilingual experience that characterize an additive form of binguality may help to identify the important features that shape the harmonious development of the deaf child. Furthermore, because of the deaf child's unique situation of language acquisition, research results pertaining to successful second language teaching programs which lead to functional bilingualism could shed some light on our understanding of language acquisition in the deaf child.

The Early Studies on Bilingual Development

Until the early 1960s bilingual development was traditionally viewed as something to be avoided at all costs because of the presumed negative consequences for the child's overall development. Early studies on the relationship between bilinguality and cognitive development supported the idea that bilingual children suffered from academic retardation, had lower IQ scores, and were socially maladjusted as compared to their monolingual peers (Hamers & Blanc, 1989). Much of this early research was biased by a prejudice against bilingualism which was in itself blamed for the relatively lower academic achievement of bilingual children. Examples of this early research are the studies by Pintner and Keller (1922), who reported a linguistic handicap in bilingual children, and Saer (1923), who spoke of mental confusion in the bilingual's cognitive functioning. (For a critical review, see Darcy, 1953, and Peal & Lambert, 1962.)

Early models of bilingual development (e.g., Macnamara, 1966) postulated that bilingualism inevitably led to a diminished functioning in the two languages. They did not account for the fact that many bilingual children achieve a high level of competence in both languages and can even surpass their monolingual counterparts in each language. Neither did it account for the early research results stemming from bilingual children's biographies written in the first half of the century, e.g., Ronjat (1913) and Leopold (1939–1949). These observations pointed to a harmonious development of the bilingual child including cognitive advantages, such as a more abstract conception of language, sustained attention for content rather than form, and a greater capacity for dissociating the word from its referent.

A number of criticisms may be leveled at the early psychometric studies: the bilingual subjects were often not comparable with the monolingual controls in terms of socioeconomic background, education, or proficiency in the language of testing; bilingualism was often ill defined; and tests were often administered in the subjects' weaker language. These variables have been better controlled in the more recent studies.

Bilingual Development: The State of the Art

A large body of research on bilingual development and second language acquisition has been conducted in Canada. As a result of their history and demography both the province of Quebec and Canada as a whole have to manage a growing multilingual and multicultural population. It is no wonder that in this context, special attention is given to bilingual development, second-language acquisition, and innovative approaches to second-langauge teaching and bilingual education.

Cognitive Development of Bilingual Children

It is in the general framework of the research and the sociopolitical context of the 1960s that Peal and Lambert (1962) published their monograph entitled "The Relation of Bilingualism to Intelligence," now considered a landmark in research on bilingualism. Comparing English-French bilingual elementary school pupils in Montreal with their monolingual counterparts in each language, the authors found that the bilinguals scored higher on verbal and non-verbal intelligence tests. Contrary to the earlier studies, potential methodological faults were carefully attended to: Groups were matched for age, sex, and socioeconomic level; and subjects were controlled for language proficiency, bilinguals having to achieve high scores in both languages and monolinguals having to score very low in one of the languages. The bilingual group scored significantly higher than the monolingual controls for most of the measures. The authors suggested that the higher intelligence scores of the bilinguals could be attributed to greater mental flexibility and a greater facility in concept formation; they attribute this to the bilingual's ability to manipulate two symbolic systems and thus analyze underlying semantic features in greater detail.

Cognitive Advantages of Bilinguals

Since the Peal and Lambert study numerous empirical studies, both in Canada and around the world, with different language combinations, have detailed the various aspects of the cognitive advantages of the bilingual child: a greater ability in the reconstruction of perceptual situations (Balkan, 1970, with French-English bilinguals in Switzerland); superior results on tests of verbal and non-verbal intelligence and of verbal originality and divergence (Cummins & Gulutsan, 1974, with English-

Ukrainian bilinguals in western Canada); a greater sensitivity to semantic relations between words (Ianco-Worrall, 1972, with English-Afrikaans bilinguals; Cummins, 1978, with English-Irish bilinguals); higher scores on concept formation tasks (Liedtke & Nelson, 1968, with English-German bilinguals); and better performance in rule-discovery tasks (Bain, 1975, with English-French bilinguals in western Canada; Bain & Yu, 1978, with French-Alsatian bilinguals in France, German-English bilinguals in Germany, and English-French Canadian bilinguals).

Bilinguals show a greater degree of divergent thinking (Scott, 1973, with French-English bilinguals in Montreal; Carringer, 1974, with English-Spanish bilinguals) and of creative thinking (Torrance, Gowan, Wu, & Aliotti, 1970, with Chinese-English bilingual children in Singapore) and outperform monolinguals on traditional school tests (Gorrell, Bregman, McAllistair, & Lipscombe, 1982, with Spanish-English and Vietnamese-English bilinguals). They are also superior in verbal transformation and symbol substitution tasks (Ekstrand, 1981, with Swedish-Finnish bilinguals) and have a greater facility in solving non-verbal perceptual tasks, in performing grouping tasks (Ben-Zeev, 1972, 1977, with English-Hebrew bilinguals), in following complex instructions in perceptual-motor coordination (Powers & Lopez, 1985, with Spanish-English bilinguals), and in analogical reasoning tasks (Diaz & Kingler, 1991). To sum up, the cognitive advantages linked to bilingual experience seem to be mainly at the level of a higher creativity and reorganization of information.

These observations have been further confirmed by a number of studies of bilingual children who speak various combinations of Indo-European and non-Indo-European languages in Third World and in Western countries. Although creativity differences between bilinguals and monolinguals seem to be universal, some specific aspects of creativity are influenced by cultural particularities. Okoh (1980), for example, comparing the development of bilingual children in Nigeria (several African languages and English) and in Wales (Welsh-English) with matched monolinguals in both countries, found that all bilinguals scored higher for divergent thinking and verbal creativity; but on non-verbal creativity tests the Welsh bilinguals scored higher than the Nigerian bilinguals, who did not differ from the monolinguals. Cultural variations in the type of cognitive tasks on which bilinguals show an advantage have also been noted in a study comparing Spanish-English and Vietnamese-English bilinguals (Gorrell, Bregman, McAllistair, & Lipscombe, 1982).

The conclusions that bilingual children may be potentially more creative than monolinguals are further supported by experiments in India, conducted with bi- and monolingual children from the same tribal cultural background. Kond children in Orissa, bilingual in Kui (a Dravidian tribal language) and Oriya (the Indo-European state language) scored significantly higher than matched Oriya-monolingual Konds on metalinguistic ability, Raven's Progressive Matrices, and Piagetian conservation tasks (Mohanty & Babu, 1983; Pattnaik & Mohanty, 1984), and were better at detecting syntactic ambiguity (Babu, 1984). These results are interpreted as a manifestation of a higher metalinguistic ability and cognitive flexibility; thus, bilingual experience may result in the development of a greater ability to reflect on language.

When equated for cognitive functioning, bilinguals may possess better verbal abilities than monolinguals. The studies mentioned above report bilinguals as superior in a variety of verbal tasks: analytic processing of verbal input; analytical reasoning; verbal creativity; awareness of the arbitrariness of language and of the relationship between word, referent, and meaning; and perception of linguistic ambiguity. Compared to their monolingual counterparts, bilinguals achieve better in tests of first-language syntax, complex syntactic structure, and first-language composition; they are more apt at analyzing structural ambiguity and perform better on problem-solving tasks (for a review of the literature, see Hamers & Blanc, 1989). To sum up, bilingual children have greater metalinguistic competence and better-developed creative processes. The causal link between bilingual experience and cognitive development has been in recent years fairly well assessed (Tucker, 1991; Reynolds, 1991): in short, bilinguals perform better because they had a bilingual experience.

Negative Effects of Bilingual Development

Not all studies report cognitive advantages linked with bilinguality. A few still mention an intellectual handicap. For example, Tsushima and Hogan (1975) found lower scores on verbal ability tests among Japanese-English children than among monolinguals matched for non-verbal intelligence. Finnish migrant children, attending Swedish comprehensive schools, obtained scores on literacy skills in their first language (L1) and second language (L2) below the Finnish and Swedish norms (Skutnabb-Kangas & Toukomaa, 1976). In this case development of the mother tongue prior to migration was related to achievement in both languages. From these findings the authors postulated that competence in the mother tongue had to be sufficiently established before the child could successfully acquire a second language.

These more recent studies indicating negative effects cannot be faulted on the ground of methodological weakness; for this reason we must find an explanation which takes into account the negative as well as the positive consequences of early bilingual experience. In other words, we must inquire into the nature of the advantages and disadvantages linked to bilinguality.

Negative consequences of bilingual experience are often described in terms of a cognitive deficit. The notion of semilingualism has been used to describe the child who fails to reach monolingual proficiency in literacy skills in any language and seems unable to develop a linguistic potential (Skutnabb-Kangas & Toukomaa, 1976). Semilingualism is defined as a handicap which prevents the child from acquiring the linguistic skills appropriate to his original potential in any language. It does not imply failure to communicate in ordinary everyday life, since children labeled as semilingual are judged to be quite fluent; but this fluency is alleged to be superficial and to mask a deficit in the knowledge of the structure of both languages.

The notion of semilingualism as an explanatory device has, however, been criticized on the following grounds: First, the notion is ill defined; "linguistic potential" is unexplained; in addition, the deficit is only measured by comparison with standardized norms obtained through traditional psychometric tests and academic results (Brent-Palmer, 1979). From these, no conclusion can be drawn as to the existence of a linguistic/cognitive deficit; rather, there is enough counterevidence which suggests that sociocultural factors are responsible for poor normative linguistic achievement and scholastic results (Troike, 1984). Many immigrant groups who also come from a different cultural background, but who do not have to face depressed socioeconomic conditions, perform linguistically and cognitively at least as well as monolinguals. As Troike (1984) points out, if a linguistic handicap resulting from bilingual experience were responsible for poor results on linguistic tests and academic tasks, then Hispanic Americans, who are socioeconomically more deprived than White Americans from an Anglo-Celtic background but less than Black Americans, should perform worse on language tests than both of these groups. This is, however, not the case: The Hispanics perform worse than the Whites but better than the Blacks. It becomes then difficult to implicate language proficiency as an explanatory factor for poor performance. Poor performance of bilingual children seems to be confined to socioeconomically depressed minority children. In order to explain this we have to look more into the nature of the bilingual's cognitive advantages and into the sociocultural context which fosters or hinders additive bilinguality.

The Nature of the Bilingual's Cognitive Advantages

Most studies reporting the positive consequences of bilingual experience also report that bilinguals develop a higher awareness of the arbitrary nature of linguistic signs. According to Segalowitz (1977) the interiorization of two languages results in a more complex, better-equipped mental calculus enabling the child to alternate between two systems of rules; the bilingual's increased capacity for dissociating signifier from signified could thus be a manifestation of a more general cognitive ability to analyze the underlying conceptual characteristics in information processing (Genesee, 1981). For Ben-Zeev (1977) the cognitive advantages stem from mechanisms developed originally to overcome a potential interference arising from a bilingual environment; these mechanisms, generalized to other information processing tasks, will benefit the child's overall cognitive growth.

Cummins's Model

Cummins (1976, 1979, 1981) attempted to explain the contradictory positive and negative results in the following way. One has to assume, first, a developmental interdependence hypothesis and, second, a minimal threshold of linguistic competence hypothesis. The first hypothesis suggests that competence in a second language is a function of competence in the mother tongue, at least at the beginning of exposure to the second language. The threshold hypothesis implies that a first language competence threshold has to be attained in order to avoid a cognitive deficit linked to childhood bilinguality and that a second language competence threshold must be exceeded if bilinguality is to influence cognitive functioning positively.

According to Cummins the twofold threshold hypothesis explains the apparently contradictory results from the different studies. The first threshold must be reached in order to avoid an intellectual handicap as a consequence of childhood bilingual experience; if this lower threshold is not attained, a below-normal level of competence in both languages might result. Above the first threshold and below the second a handicap will be avoided. But it is only when the second threshold is exceeded that bilingual experience can have a positive effect on cognitive processing and that competence in both languages will tend toward balance. The empirical evidence in support of this construct can be summarized as follows: Fluent bilinguals outperform non-fluent bilinguals on cognitive tasks (e.g.,

Hakuta & Diaz, 1984; Diaz & Kingler, 1991). The language competence, which varies according to the children's stage of cognitive development, seems to act as an intervening variable which will determine the effect of bilingual experience on future cognitive development.

Cummins's other hypothesis, that of developmental interdependence, postulates that the level of competence in L2 is partly a function of the competence developed in L1 at the start of exposure to L2. When certain language functions are sufficiently developed in L1 it is likely that massive exposure to L2 will lead to a sound competence in L2 without detriment to competence in L1. A high level of competence in L1 is thus related to a high level of competence in L2. In support of this hypothesis, Cummins (1984) reports, for example, on the Carpinteria Spanish-language preschool program in California: Hispanic preschoolers who scored much lower on a school readiness test compared to English-speaking peers were exposed to a variety of language-enriching experiences in their mother tongue; at elementary school entry these children outperformed Spanish monolingual controls in both English and Spanish and compared favorably with English controls on readiness skills.

Although Cummins did not develop the idea that the interdependence is bidirectional, there is empirical support in favor of this from a study of Swedish children learning English in Sweden (Holmstrand, 1979): Elementary school children who already had a high competence in their mother tongue, and who started to learn a foreign language at an early age, improved their competence in their mother tongue more than peers who did not have exposure to a foreign language. This then suggests that the interdependence hypothesis works in both directions and that language training in one language might be helpful for attaining a higher level of competence in the other language.

Cummins suggests that cognitive academic proficiency can be conceptualized along two independent continua: The first relates to the degree of contextual support available for expressing and receiving meaning (from context-embedded to context-reduced); the second refers to the degree of cognitive involvement in the verbal activity (from cognitively undemanding to cognitively demanding). Thus, a verbal task may be cognitively demanding or not and, at the same time, be more or less context-embedded. Linguistic demands of the school rely on context-reduced and cognitively demanding language behavior. Most of the studies reporting negative consequences of early bilingual experience are concerned with measures of context-reduced and cognitively demanding behavior of children who may not have developed the necessary underlying proficiency.

Bilingual Development, Literacy, and Metalinguistic Awareness

Instruction that develops first-language literacy skills is not developing only these skills, it is also developing a deeper conceptual and linguistic competence that is strongly related to the development of general literacy and academic skills. In other words, there is a common cognitive proficiency underlying behavior in both languages. The interdependence or common underlying proficiency principle implies therefore that experience with either language can promote development of language-cognitive skills, given proper motivation and exposure to both languages.

When bilingual development does not result in cognitive advantages, it is always in cases where the children did not possess the skills prerequisite for literacy. It might well be that here we are dealing with a literacy or a metalinguistic problem, not a linguistic competence threshold: Metalinguistic awareness is different from ordinary linguistic communication in the sense that it calls on different cognitive skills, and bilingual children differ from monolingual children on literacy and metalinguistic tasks (Bialystok & Ryan, 1985).

Cummins's model is relevant insofar as it attempts to explain apparently contradictory evidence; it is also useful in providing a model for bilingual education, specifically in the case of ethnolinguistic minority children. Applied to the case of the deaf children it might give some useful insight in the elaboration of bilingual (signed-spoken language) programs. However, some specific problems arise in this case and some important questions have to be answered before borrowing a model from bilingual education. How does one cope with the problem of developing literacy skills in the deaf child's first language? To what extent have deaf children developed conceptual skills and metalinguistic awareness? Can we speak of the deaf child's linguistic development in terms of a first and a second language?

The Sociocultural Context of Bilinguality: Lambert's Model

Lambert (1974, 1977) was the first to suggest that the roots of bilinguality are to be found in the social psychological mechanisms involved in language behavior, particularly in the perception of the relative status of both languages. He drew attention to the fact that different types of bilinguality may result according to the sociocultural context in which bilingual experience occurs. He distinguishes between an additive and a subtractive form of bilinguality. In its additive form bilingual development is such that both languages and cultures will bring complementary positive elements to the child's overall development; this situation is found when both the community and the family attribute positive values to the two languages; the learning of an L2 will in no case threaten to replace L1.

Subtractive bilinguality, on the other hand, develops when the two languages are competing rather than complementary; this form evolves when an ethnolinguistic minority rejects its own cultural values in favor of those of an economically and culturally more prestigious group. In this case, the more prestigious L2 will tend to replace L1 in the child's repertoire. This happens when a minority child is schooled through an L2 that is socially more prestigious than his own mother tongue. The degree of bilinguality will reflect some stage in the subtraction of the ethnic language and the associated culture, and their replacement with another (Lambert, 1977, p.19). This subtraction will manifest itself at several levels and will influence intellectual development and personality; language competence which first developed via the mother tongue will be affected.

Lambert's views explain why a cognitive advantage linked to bilingual experience is found primarily either among bilingual children from mixed-lingual families or among children from a dominant social group who receive their schooling through the medium of a less prestigious L2; while the subtractive form is met among children from ethnolinguistic minorities schooled through a dominant, more prestigious L2. In the additive case, the two languages receive important positive values from the community and consequently from the child himself, whereas in the subtractive condition L1 is little valorized compared to L2. Lambert's model insists on the role played by the sociocultural environment in the development of bilinguality. This is in accordance with more general views of child development. It is therefore crucial to focus on the sociocultural environment in which bilingual development occurs and to understand its role in the development of bilinguality.

By pointing out the relevance of the sociocultural environment Lambert stresses the role played by social psychological mechanisms in bilingual development, particularly those involved in the internalization of societal values. Lambert also introduces the notion of an interdependence hypothesis, but at the level of the internalization of social/cultural values: It is the relative status between the two languages and its internalization that will determine the nature of bilinguality.

The Sociocultural Interdependence Hypothesis

The sociocultural interdependence hypothesis is supported by empirical evidence: Several studies (e.g., Long & Padilla, 1970; Bhatnagar, 1980) demonstrate that pupils obtain better academic results when their low-status L1 is valorized and fully used than when L1 is neglected in the home; school results and language proficiency in both languages improve also when the mother tongue is valorized and used in the school system (Dubé & Hébert, 1975). There is also ample evidence, stemming from research on immersion programs, that when a child is a member of a dominant ethnolinguistic group, schooling through the medium of L2 may be a way to develop high bilinguistic skills, possibly with positive cognitive effects.

Lambert's approach has the merit of drawing attention to the social roots of bilingual outcome and to the fact that the equations bilinguality = cognitive advantage and bilinguality = cognitive deficit are both possible. Under the right conditions bilingual experience may have positive effects on cognitive processes; under adverse sociocultural conditions bilingual experience may hinder cognitive growth. With regard to the deaf child this approach points to the necessity to evaluate the sociocultural environment in which the bilingual deaf child evolves and the relative status of both languages (signed versus spoken).

The Social-Cognitive Interaction Model

We still know very little about the intervening sociopsychological mechanisms between sociocultural environment and intellectual functioning. Lambert's model draws attention to the existence of a relationship; it does not, however, explain how this relationship evolves.

In a first model (Hamers & Blanc, 1982, 1987) we suggested that the child becomes cognizant of the social reality, including language, through interactions with significant others in his social network. The process of socialization, the formal and functional models of language use in the social network, and the values attributed to the languages and language behavior, all play an important role in the representation the child will have of language. Language use and socio-affective values of the child's microsocial world will determine the type of bilinguality the child will develop. We assume that there is a constant interaction between network characteristics, language use, language valorization in the network, and the type of bilingual development. This approach receives some support from our most recent research on the role of social network in bilingual development. For example, immigrant children in Quebec become more balanced bi- or trilinguals when the family network not only maintains the heritage language, but does so for literacy-oriented tasks; the quality of the relation with the primary socializers also plays an important role (Hamers, 1992, 1994).

To summarize our approach (see Hamers, 1988), we suggested that, in order for a child to benefit from an early bilingual experience: (1) The two languages have to be used and valorized by relevant others in the child's social network; (2) the functions that language serves have to be fully developed, regardless of the language or languages used; and (3) the child must develop a positive social representation of the language functions in general and of both his languages.

The identification of all the conditions that are favorable to an additive form of bilinguality is still a long way off. If it seems that these conditions are dependent on the relative status of each language in the child's environment, to what extent is the child's perception of these social factors more important than those very factors? We have, for example, some evidence from Africa that in the development of bilinguality, the child's social perception of both languages plays a more important role than the social reality (Da Silveira & Hamers, 1990).

More recently (Hamers & Blanc, 1989) we suggested that additive bilinguality is attained, provided that the child's social network permits the development of both a high degree of cognitive functioning of language (defined in terms of control and analysis leading to metalinguistic awareness, as proposed by Bialystok & Ryan, 1985) and a high degree of valorization of both languages, whereas for a subtractive form to develop there must be a combination of a low cognitive functioning with a low degree of valorization of language in general and of the child's L1. Therefore, the crucial question might be how to create additive conditions when they do not exist.

This question can be extended to the situation of the deaf child. One major difficulty stems from the fact that the deaf child's L1 is often ill defined. The vast majority of deaf children (Mayberry & Fischer, 1989) are born into hearing families, totally unfamiliar with sign language; in the best of the cases one of his parents will learn ASL as a second language, while the child acquires it as L1. In the latter case the child's functional and formal model of ASL will be that of a more or less fluent L2 signer. In contrast to the hearing child, the deaf child often acquires sign language outside the home, at an age at which he or she is already language-deprived compared to his or her hearing peers. The deaf child is often in a unique situation where his mother tongue will be taught as a second language. Are these conditions sufficient to develop a high degree of cognitive functioning? Furthermore, to what extent is the ASL valorized around the child, as compared to the spoken language?

One crucial question asked in the case of bilingual minority children is: To what extent can an additive form of bilinguality develop in a subtractive context? In other words, how determining is the sociocultural context for the outcome of bilinguality and how well can the individual develop strategies and social psychological mechanisms that can modify the influence of the social context?

Evidence stemming from research with Francophone minority children in New Brunswick and in western Canada (Landry & Allard, 1990) points to the important role the school can play in a subtractive environment, by giving a maximum support to the minority language. If, in addition to favorable school attitudes, cultural beliefs in the child's network are positively oriented toward the minority language, additive bilinguality can develop in a subtractive context (Landry & Allard, 1990). Landry & Allard (1988) insist also on the fact that the additive-subtractive distinction is more relevant to socio-affective than to cognitive development. A high level of additivity includes a high level of competence in both the communicative and cognitive uses of both languages.

All the environmental factors that enable the child to reach the competence necessary for developing additive bilinguality have yet to be identified. We still lack adequate theoretical models to account for individual and social factors and explain their causal relationship. One important set of empirical data which can shed some further light on bilingual development is provided by research in bilingual education and second-language acquisition.

Bilingual Education and Second-Language Acquisition in Canada

When we speak of bilingual education it must be understood that we refer to any system of school education in which, at a given moment and for a varying amount of time, instruction is planned and given in at least two languages (Hamers & Blanc, 1989). It differs from submersion, in which the child is given instruction in a non-maternal language and no provision is made for the L1, and from the core programs in which an L2 is taught as a subject matter for a limited number of hours. Most bilingual programs fit into one of three categories: (1) instruction is given in both languages simultaneously; (2) instruction is given first in L1; the pupil is taught until able to use L2 as a means of learning; and (3) the largest part of instruction is given through L2; L1 is introduced at a later stage, first as a subject, later as a means of instruction. According to its goal, bilingual education can be divided into (1) compensatory programs in which the child is first schooled through his or her mother tongue in order to be better integrated in the mainstream; (2) enrichment programs normally developed for the majority children, which aim at developing an additive form of bilinguality; and (3) group maintenance programs in which the language and culture of the minority child are preserved.

The Canadian Immersion Programs

Immersion is very different from traditional L2 approaches; it simply means that a group of L1 children receive all or part of their schooling through the medium of L2. It is based on two premises: (1) that an L2 is learned in the same way as an L1 and (2) that a language is best learned in a stimulating context which enhances the language functions and exposes the child to the natural forms of a language (Hamers & Blanc, 1989). An immersion program involves a switch of languages between home and school and is designed for a child from the dominant group. These programs were first developed for Anglophone children in Quebec (a minority in the province but part of the Canadian majority); in the 1960s, the Anglophones, anticipating the sociopolitical evolution of the province and acknowledging the necessity for their children to master French as a working language, were displeased with the poor results obtained with core programs and demanded a more efficient approach to the mastering of French (Lambert & Tucker, 1972).

The original St. Lambert project, which originated in Montreal, served as a model for all later immersion programs: the Anglophone child is introduced to schooling exclusively through French; English is introduced during the third year, first as a subject matter and gradually as a means of instruction; by the end of the elementary school, both languages are used on a fifty-fifty basis. Besides this early immersion, variations have been developed such as late, total, and partial immersion. Large-scale evaluations have been conducted on immersion programs (for a review see Hamers & Blanc, 1989; Genesee, 1991).

The main results of immersion programs can be summarized as follows: When compared to pupils in regular English schools, immersion pupils show no signs of deficits in mother tongue development; achievement in English is not related to the amount of exposure they had to English; the overall academic achievement is comparable; and they develop a functional command of French that surpasses results obtained with all other forms of second-language teaching. They do not, however, reach native-like production skills in French, unless they come into contact with native speakers. Teaching methods might be partly responsible for the lack of expressive abilities. Apparently, immersion children lack the necessary social motivation to develop nativelike competence (Hamers & Blanc, 1989). Lambert (1991) argues that some pupils do not progress beyond a functional mastery of French because closer identification could be threatening to their own cultural identity.

Although immersion programs do not in most cases lead to balanced bilinguality, they have proven beyond doubt that children can learn in a bilingual context without any loss in their academic achievement. However, immersion appears mainly as an ideal solution for the ethnolinguistic majority child whose culture and first language are valorized in the community and who has already reached a high level of analyzed language by the time she or he goes to school. This description does not fit the deaf child who lacks both a highly valorized first language and a high level of analyzed language. We therefore now turn to the education of minority children.

Second-Language Approaches for the Francophones in Canada

French is very much a minority language on the North American continent. In the coercive legal context of Quebec it maintains itself, but it loses ground everywhere else in the country (Hamers & Hummel, 1994). Outside Quebec the Francophone minorities generally apply group maintenance programs; English, usually already mastered by the Francophone child before she or he starts school, will be taught in French schools as a core program. To develop these children as bilinguals, intensive mother tongue teaching is seen as more important than L2 teaching: For example, Franco-Manitoban children who had a bilingual program of 20% English and 80% French, were as good in English but much better in French skills than their counterparts who had 80% English and 20% French (Hébert, 1976). These results are in line with findings in other countries (e.g., the Motet Program in the United Kingdom, Fitzpatrick, 1987; the Carpinteria program in the United States; see Hamers & Blanc, 1989, for a review). The educational problems encountered by the Francophone minorities outside Quebec do not differ from those encountered by other ethnolinguistic minorities.

However, Quebec Francophones, especially those in the unilingual regions of the province, and Quebec immigrants also have strong claims for efficient ESL teaching. Immersion is ruled out for them because of the danger of assimilation to the Anglophones and because immigrants are required by law to attend the French schools. One approach, which, when combined with ESL core programs, has given positive results in raising children to a higher level of bilingual competence, is that of exchange programs. Although there is a tremendous variety in these programs, the main idea is that Francophone and Anglophone children should spend some time together (which can vary from several months in each other's home and school to short meetings between two classes) using each other's language for different purposes. Evaluation of these exchange programs shows that when the programs meet certain criteria and when both languages are used and considered on an egalitarian basis, the children's attitudes toward the L2 and their bilingual skills greatly improve. Here again, a situation was created where languages respond to a social or cognitive need; again, both languages are equally valorized around and with the child.

Whereas this seemed a solution easy to apply in the Quebec context, it might appear as rather utopian in the case of the deaf child: It would mean that some hearing children would have to be willing to become bilingual in signed and spoken languages and that both deaf and hearing children would evolve in a school environment where both languages were used on an egalitarian basis and were equally valorized. The applicability of such a solution has to be considered.

Bilingual Education for Minority Children

When discussing bilingual education for minority children, two important contextual aspects must be kept in mind: (1) They come from little-valorized mother tongue backgrounds and (2) because they often belong to socially deprived communities their literacy-oriented skills are generally less well developed.

In the past twenty years Canadian and Quebec schools have undergone a massive reorientation with regard to minority children. Multicultural educational policies have been developed in order to realize the potential of children who are not from an English or French background. Although the primary concern still is to improve the teaching of the official language, greater attention has been paid to all adjustment problems of the immigrant child (Cummins, 1984). As the research results on bilingual education indicate the importance of L1 maintenance for the minority child, two major programs have been established: (1) the Heritage Language Program in Ontario and (2) the Programme d'Enseignement des Langues d'Origine in Quebec. At first, heritage languages were taught outside regular school hours, but the general trend is to include the heritage language as a subject in the school curriculum.

There are also several programs in which the heritage language is used as a medium of instruction. These programs either are transitional programs (e.g., the Italian program in Toronto; see Shapson & D'Orey, 1984) or aim at linguistic enrichment (e.g., the French-English Hebrew trilingual program – Genesee, Tucker, & Lambert, 1978; or the Ukrainian immersion in Alberta – Cummins, 1984). Enrichment programs, in contrast to compensatory programs, aim at the personal, emotional, and cognitive benefits of becoming fluently bilingual and of participating in two cultures; they include immersion programs for the majority and maintenance programs for the minority child.

Conclusions

The study of bilingual development has evolved dramatically in the last 30 years. From the conception that the bilingual is someone whose speech shows interferences, who is at worst cognitively deficient and at best the sum of two monolinguals, we have moved to the conception of an integrated person, as Grosjean (1985) puts it: a unique and specific speaker-hearer, a communicator of a different sort for whom bilingual experience enhances cognitive functioning. We have both better theoretical constructs and a larger empirical data bank on bilingual development. Goodz (1989), for example, has defined the kind of linguistic behavior in the mixed family that will make a child a perfectly balanced bilingual even before entering school. This type of research might help in building guidelines for defining the deaf child's mother tongue.

We are also more aware of the nature of the cognitive advantages of bilinguality. Why is it then that all children cannot benefit from bilingual experience? Research on bilingual education demonstrates that bilingual programs viewed as enrichment programs create the necessary conditions for additive bilinguality. For the child to benefit from a bilingual experience both languages must be valorized around him. How this is done must be assessed by those who plan language education. Does education aim at functional bilinguality in the majority child, assimilation of the minority child into the mainstream culture, integration of the minority child – including the deaf child – in a pluralistic society, or bilinguality for all children? When the child's home language is the dominant language in the society and when it is valorized by the family environment in terms of literacy skills, as well, an immersion program is a solution for reaching functional bilinguality; if the immersion program is planned at an early age, the child can develop an additive form of bilinguality in addition to becoming functionally bilingual.

The picture is different for the minority child. There are many indications that the minority child benefits from being introduced to literacy in his or her mother tongue; but this is too often ignored or impossible. Too many educators still believe in the myth of the bilingual handicap and are convinced that the earlier the child is introduced to a prestigious L2 the better he or she will develop academically. Bilingual education programs and mother tongue teaching in the early school years have been shown to benefit the minority child and improve academic achievement. Time spent on L1 does not slow down proficiency in L2; but it increases the language skills in the mother tongue. However, the linguistic mismatch hypothesis advocated by the UNESCO (1953) declaration that advocates the right of all children to L1 education is an oversimplification. That a child can develop an additive form of bilingualism while literacy is taught via an L2 has been proven by the results of immersion.

One of the major differences between bilingual programs for majority and minority children lies in their final goals: functional bilinguality versus mainstream assimilation. When functional bilinguality is promoted in the minority child, as when the family and the social environment valorize the mother tongue sufficiently to maintain it, academic achievement is improved. Functional and additive bilinguality can be attained for all children provided that both languages are highly valorized and used for all functions with and around the child. If the deaf child can to a certain extent be compared with his ethnolinguistic minority counterpart, at least as far as the low status of the L1 is concerned, how can an environment be created in which both the signed and the spoken language are equally and highly valorized?

The social context in which the deaf child acquires language differs greatly from that of the hearing child, even if a certain number of parallels can be drawn; one major difficulty stems from the definition of the deaf child's mother tongue. If mother tongue and home language play such an important role in the development of additive bilinguality, how do we create additive conditions for the hearing-impaired child who is severely impoverished in early communication from birth onward? What relevant information the deaf community can draw from the field of research in bilingualism is, however, for themselves to evaluate.

References

Babu, N. (1984). Perception of syntactic ambiguity by bilingual and unilingual tribal children. *Psycho-Lingua, 14,* 47–54.

Bain, B. (1975). Toward an integration of Piaget and Vygotsky: Bilingual considerations. *Linguistics, 16,* 5–20.

Bain, B., & Yu, A. (1978). Toward an integration of Piaget and Vygotsky: A cross-cultural replication (France, Germany, Canada) concerning cognitive consequences of bilinguality. In M. Paradis (Ed.), *Aspects of Bilingualism.* Columbia, SC: Hornbeam Press.

Balkan, L. (1970). *Les effets du bilinguisme français-anglais sur les aptitudes intellectuelles.* Brussels: AIMAV.

Ben-Zeev, S. (1972). *The influence of bilingualism on cognitive development and cognitive strategy.* Unpublished Ph.D. dissertation, University of Chicago.

(1977). Mechanism by which childhood bilingualism affects understanding of language and cognitive structures. In P.A. Hornby (Ed.), *Bilingualism: Psychological, social and educational implications* (pp. 29–55). New York: Academic Press.

Bhatnagar, J. (1980). Linguistic behavior and adjustment of immigrant children in French and English schools in Montreal. *International Journal of Applied Psychology, 29,* 141–158.

Bialystok, E. (1991). Introduction. In E. Bialystok (Ed.), *Language processing in bilingual children* (pp. 1–9). Cambridge: Cambridge University Press.

Bialystok, E., & Ryan, E. B. (1985). A metacognitive framework for the development of first and second language skills. In D. L. Forrest-Pressley, G. E. MacKinnon, & T. G. Waller (Eds.), *Metacognition, cognition and human performance* (Vol. 1, pp. 207–252). New York: Academic Press.

Brent-Palmer, C. (1979). A sociolinguistic assessment of the notion "immigrant semilingualism" from a social conflict perspective. *Working Papers on Bilingualism, 17,* 135–180.

Carpinteria Unified School District. (1982). *Title VII evaluation report 1981–1982.* Carpinteria, CA: Unpublished Report.

Carringer, D. C. (1974). Creative thinking abilities of Mexican youth: The relationship of bilingualism. *Journal of Cross-Cultural Psychology, 5,* 492–504.

Cummins, J. (1976). The influence of bilingualism on cognitive growth: A synthesis of research findings and explanatory hypotheses. *Working Papers on Bilingualism, 9,* 1–43.

(1978). Bilingualism and the development of metalinguistic awareness. *Journal of Cross-Cultural Psychology, 9,* 139–149.

(1979) Linguistic interdependence and the educational development of bilingual children. *Review of Educational Research, 49*, 222–251.

(1981). The role of primary language development in promoting educational success for language minority students. In *California State Department of Education. Schooling and Language Minority Students: A Theoretical Framework*. Los Angeles: Evaluation, Assessment and Dissemination Center.

(1984). *Bilingualism and special education: Issues in assessment and pedagogy*. Clevedon, England: Multilingual Matters 6.

Cummins, J., & Gulutsan, M. (1974). Some effects of bilingualism on cognitive functioning. In S.T. Carey (Ed.), *Bilingualism, Biculturalism and Education* (pp. 129–136). Edmonton: University of Alberta Press.

Darcy, N. T. (1953). A review of the literature on the effects of bilingualism upon the measurement of intelligence. *Journal of Genetic Pyschology, 82*, 21–57.

Da Silveira, Y. I. & Hamers, J. F. (1990). Scolarisation et bilingualité en Afrique: un défi? *Langage et Société, 52*, 23–58.

Diaz, R. M., & Kingler, C. (1991). Towards an explanatory model of the interaction between bilingualism and cognitive development. In E. Bialystok (Ed.), *Language processing in bilingual children* (pp. 167–192). Cambridge: Cambridge University Press.

Dodson, K. (1981). A reappraisal of bilingual development and education. In H. Baetens Beardsmore (Ed.), *Elements of bilingual theory* (pp. 14–27). Brussels: Vrije Universiteit te Brussel.

Dubé, N. C., & Hébert, G. (1975). *Evaluation of the St John Valley Title VII Bilingual Education program, 1970–1975*. Unpublished report. Madawaska, ME.

Ekstrand, L. H. (1981). Theories and facts about early bilingualism in native and migrant children. *Grazer Linguistische Studien, 14*, 24–52.

Fischer, S. D. (1978). Sign Language and creoles. In P. Siple (Ed.), *Understanding language through sign language research* (pp. 309–331). New York: Academic Press.

Fitzpatrick, F. (1987). *The open door*. Clevedon, England: Multilingual Matters.

Genesee, F. (1981). Cognitive and social consequences of bilingualism. In R. C. Gardner & R. Kalin (Eds.), *A Canadian social psychology of ethnic relations*. London: Methuen.

(1991). Second language learning in school settings: Lessons from immersion. In A. G. Reynolds (Ed.), *Bilingualism, multiculturalism, and second language learning: The McGill conference in honour of Wallace E. Lambert* (pp. 183–202). Hillsdale, NJ: Lawrence Erlbaum.

Genesee, F., Tucker, G. R., & Lambert, W. E. (1989). The development of ethnic identity and ethnic role taking skills in children from different school settings. *International Journal of Psychology, 13*, 39–57.

Goodz, N. (1989). Parental language mixing to children in bilingual families. *Infant Mental Health Journal, 10*, (1) 25–40.

Gorrell, J. J., Bregman, N. J., McAllistair, H. A., & Lipscombe, T. J. (1982). A comparison of spatial role-taking in monolingual and bilingual children. *Journal of Genetic Psychology, 140*, 3–10.

Grosjean, F. (1980). Psycholinguistics of sign language. In H. Lane & F. Grosjean

(Eds.), *Recent perspectives on American Sign Language* (pp. 33–54). Hillsdale, NJ: Lawrence Erlbaum.

(1985). The bilingual as a competent but specific speaker-hearer. *The Journal of Multilingual and Multicultural Development, 6,* 467–477.

Hakuta, K., & Diaz, R. (1984). The relationship between bilingualism and cognitive ability: A critical discussion and some new longitudinal data. In K.E. Nelson (Ed.), *Children's Language* (Vol. 5, pp. 319–344). Hillsdale, NJ: Lawrence Erlbaum.

Hamers, J. F. (1987). The relevance of social network analysis in the psycholinguistic investigation of multilingual behavior. In M. Blanc & J. F. Hamers (Eds.), *Theoretical and methodological issues in the study of languages/dialects in contact at the macro and micro-logical levels of analysis.* Quebec: International Center for Research on Bilingualism.

(1988). Un modèle socio-psychologique du développement bilingue. *Langage et Société, 43,* 91–102.

(1991). L'ontogénèse de la bilingualité: Dimensions sociales et trans-culturelles. In A.G. Reynolds (Ed.), *Bilingualism, multiculturalism and second language learning: The McGill conference in honour of Wallace E. Lambert* (pp. 127–144). Hillsdale, NJ: Lawrence Erlbaum.

(1992). Réseaux sociaux, attitudes parentales et développement multilingue. *Revue de linguistique et de didactique des langues, 6,* 69–92. Grenoble: Université Stendhal.

(1994). Développement bilingue, usage langagier, réseaux sociaux, valorisation et croyances langage. In J. Blomart and B. Krewer (Eds.), *Perspectives de l'interrculturel* (pp. 285–312). Paris: Editions de l'Harmattan.

Hamers, J. F., & Blanc, M. (1982). Towards a social-psychological model of bilingual development. *Journal of Language and Social Psychology, 1,* 29–49.

(1983). Bilingualité et Bilinguisme. *Série Psychologie et Sciences Humaines, 129.* Brussels: Mardaga.

(1987, July). *Social psychological foundations of bilingual development.* Paper presented at the Third International Conference on the Social Psychology of Language, Bristol, England.

(1989). *Bilinguality and Bilingualism.* Cambridge: Cambridge University Press.

Hamers, J. F., & Hummel, K. (1994). The Francophones of Quebec: Demolinguistic realities, language policies and language use. In R. Bourhis (Ed.), *International Journal of the Sociology of Language. Special issue on Canada, 6,* 127–152.

Harley, B., & Swain, M. (1977). An analysis of verb form and function in the speech of French immersion pupils. *Working Papers on Bilingualism, 14,* 31–46.

(1978). An analysis of verb system used by young learners of French. *Interlanguage Studies Bulletin, 3,* 35–79.

Hébert, R. (1976). *Rendement académique et langue d'enseignement chez les élèves Franco-Manitobains.* Saint-Boniface, Manitoba: Centre de Recherches du Collège universitaire Saint-Boniface.

Holmstrand, L. E. (1979). The effect of general school achievement of early commencement of English instruction. *Uppsala Reports on Education, 4,* 1–15. Uppsala: University of Uppsala Department of Education.

Ianco-Worrall, A. D. (1972). Bilingualism and cognitive development. *Child Development, 43,* 1390–1400.

Lambert, W. E. (1974). Culture and language as factors in learning and education. In F. E. Aboud, & R. D. Meade (Eds.), *Cultural factors in learning* (pp. 214–229). Bellingham: Western Washington State College.

(1977). Effects of bilingualism on the individual. In P. A. Hornby (Ed.), *Bilingualism: Psychological, social and educational implications* (pp 15–27). New York: Academic Press.

(1987, November). Persistent issues in bilingualism. Paper presented at the Symposium on the Development of Bilingual Proficiency. Toronto: OISE.

(1991). "And then add your two cents' worth." In A. G. Reynolds (Ed.), *Bilingualism, multiculturalism and second language learning: The McGill conference in honour of Wallace E. Lambert* (pp. 217–249). Hillsdale, NJ: Lawrence Erlbaum.

Lambert, W. E., & Tucker, G. R. (1972). *Bilingual education of children: The St. Lambert experiment.* Rowley, MA: Newbury House.

Landry, R., & Allard, R. (1988, August–September). *Ethnolinguistic vitality beliefs and language maintenance and loss.* Paper presented at the International Conference on Maintenance and Loss of Ethnic Minority Languages. Noordwijkerhout, The Netherlands.

(1990). Contact des langues et développement bilingue: un modèle macroscopique. *Revue canadienne des langues vivantes, 46,* 527–553.

Lane, H. (1988). Is there a psychology of the deaf? *Exceptional Children,* (55)1, 7–19.

Leopold, W. F. (1939–1949). *Speech development of a bilingual child.* (Vols. 1–4). Evanston, IL: Northwestern University Press.

Lidell, S. (1984). THINK and BELIEVE: Sequentiality in American Sign Language. *Language, 60,* 372–399.

Liedtke, W. W., & Nelson, L. D. (1968). Concept formation and bilingualism. *Alberta Journal of Education Research, 14,* 225–232.

Long, K. K., & Padilla, A. M. (1970). *Evidence for bilingual antecedents of academic success in a group of Spanish-American college students.* Unpublished Research Report. Bellingham: Western Washington State College.

Macnamara, J. (1966). *Bilingualism and primary education.* Edinburgh: Edinburgh University Press.

Mayberry, R. I. & Fischer, S. D. (1989). Looking through phonological shape to lexical meaning: The bottleneck of non-native sign language processing. *Memory and Cognition, 17* (6), 740–754.

Mohanty, A. K., & Babu, N. (1983). Bilingualism and metalinguistic ability among Kond tribals in Orissa, India. *Journal of Social Psychology, 121,* 15–22.

Moores, D. (1982). *Educating the deaf: Psychology, principles, practices.* Boston: Houghton Mifflin.

(1990). Cultural pluralism, cultural particularism, and deafness. *American Annals of the Deaf, 135* (5), 341.

Okoh, N. (1980). Bilingualism and divergent thinking among Nigerian and Welsh school-children. *Journal of Social Psychology, 110,* 163–170.

Pattnaik, K., & Mohanty, A. K. (1984). Relationship between metalinguistics and cognitive development of bilingual and unilingual tribal children. *Psycho-Lingua, 14,* 63–70.

Peal, E., & Lambert, W. E. (1962). The relation of bilingualism to intelligence. *Psychological Monographs, 76*, 1–23.

Pintner, R., & Keller, R. (1922). Intelligence tests for foreign children. *Journal of Educational Psychology, 13*, 214–222.

Powers, S., & Lopez, R. L. (1985). Perceptual, motor and verbal skills of monolingual and bilingual Hispanic children: A discriminant analysis. *Perceptual and Motor Skills, 60*, 999–1002.

Reynolds, A. G. (1991). The cognitive consequences of bilingualism. In A. G. Reynolds (Ed.), *Bilingualism, multiculturalism, and second language learning: The McGill conference in honour of Wallace E. Lambert* (pp. 145–182). Hillsdale, NJ: Lawrence Erlbaum.

Ronjat, J. (1913). *Le développement du langage observé chez un enfant bilingue.* Paris: Champion.

Saer, O. J. (1923). The effects of bilingualism on intelligence. *British Journal of Psychology, 14*, 25–28.

Scott, S. (1973). *The relation of divergent thinking to bilingualism.* Unpublished research report. Montreal: McGill University.

Segalowitz, N. (1977). Psychological perspectives on bilingual education. In B. Spolsky & R. Cooper (Eds.), *Frontiers of bilingual education* (pp. 119–158). Rowley, MA: Newbury House.

Shapson, S., & D'Oley, V. (Eds.). (1984). *Bilingual and multicultural education: Canadian perspectives.* Clevedon, England: Multilingual Matters, 15.

Siple, P. (Ed.). (1978). *Understanding language through sign language research.* New York: Academic Press.

(1982). Sign language and linguistic theory. In L. Obler & L. Menn (Eds.), *Exceptional language and linguistics.* (pp. 313–338). New York: Academic Press.

Skutnabb-Kangas, T., & Toukomaa, P. (1976). *Teaching migrant children's mother tongue and learning the language of the host country in the context of the sociocultural situation of the migrant family.* Tampere: UNESCO Report, University of Tampere, Research Reports, 15.

Torrance, A. P., Gowan, J. C., Wu, J. M., & Aliotti, N. C. (1970). Creative functioning of monolingual and bilingual children in Singapore. *Journal of Educational Psychology, 61*, 72–75.

Troike, R. C. (1984). SCALP: Social and cultural aspects of language proficiency. In C. Rivera (Ed.), *Language Proficiency and Academic Assessment* (pp. 44–54). Clevedon, England: Multilingual Matters, 10.

Tsushima, W. T., & Hogan, T. P. (1975). Verbal ability and school achievement of bilingual and monolingual children of different ages. *Journal of Educational Research, 68*, 349–353.

Tucker, G. R. (1991). Developing a language-competent American society: The role of language planning. In A.G. Reynolds (Ed.), *Bilingualism, multiculturalism, and second language learning: The McGill Conference in honour of Wallace E. Lambert* (pp. 65–80). Hillsdale, NJ: Lawrence Erlbaum.

UNESCO (1953). *The use of vernacular languages in education.* Paris: UNESCO.

Woodward, J. (1973). Some characteristics of pidgin sign English. *Sign Language Studies, 3*, 39–46.

PART II

Psychosocial, Cognitive, and Language Experiences of Deaf People

CHAPTER FIVE

From the Cultural to the Bicultural: The Modern Deaf Community

CAROL A. PADDEN

Almost as stunning as the changes in the deaf community in the last thirty years have been changes in the last *five* years. Thirty years ago, Deaf people generically referred to their language as "the sign language"; it is now renamed "American Sign Language," standing in contrast to the also renamed British Sign Language, French Quebec Sign Language, Thai Sign Language, and the myriad national sign languages of the world. The activities of their everyday life were called "the deaf way," or "the deaf world"; they are now called "Deaf culture." The last five years have seen even newer vocabulary take hold, from calls for rights of Deaf people as a "linguistic minority" to schools that can educate the "bicultural" Deaf person.

Without doubt, the new vocabulary perplexes and distresses the larger public. Intense debates have erupted between the fields of medicine and education and the "cultural activists" of the deaf community. Two prominent national magazines, the *Atlantic Monthly* and the *Los Angeles Times Weekly Magazine* have featured Deaf cultural activism as a major story (Dolnick, 1993; D'Antonio, 1993). Both chose the most extreme of

Carol A. Padden (Ph.D., Linguistics, University of California, San Diego) is Associate Professor of Communication at the University of California, San Diego, where she teaches courses on language, culture, and media, including reading and writing. She grew up in the shadow of Gallaudet University; her parents are graduates of Gallaudet and taught there for many years. She is Deaf, as are all members of her family except for her daughter. She is the coauthor with Tom Humphries of the well-known *Deaf in America: Voices from a Culture* (1988, Harvard University Press). Her address is: Department of Communication, 0503, University of California, San Diego, La Jolla, CA 92093.

clashes, a debate between Deaf people, doctors, and hearing parents over cochlear implants and whether the devices are being overprescribed to young deaf children. Deaf people are described as challenging the ulterior motives of doctors and hearing parents. Hearing parents of deaf children in response accuse Deaf people of unnatural and unnecessary claims to cultural rights.

My goal here is to review the newest rhetoric of the American deaf community, especially with respect to the terms "cultural" and "bicultural." When I refer to "the deaf community," I refer to an abstract collection of ideas and activities spread out over many smaller communities of deaf people stretched out over the physical and ethnic geography of the United States.[1] In an earlier paper of mine (Padden, 1980), I describe the deaf community as made up of not only Deaf people – those who commit to the use of American Sign Language – but also other active participants in the community, hearing relatives and spouses of Deaf people and their signing co-workers and friends. I retain this basic definition. Deaf communities in Washington, D.C.; New York; Chicago; and San Francisco each participate locally as well as nationally in a broader plan to assert cultural rights of Deaf people. I am interested in local plans as well as those addressing a national agenda. I am particularly interested in two institutions that have felt the impact of the new rhetoric most acutely: the school and the workplace.

A History of "Deaf Culture"

In culture studies today, a great deal of interest has been directed to societies changing in the face of modern pressures. From Indonesia (Siegel, 1986) to Native Americans in Connecticut (Clifford, 1988), it is clear that the nature of the modern world is constantly shifting and changing. Immigration and efforts at integration have created new opportunities of coexistence; groups of people coexist in ways they never have before. Deaf people are no exception. Just as Indonesia is forced to face the modern world, Deaf people today coexist with hearing people in very different ways than they did thirty or even five years ago. Their language and

---

[1] Communities often disagree over the details of cultural representation – for example, the disagreement between white and black Deaf communities over whether performances of signing songs (a signed version of lip-synching) are legitimate. Black Deaf people have argued that signing songs is more acceptable in their communities.

rhetoric reflect the pressures of modern integration, brought about by profound changes in their schools and work lives.

Living Among Others

The debate over whether Deaf people constitute a true "cultural" group still rages on several fronts, not only in the media for the larger public, but even within deaf communities. A large part of the debate concerns the peculiar facts of transmission within the group. Clearly there is not the conventional line of transmission, from parent to child, that is part of one of the more comfortable and popular definitions of a culture.

First, although Deaf people are far more likely to marry other Deaf people, only a small number of such unions will produce deaf children. In a classic survey of 4,471 Deaf couples conducted in the nineteenth century, only 8.6% of their offspring were deaf (Fay, 1896). Studies of inheritance in Deaf families since this time have shown little deviation from these figures (Schein & Delk, 1974; Arnos et al., 1992). The oft-reported figure that less than 10% of all deaf children have parents who are also deaf attests to the tenuous and imperfect transmission of Deaf culture from one generation to the next. Deaf people are far more likely, indeed ten times more likely, to produce hearing children than children like themselves. Furthermore, Deaf people are far more likely to have hearing parents and relatives than they are to have families who are Deaf. Indeed, Deaf people always have hearing relatives, often in their immediate families.

At the same time, Deaf people are different from other disabled groups in terms of transmission. Inherited deafness is more frequent than inherited blindness. Unlike deafness, blindness tends more to be an acquired condition, often taking place late in life. Total or near-total deafness is more likely to occur early in life than blindness (Gearheart, Mullen, & Gearheart, 1993).[2] Additionally, it has been estimated that of all children born deaf today, 62% of them are deaf from genetic causes (Marazita, Ploughman, Rawlings, Remington, Arnos, & Nance, 1993).

The relative frequency of deafness over generations has resulted in a fairly stable history organized in large part around institutions such as the school, the club, and the church. Deaf people themselves have founded schools (for example, the Indiana School for the Deaf, founded in 1843,

---

[2] The exact incidence of genetic blindness is difficult to determine. It has been reported that the *prevalence* (or number of cases) of blindness in school age children is 0.04% as against deafness in 0.5% of school age children. Gearheart et al., 1993.

and the Arizona School for the Deaf, in 1911), local clubs, national organizations, and religious groups. But these entities almost always exist within
the control of the state. Schools for the deaf may be enclaves at the center of
their community, but the schools are under the control of the state government. Deaf organizations may have their own building or even operate a
small business, but their licenses and regulations belong to the larger
society. There are no towns or even blocks or areas of a city entirely
occupied by Deaf residents anywhere in North America. Unusual island
communities of Deaf people such as on Martha's Vineyard may have had
larger than usual numbers of Deaf people, but hearing relatives and fellow
islanders have coexisted with them (Groce, 1985). Deaf people cannot
avoid working with others and living in buildings and using objects
designed by others. Their lives are undeniably infiltrated, in large part, by
others.

Deaf people have always had to coexist with hearing people, but what
is remarkable about the last thirty years, and especially the last five, has
been how the terms of that coexistence have changed. The ways that Deaf
people coexist with hearing people in their schools and workplaces have
changed dramatically in this period of time. The new vocabulary of "cultural" and "bicultural," I would argue, consists of modern ways to recognize the boundaries between Deaf and hearing people, and to imagine
what these boundaries should be.

The School

Given the patterns of transmission across generations, the school,
and not the family, becomes a major socializing agent for deaf children.
The traditional means of schooling deaf children in the first part of this
century was the residential school where deaf children not only were
introduced to classrooms with other deaf children, but also in many instances lived in a boarding arrangement for long periods of time. A single
residential school was expected to serve an entire state or a large region of
a state, and was often located in the middle of the state, as in Frederick,
Maryland, or Colorado Springs, Colorado. The long-term separation of
deaf children from their families and neighborhoods created the basis of
the many deaf school communities of the United States. Today, Deaf adults
identify each other by the city and the state in which they attended school
more often than by the city in which they were born. ("Where are you
from?" "Frederick.")

In this sense, then, the school and its grounds have served as "island communities." The typical residential schools, founded since the 1800's – indeed, the ones judged to be among the most beautiful – were those that fulfilled the "asylum" prototype of large buildings situated on pastoral grounds, often within walls. Travel outside the walls of the school was carefully controlled, in the interests of protecting the children. A graduate once described his years at a residential school as not dissimilar to living in a minimum security prison. There were no high barbed-wire fences, but the boundaries could not be breached, either by the deaf children or by outsiders. The result was the creation of a bounded community headed by teachers and school administrators. The school reflected the community boundaries, the careful separation of deaf children from the public, and protection from outside hearing people.

Beginning in 1970, spurred in part by a social trend toward deinstitutionalization and subsequent disenchantment with expensive asylums, deaf children began attending different kinds of schools. Instead of choosing residential schools, many parents responded to the opening of public schools to disabled students, prompted by the enactment of Public Law 94142, and placed their deaf children in local public schools (Moores, 1987). Between 1970 and 1978, enrollment in public residential schools dropped by 9.8% (Schildroth, 1980). In the next six years, the decline was accelerated: 22.5% fewer deaf students attended residential schools between 1979 and 1985. In this same period, there was an increase of 16% in local school attendance by deaf children (Schildroth, 1988).[3]

The shifting of demographics of deaf children away from the traditional residential school had an impact on the deaf community's sense of boundaries. Instead of designated pastoral spaces, deaf children found themselves among other children, in local public schools. With the disappearance of the residential school boundaries, new anxieties arose among community members who lived through the transition from the traditional school to the integrated school. Boundaries are no longer determined by actual walls, but by other means, less physical and more psychic.

The Workplace

In another work, I asked what precipitated such a profound change in the ways Deaf people talked about themselves and their language (Pad-

---

[3] It should be noted that between 1970 and 1983, there was a steady decline in total numbers of the hearing-impaired (Allen, 1992). Because of a rubella epidemic, an unusually large number of deaf children entered schools in the years 1964–1965; these children began leaving schools at the time these surveys were taken.

den, 1990). Why did they change the name of their language from "the sign language" (Burnes, 1950) to "the American Sign Language" (Stokoe, Croneberg, & Casterline, 1965) to "ASL"? There were several influences, one of which was the expanding of research into deaf people's lives and their sign languages. The fields of psychology, linguistics, and anthropology undertook research on topics ranging from structural properties of sign languages, acquisition of sign languages in young deaf children, and the sociology of deaf people. The effect of science's interest in sign language and Deaf culture was to cast legitimacy on them.

But these are influences from outside rather than within the community. What changes took place to bring the community to a different standard of self-description? I have argued that another profound influence has been changes in the work lives of Deaf people. They took up different kinds of occupations, as a result splintered their communities into middle-class and working-class groups (popularly called "grassroots Deaf"), and strove for different kinds of ambitions than the previous generation of Deaf people.

Until about the middle 1960s, the primary occupations for deaf people in the United States were either the "solitary" trades (shoe repair, upholstery, printing, or factory assembly) or as teachers or dormitory supervisors at residential schools (Crammatte, 1987; Cronenberg & Blake, 1966; Braly & Hall, 1935). Teaching at that time had little of the trappings of "professional" life: There were few qualifications other than a college degree, and sometimes not even that was required. Deaf people were insulated from the ranks of management; nearly none were elevated to principals or supervisors in their schools. The working-class standard within the community was so predominant that it was entirely appropriate and common for deaf teachers to moonlight as printers at local newspapers or upholsterers to supplement their small teaching incomes.

There were several consequences of the emergence of professionalization within the deaf community, the most significant of which was new social tensions between the middle class and the working class within the community. Teachers and other professionals no longer moonlighted in blue-collar jobs; they fled the Deaf clubs and the bowling alleys, leaving behind the working class. Deaf clubs in the United States today have nowhere near the popularity they enjoyed in the 1940s and 1950s, when they were packed every weekend night. After World War II, the Los Angeles Club of the Deaf was at the height of its strength; it owned a building in the center of town and was the political and social center of the deaf community. It is now defunct, its social and political functions distributed elsewhere in the community (DeBee, 1985).

The flight of Deaf people from the traditional club has variously been blamed on television, the videocassette recorder, and the telephone. As the argument goes, as Deaf people turn to more private pursuits, they lose interest in the traditional group activities. I see the changes as stemming from the rise of the Deaf middle class in the United States, causing new tensions in deaf communities. Along with the new economic lives of the Deaf middle class came a desire for the trappings of middle-class life: to conduct one's business by telephone instead of the traditional face-to-face encounter and to participate in the consumption of television and all it promises. The Deaf middle class has pushed for closed-captioning of television programs and telephone relay services allowing them to telephone hearing individuals through an intermediary, the telephone relay agent. With the diminished role of the Deaf club, it became important to seek out a way to describe group cohesiveness, the reason for such a strong sense of group membership, even if many Deaf people no longer went to clubs.

The "Cultural" Definition

In an edited volume published by the National Association of the Deaf (Garretson, 1991), authors were asked to preface their articles with brief biographies of themselves. Older deaf authors followed tradition and described themselves in medical terms, how they became deaf and at what age. One said he "became deaf from spinal meningitis at the age of five"; another reported that he "began to lose his hearing from German Measles when he was nearly six, becoming totally deaf at the age of eight."

In sharp contrast, a younger group of authors omitted such references and reported instead that they were "born deaf to deaf parents." One wrote that she was "the oldest of three daughters of a Deaf family," and another listed a comedy talk show on Deaf culture as a recent career accomplishment. With the adoption of the "cultural" came a conscious rejection of the medicalized self.

To use a cultural definition is not only to assert a new frame of reference, but to consciously reject an older one. The medical definition is predicated on repair and replacement; it sees the past as littered with failure and ignorance. The cultural subscribes to an ideal of equality, that all languages and cultures are equal because they are adaptations to the conditions of life. The cultural sees the past as a rich resource, making the present possible. Certainly the richest resource of the Deaf community is its sign language, ASL, made possible by its preservation across generations of Deaf people (Kannapell, 1989; Woodward, 1982; Padden & Humphries, 1988; Bienvenu, 1991).

But the cultural definition continues to perplex many. If Deaf people are indeed a cultural group, why then don't they seem more like the Penan of the island of Borneo, or the Huichol of Mexico? In open forums, professional anthropologists have been invited to offer their perspectives on whether Deaf people and their culture constitute a "true culture."[4] Deaf people lack their own burial rites (unless one counts the intensely personal testimonials that are the hallmark of a good Deaf funeral), do not wear traditional clothing, and do not have distinctive food (but they seem to engage in different eating behaviors). How can they be truly called "cultural"?

The type of cultural definition that notes food, burial habits, clothing, or the like rests on a view of culture as carefully bounded and carefully separate from other influences. But in the modern world groups coexist and are influenced by each other. Deaf people's demands for a new definition of themselves are not unlike the demands of the Wampanoag Indians of Massachusetts, who went to federal court in 1977 asking for the right to sue for lost lands (Clifford, 1988). The Indians were residents of Mashpee, "Cape Cod's Indian Town," and as part of their petition to the court portrayed themselves as descendants of earlier tribes dating back to the seventeenth century. Like Deaf people, the Wampanoag live among others, even marry others. Their daily rites may not seem very different from their white neighbors, yet they have a name for themselves and they share certain beliefs about each other.

The issues that Deaf people debate have a great deal to do with boundaries between themselves and others, about exclusivity and authenticity. The issue of exclusivity comes up in the question whether Deaf people constitute a "real culture" or "just a subculture." Since they do not bury their own dead or have unique food rituals, they should be a subculture, or subsumed under the category of American culture. The issue is less about which of the two is the right definition, or the better definition, than about the consequences of one definition or another. The term "subculture" to non-academics suggests subordination.

---

[4] A recent example was a keynote address by J. Jorge Klor de Alva at the annual Conference of Educational Administrators Serving the Deaf (CEASD) in April 1994.

Authenticity likewise involves the power to define. A deaf person by medical standards is one who is "severely to profoundly deaf," or who attains a certain score on a test of hearing. A Deaf person is one who knows the language and knows the ways of the group. An authentic Deaf person would be someone who has Deaf parents, attended a school for deaf children, and the informal list continues: attended Gallaudet University, has deaf children, married another Deaf person. The obvious, of course, is that such individuals have some kind of hearing impairment, but the categories of hearing measurement are subordinated to community and family affiliation.

In academic life, definitions of "culturally Deaf" are suspect as potentially stereotypic, but within the group they serve to reassure insiders and dismay outsiders. The reality of the "authentic" Deaf person is one that holds for just about any modern individual – it is an ideal. Not surprisingly, such individuals are not numerous. History and shifting institutional priorities have changed where deaf children attend school, bringing them into contact with different educational practices and different groups of people. It is more likely now than in the past for a Deaf person to attend institutions other than Gallaudet. What seems to be at issue here is whether the person has authentic loyalties (Kannapell, 1989), a commitment to the language and cultural ideals of the group.

The "Bicultural" Definition

The term "bicultural" has only recently appeared on the scene in the community of Deaf people. Other than a logical extension of the cultural, what purpose does the term serve? To what does it refer? In a "Statement of Mission and Values" issued by the California School for the Deaf in Fremont (1993), the school lists ten tenets, including: "every [deaf] student has a right to an educational environment where he or she is able to understand others and be understood by others," and "staff members should be competent in American Sign language and have an understanding of and appreciation for Deaf culture."

It seems that the emerging intention of the term "bicultural" is not to be competent in two cultures, as bilingualism is to be competent in two languages, at least in its traditional definition (Grosjean, 1992), but to negotiate tensions between competing and profoundly contradictory beliefs, lives, and activities, those that are embedded in the lives of hearing people on one hand and those of Deaf people on the other. The term "bicultural" is being used to describe a way of conceiving boundaries between Deaf and hearing people in a world where the residential schools and the Deaf clubs of the past no longer exist.

The "Bicultural Self"

In our book on Deaf culture (Padden & Humphries, 1988), we described the everyday talk of Deaf people as marked by a certain style of self-reference, a way of positioning the self relative to others. One example came from a conversation about an acquaintance who was VERY HARD-OF-HEARING.[5] It was understood that the person in question was someone who could hear very well, exactly the opposite of the sign's literal English translation.

As we studied this thread of significance, we found another related term. Someone who is A-LITTLE HARD-OF-HEARING is one who does not hear well at all, again the opposite of its English translation. What the two phrases together reveal is a network of meaning in which DEAF is seen as a central state of being, and to be A-LITTLE is to be a slight departure from this central state. VERY, on the other hand, represented a large departure, toward the more distant and opposing pole, HEARING. We proposed the idea of a "different center," around which ideas and beliefs are organized in ways shared by Deaf people.

More generally, the signs DEAF and HEARING are not only labels of hearing condition, but are actively used in everyday talk as labels of position. At times the labels are used without reflection, as in VERY HARD-OF-HEARING, and other times consciously and deliberately. A running joke at schools for the deaf is to refer to the opposing, or visiting, Deaf football team as HEARING. The labels are usually recognized as mistakes, but participants revel in these extensions of meaning.

These labels often surface in subtle shadings of common talk. Recently I was at a gathering of family members discussing land that they were considering buying. The father explained that the developer planned to build a home next to his son's. The son corrected him and said that the developer actually planned to build elsewhere and the lot next door would be occupied by "someone hearing." The comment is odd, stating the obvious. Every lot in the area will be built on by a hearing family. What

---

[5] I follow the standard convention of representing ASL signs with capitalized English glosses.

the son meant was that someone outside the known set, in this case other than the son's family and the developer, would occupy that land. DEAF means "known," "of the set," and HEARING means "not known," "not of the set."

To invoke the labels of DEAF and HEARING is to call up a web of relationships between what is central and what is peripheral, what is known and what is not known, and what is familiar and what is foreign. To talk of these terms is to offer a counterbalance between two large and imposing presences in Deaf people's lives – their own community and the community within which they must live, among hearing people. For Deaf people the poles of everyday life are the language and ways of the community within the language and ways of others, the English-talking society of North America.

These ways of conceiving the self also can be seen in what I call "urban folk tales," following Brunvand's (1989) coining of the term to describe popular but rarely verifiable stories of Deaf Americans. The tales tell of the dangers of living as a Deaf person in an almost entirely hearing world. In one widely circulated version, a Deaf man is mistaken for a fugitive and chased on foot by an FBI agent (or an agent of the CIA or Secret Service) who calls out to him to stop or he will shoot. The Deaf man fails to hear and is indeed shot and killed. The story is said to have appeared on the front page of the Chicago (or Seattle or Los Angeles) newspaper. The tale is a popularized fantasy of an unprotected and innocent Deaf citizen suffering at the hands of a faceless official hearing person.

The same fears and worries also color how real-life events are told. Several years ago a prominent Deaf man was found shot at pointblank range in the basement garage of his high-rise apartment building. His wife had gone up to their apartment alone while he unloaded the trunk of their car. When he failed to appear, she went down to investigate and found him dead. The shooter was never apprehended and the murder remains unsolved. The case was extensively discussed, reviewed, and speculated upon. A robber must have shouted to him to turn around, many believed, and when he failed to respond, shot him dead. It is of course entirely possible that he died while trying to resist the robber; indeed, many hearing victims are shot in this way. But it was far more meaningful to speculate that he died at the hands of someone relentlessly hearing.

The stories and anecdotes tell of ways of positioning self and other, and tell how to make sense of the actions and activities of people's lives. The material of language, words and signs, exist as points of reference, as they contemplate the irreducible tensions of their lives.

Reorganization of Boundaries

The School

In recent years, not only did enrollments decline at residential schools, but fewer children boarded at the schools (Schildroth, 1980). Month-long stays are no longer permitted; today children who board at residential schools typically return home each weekend to their families. The classic school for deaf children of a generation ago no longer exists, as its boundaries have become more permeable. In this context, debates rage over whether the modern pattern of schooling for deaf children ensures a good education (Commission on Education of the Deaf, 1988). Leaving aside the question of whether the current model is beneficial or not, what has been the impact of this changed style of schooling on the deaf community? At least one impact has been a heightened sense of boundaries, expressed in the form of debates over languages and cultures. In this sense, the debates make explicit what did not have to be said a generation ago.

The vocabulary of languages and cultures has found its way into the school in the form of calls for educational reform. A number of schools have proposed new "bilingual-bicultural" programs in which the school aims to educate children in two languages, ASL and English, and in two cultures, those of the larger society and of Deaf people. Not surprisingly, most of the schools calling for this kind of reform are residential schools, historically educational havens for young deaf children. Teachers are encouraged to restructure curriculum and classroom practice to reflect a new emphasis on culturally relevant education for deaf children. The reform movement has taken on a name, "Bi-Bi," and has given rise to newsletters, workshops, and conferences around the country.

As part of our research project studying early reading and writing in young deaf children, our group visited a Bi-Bi residential school and observed activities in classrooms. We wanted to know how a philosophy centered on notions of language and culture would be translated into classroom practice. In a third grade classroom we found the first indications of this fairly new effort, in which aspects of the new curriculum and new teaching practice were manifested in the teacher's depiction of distance and relationship between ASL and English and their respective cultures. In much the same way that the community talks of what is known and familiar and then what is not known and distant, teachers in

Bi-Bi classrooms extend these metaphors of explanation into classroom practice.

We videotaped and transcribed a Deaf teacher explaining to her students how to carry out an experiment described in a textbook on science. The teacher had previously explained to us that many of her students were only barely able to read the textbook, so she would need to adapt the activity of reading to accommodate them. The task was to do science, but the teacher saw her task as broader than just science, to include reading and acquisition of scientific knowledge. The teacher needed to teach the specialized, not obvious knowledge of science – in this case, whether vinegar introduced into baking soda will cause a gaseous emission and hence a chemical change.

Her strategy was to make transparencies of the relevant pages in the science textbook and invite the students to read lines from the page with her. As she read each line, she began a mode of explanation that moved between the textbook and the resources of sign language. Broadly, her style of explanation drew from vernacular forms of talk used in the Deaf community but adapted for use in the classroom. We call this adapted style of talk "school ASL" (Sterne, 1993) because it has a number of features that seem specific to the context of instruction around and with English. Some of these elements involve purposely distancing scientific concepts through English fingerspelling and other linguistic devices, drawing comparisons between known popular elements and new scientific elements, and drawing equivalences between ASL and other systems of English.

Distance. Fingerspelling is usually described as a device in ASL for representing written English in manual form with handshapes forming letters of the alphabet. What is rarely acknowledged is how the system of fingerspelling has come to signify a relationship between ASL and English. The science teacher frequently fingerspelled, and she often did it as a way of purposely highlighting scientific vocabulary to show its distance from everyday concepts in ASL. One example was the teacher's careful explanation of the scientific concept of "problem":

SAME MATH, KNOW STORY, WRITE, SAY: [role shift]: "SUPPOSE [you] HAVE 8 APPLE, THEN [you] TOSS-OUT 4 APPLE TOSS-OUT 1. HOW MANY APPLE [you] HAVE REMAIN?"
[Just like in Math, you know the story that goes (in written English), "Suppose you have 8 apples, then you throw away 4, how many apples do you have left?"]

4, RIGHT. SAME 1 PROBLEM [false start] P-R-O-B-L-E-M. THAT P-R-O-B-L-E-M
[points to class] FIGURE-OUT, ANSWER. QUESTION. PROBLEM NEGATIVE? NO.
ONLY QUESTION.
[*Four, that's right. Just like the idea of problem, I mean "problem." A problem is
what you need to figure out, to answer. A question. Is a problem a negative thing?
No, it's just a question.*]

The teacher made a point of fingerspelling the word "problem" so as to
distinguish it from the common definition of problem of a personal
difficulty or struggle. By fingerspelling the word, the teacher had effectively distanced it from the common known definition, thus establishing
its special scientific meaning.

In another example, the teacher is reading from the screen the list of
materials needed for the experiment and then she turns to the class:

WHAT F-U-N-N-E-L-S? F-U-N-N-E-L-S . . . [picks up funnel from table] F-U-N-N-
E-L [displays funnel] WHY USE IT?
[*What are funnels? Here's a funnel. . . . For what purpose is this used?*]

As she fingerspells, the teacher displays a countenance of puzzlement. She
wrinkles her nose as she fingerspells the word "funnel" and moves her
hand to one side so as to look at it. The discourse device serves to distance
the word, set it up as alien and unknown. The teacher has effectively
marked an English word, a tool in a science experiment. In a way, the
teacher has mimicked her children's view that things English are often
foreign and difficult to comprehend.

Linking. The teacher then proceeds to demonstrate how foreign
things can be understood. She turns next to baking soda, a necessary
ingredient in the experiment, but senses that her students may not know
the term "baking soda." She explains:[6]

B-A-K-I-N-G S-O-D-A, B-A-K-I-N [while pointing to words on overhead
projection], THAT SAME [picks up box of baking soda and points to "baking
soda" on box while mouthing "baking soda"].
[*Now baking soda, baking – right here on the screen is the same thing as this box in
my hand.*]

---

[6] Fingerspelled words are represented by capital letters separated by hyphens. Fingerspelled loan signs are represented in glosses with an initial # sign. "CL:" means a single
classifier predicate. "Over time" is a notation showing aspectual inflection on the
predicate.

SEE THAT BEFORE, CL:arm&hammer logo? THINK #ALL, MAYBE #ALL HAVE, [points to box] HOME IN COLD, R-E-F, CL:[puts box in fridge]. box-ABSORB, SMELL TERRIBLE, [points to box] box-ABSORB-over time, CAN.
[*You've seen it before, the picture of the arm and biceps? I think all of you, maybe all of you have this at home in your refrigerator. It absorbs bad odors in the refrigerator, over time it absorbs (odors).*]

She provides an explanation which in large part describes to the children the familiar orange box of Arm & Hammer baking soda with its emblem of an arm and biceps. She explains what it is used for, then connects it to its place on a list of materials for a science experiment. She seems to intuitively understand what a young group of children who can barely read are likely to know, and what it will take to make them understand something they do not yet know. She believes that if they cannot yet read the words on the object, in this case the box of baking soda, then the visual elements of the object will be especially salient to them.

Framing equivalences. Finally, the teacher offers ways of moving between languages and systems, from ASL to fingerspelling to print, each a stop in an interwoven system of symbols. When she introduces the experiment, she says:

#DO SCIENCE #DO SCIENCE. WILL TALK ABOUT, REMEMBER CHEMICAL CHANGE, C-H-E-M-I-C-A-L C-H-A-N-G-E [writes "chemical change" on the board]. WHAT MEAN? WHAT MEAN [points to words "chemical change" on board]?
[*What are we doing in science today? We're going to talk about – remember this idea of chemical change? Chemical change? What does it mean, what do these words here mean?*]

First she signs, then she fingerspells, and then she writes the words on the board. They are equivalent, she tells her students by example. Here's the sign, and there is an equivalent in fingerspelling, also in print. They are all connected. Her young students know the languages have equivalences, but aren't quite sure exactly how. She will be their model for moving smoothly between languages, from one world of meaning to another.

The question here is what is linked, in what form, and by what means. The systems of signing, fingerspelling, and print are not merely different languages or representations of different languages; they are markers of distance and proximity, of difference and similarity. The teacher skillfully uses the systems both to convey meaning and to convey systems of meaning – of the everyday to the scientific, of the familiar to the new.

The practice of distancing systems, then later showing they are equivalent, may draw in large part from a practice of conceiving the self in positions relative to others. The sentiment of self as intimate and other as distant reappears in numerous forms throughout the discourses of school and other activities of everyday life. To the outsider, the subtle countenances of puzzlement and distancing might seem small, but they comprise active ways of positioning, from belief to practice. In the world of the other is English and, for young deaf children, science and the practices of the larger society. The teacher plays the role of modeling a "bicultural" life, showing how to link the parts together and how to understand them relative to one another. In knowing what is distant and not understood, she teaches students how to understand English, science, and other practices of the larger society.

The Workplace

I have pointed to a number of important shifts in the work lives of Deaf people, from essentially a one-class community to a split working-class and middle-class community (Padden, 1990). Among the more important of these changes has been the growth of a professional class in the Deaf community, from teachers of deaf children to sign language teachers and the social service professionals.

The professional class began to emerge in the 1960s, following a larger trend toward specialization and professionalization in education. No longer would a high school or college degree suffice; teachers needed certificates and master's degrees. New specialties were offered for "RCDs" (rehabilitation counselors for the deaf), along with degrees in "elementary education," "post-secondary education", and so on, highlighting the burgeoning industry of special education in the 1970s and 1980s. Indeed, one of the major workplaces for Deaf people is the school.

In addition, as public interest in ethnic diversity increased, the demand for adult classes in ASL exploded, to an estimated 50,000 new students each year in the language (*San Diego Tribune*, January 27, 1989), with classes in colleges and universities and, in increasing numbers, even high schools. A new industry of sign language teaching emerged, with a demand for teachers of ASL and sign language interpreting.

Coming at the tail end of these changes in Deaf people's work lives was an event many have pointed to as a profound turning point in the Deaf community, the "Deaf President Now" movement. In 1988, the students at

Gallaudet University organized a large and visible protest of its Board of Trustees' appointment of a new hearing president (Gannon, 1989). They presented a list of five demands to the Board, including the replacement of the president with a deaf person and a change of balance of representation on the Board to a majority of deaf people. Some have likened the protest to a revolution, but I have claimed (Padden, 1990) that while it was a momentous event, it was largely a revolution of the middle class. The Deaf middle class demanded a reorganization of its workplace to accommodate Deaf people as managers, administrators, even presidents and CEOs.

Not surprisingly, issues of bilingualism and biculturalism have been deeply intertwined in the protest and its aftermath. The university, and many other workplaces involving Deaf and hearing people, continue an internal debate on a variety of issues related to language use in the workplace and how deeply they should change to accommodate "cultural differences" between hearing and Deaf people. In the universities, as anywhere else in the community, it is less clear than before where the boundaries of Deafness are, or what they mean.

The anxiety over boundaries is partly class-related. When the Deaf middle class left the Deaf clubs, they took a certain amount of class anxiety with them, reflected in the nostalgic ways in which they talk today about the clubs, sports events, and the churches. The "real" culture, as it was in the old days, is said to live on in the occasional meetings of the Union League in New York City, or in the covert betting behind the courts at the annual American Athletic Association of the Deaf Basketball Tournament. But the reality is that Deaf clubs attract far fewer attendees than they did thirty or forty years ago, if they still exist at all, and their impact on the professional class of Deaf people is more nostalgic than political or social. The class divide is wide and difficult.

As the professional class left the clubs and saw their schools change, they have found themselves marooned with uncertain boundaries in rapidly changing workplaces and social spaces. This is why, in the place of the schools and clubs of the past, there is a great deal of interest in languages and cultures, particularly in how they represent differences and distances.

The "Bicultural" Deaf Community

To talk of the "bicultural" is not to talk about an additive state, to be of two cultures, but more about states of tensions. Deaf people coexist, indeed work, with hearing people in different ways today than they did thirty or forty years ago. Their changing work lives have given rise to a new vocabulary that maps out, more carefully and consciously than before, differences in languages and cultures. The new vocabulary draws from the traditions of language study and cultural anthropology, borrowing from them the essential features of linguistic and cultural relativism, of legitimacy across languages and cultures. As the familiar walls of the deaf school began to crumble and Deaf clubs were reconstituted into working-class social sites, the middle-class professional Deaf people began to imagine new ways of representing themselves, largely in the form of calls for cultural ways of living and bicultural schools and workplaces. As the community travels through the modern world, there will most certainly be even newer vocabulary, seeking to stake out and mark the community's place in a continually changing world.

Acknowledgments

We acknowledge the generous support of grants from the Spencer Foundation and the U.S. Department of Education to Carol Padden and Claire Ramsey in the preparation of this chapter.

References

Allen, T. (1992). Subgroup differences in educational placement for deaf and hard of hearing students. *American Annals of the Deaf, 137*(5), 381–388.

Amos, K., Israel, J., Wilson , M. P., & Devlin, L. (1992). Genetics of hearing disorders. *Clinics in Communication Disorders, 2,* 20–34.

Bienvenu, M. J. (1991). Can Deaf people survive "deafness?" In M. Garretson (Ed.)., *Perspectives on deafness: A Deaf American monograph,* 41 (pp. 21–25). Silver Spring, MD: National Association of the Deaf.

Braly, K., & Hall, P. (1935). Types of occupations followed. *The Federal Survey of the Deaf and Hard of Hearing.* Gallaudet College Normal Department in collaboration with the Office of Education.

Brunvand, J. (1981). *The vanishing hitchhiker: American urban legends and their meanings.* New York: Norton.

Burnes, B. (1950). The editor's page. *Silent Worker, 2,* 2.

California School for the Deaf, Fremont. (1993). *A statement of mission and values.*

Clifford, J. (1988). *The predicament of culture.* Cambridge, MA: Harvard University Press.

Commission on Education of the Deaf. (1988). *Toward equality: Education of the deaf.* A report to the President and the Congress of the United States.

Crammatte, A. (1987). *Meeting the challenge: Hearing impaired professionals in the workplace*. Washington, DC: Gallaudet University Press.

Cronenberg, H., & Blake, G. (1966). *Young deaf adults: An occupational survey*. Arkansas Rehabilitation Service.

D'Antonio, M. (1993, November 21). Sound & fury: The new technology that could bring hearing to the deaf is meeting passionate resistance – from those who fear losing a treasured subculture. *Los Angeles Times, 112*.

DeBee, J. (1985). *The LACD Story*. Film distributed by Beyond Sound, Los Angeles, CA.

Dolnick, E. (1993). Deafness as culture. *Atlantic Monthly, 272* (3), 37–49.

Fay, E. (1896). An inquiry concerning the results of marriages of the deaf in America. Chapter VII. *American Annals of the Deaf, 41*, 22–31.

Gannon, J. R. (1989). *The week the world heard Gallaudet* Washington, DC: Gallaudet University Press.

Garretson, M. (1991). *Perspectives on deafness: A Deaf American monograph*. Silver Spring, MD: National Association of the Deaf.

Gearheart, B., Mullen, R., & Gearheart, C. (1993). *Exceptional individuals: An introduction*. Pacific Grove, CA: Brooks/Cole Publishing.

Groce, N. (1985). *Everyone here spoke sign language: Hereditary deafness on Martha's Vineyard*. Cambridge, MA: Harvard University Press.

Grosjean, F. (1992). Another view of bilingualism. In R. Harris (Ed.), *Cognitive processing in bilinguals* (pp. 51–62). New York: Elsevier Science Pub.

Kannapell, B. (1989). Inside the Deaf community. In S. Wilcox (Ed.), *American deaf culture: An anthology* (pp. 21–28). Silver Spring, MD: Linstok Press.

Lane, H. L. (1992). *The mask of benevolence: Disabling the deaf community*. New York: Knopf.

Marazita, M., Ploughman, L., Rawlings, B., Remington, E., Arnos, K., & Nance, W. (1993). Genetic epidemiological studies of early-onset deafness in the U.S. school-age population. *American Journal of Medical Genetics, 46* (5), 486–91.

Moores, D. (1987). *Educating the deaf*. Boston: Houghton Mifflin.

Padden, C. (1980). The deaf community and the culture of Deaf people. In C. Baker, & R. Battison (Eds.), *Sign language and the deaf community: Essays in honor of William C. Stokoe* (pp. 89–103). Silver Spring, MD: National Association of the Deaf.

(1990). Folk explanation in language survival. In D. Middleton (Ed.), *Collective remembering* (pp. 190–202). Los Angeles: Sage.

Padden, C., & Humphries, T. (1988). *Deaf in America: Voices from a culture*. Cambridge, MA: Harvard University Press.

San Diego Tribune (1989, January 27). Educators in debate on language.

Schein, J., & Delk, M. Jr. (1974). *The deaf population of the United States*. Silver Spring, MD: National Association of the Deaf.

Schildroth, A. (1980). Public residential schools for deaf students in the United States, 1970–1978. *American Annals of the Deaf, 125*, 80–91.

(1988). Recent changes in the educational placement of deaf students. *American Annals of the Deaf, 133*, 61–76.

Siegel, J. T. (1986). *Solo in the new order: Language and hierarchy in an Indonesian city*. Princeton, NJ: Princeton University Press.

Sterne, S. (1993). *Implementing bilingual/bicultural education: "School ASL" and the basic skills of deaf literacy.* Working paper, University of California, San Diego.

Stokoe, W., Croneberg, C., & Casterline, D. (1965). *A dictionary of American Sign Language on linguistic principles.* Washington, DC: Gallaudet College Press.

Woodward, James (1982). *How you gonna get to heaven if you can't talk with Jesus: On depathologizing deafness.* Silver Spring, MD: T.J. Publishers.

CHAPTER SIX

Early Bilingual Lives of Deaf Children

CAROL A. PADDEN

Introduction

Deaf people join groups of people all over the world who must manage two languages, one of which is a dominant-world language and the other a minority, often unfavored language.[1] In the United States and Canada, Deaf people who use American Sign Language (ASL) as the preferred everyday language interact, often intimately, with individuals who use English – hearing teachers, relatives, and co-workers. Deaf people have many opportunities to use only ASL, but rarely can they avoid contact with English. They are more likely to have parents who use English than parents who use ASL. They are more likely to have teachers who are native speakers of English. Many have co-workers who speak only English.

Carol A. Padden (Ph.D., Linguistics, University of California, San Diego) is Associate Professor of Communication at University of California, San Diego, where she teaches courses on language, culture, and media, including reading and writing. She grew up in the shadow of Gallaudet University; her parents are graduates of Gallaudet and taught there for many years. She is Deaf, as are all members of her family except for her daughter. She is the coauthor with Tom Humphries of the well-known *Deaf in America: Voices from a Culture* (1988, Harvard University Press). Her address is: Department of Communication, 0503, University of California, San Diego, La Jolla, CA 92093.

[1] I follow a convention used elsewhere in which the capitalized form "Deaf" is used in referring to those deaf individuals whose primary everyday language is American Sign Language. The audiological condition of deafness is marked with the lowercase form "deaf."

The language lives of Deaf people involve constantly moving between languages, ASL and English, and between cultural worlds, the worlds of ASL signers and English speakers. Because ASL does not have a written system, Deaf people use written English both as a means of contact with English and as a means of storing information about themselves and their language. Deaf people recite ASL poems and make videotapes of poetry performances, but their analyses of poetry appear in written English. Deaf children in a third grade classroom read a paragraph together in English, and then explain its meaning to each other in ASL. Deaf teenagers read computer manuals in English and explain to friends in ASL how to write a short program on the computer. Hardly a day goes by without changing languages and changing channels, from signing to reading, from writing to signing, and back again.

As it turns out, we know more about ASL and about ASL signers than we do about ASL signers who also know English. Bilingualism in Deaf individuals is a difficult concept to define. Part of the difficulty is that bilingualism, as it has been used of hearing individuals who have command of two spoken languages, has been widely understood as a linguistic concept to refer to matched or "balanced" bilinguals whose command of both languages is equivalent in all domains and functions. Grosjean (1992) argues that this definition is not only idealized but misleading as well.

More often than not, individuals who have acquired and use two languages do so under different social and cultural contexts. Their skill in one language may not be matched in the other. The unevenness of their acquisition and skill is not due to lapses in language ability, but is the result of a natural consequence of the circumstances in which they are language users. Take for example a bilingual child whose father is an immigrant and whose the mother is a native of the country in which the family lives. The social opportunities for the child to use the father's language will be less public than those for the mother's language. The child uses the father's language in intimate family settings, and because the father's language is not used in school, the child will not learn that language in the context of school and as a result will not learn how to read and write in that language. The child is not an "imperfect" bilingual who speaks both languages but is able to read and write only one, but a bilingual whose life circumstances have engendered different skills in two languages.

In the current discussion about language competence in deaf individuals, some have argued that "bilingualism" is not an appropriate term for those who use American Sign Language (ASL) and English since many

Deaf individuals do not acquire or use English in spoken form; instead their interaction with English is said to be primarily through reading and writing. I would like in this chapter to echo Grosjean's observations and reframe the discussion of bilingualism in Deaf signers along different lines. Instead of inquiring in the abstract whether bilingual signers have equal competence in ASL and English, the question becomes: What are the contexts of their contact with English, and how do these contexts shape their knowledge of English?

Asking this type of question will have several consequences. First, instead of defining deaf people as a single population, it becomes important to define groups of deaf people within this population in terms of their social and cultural worlds. Their competence in English is linked to the roles they play, the worlds they move within, and the tasks they engage in. Second, deaf people's skill in English should not be matched against an abstract or idealized notion of linguistic competence. Bilingual Deaf people's competence should be viewed as developing out of a particular configuration of language experiences. Many do not speak English, but interact with it primarily in written form. Their interaction with English is by way of systems which represent English in specific ways.

As a way of understanding bilingualism in Deaf adults, I summarize here studies conducted by myself and my colleagues on a group of young Deaf children who have frequent contact with English (Padden & LeMaster, 1984; Padden, 1991, 1993, and Chapter 5 of this volume). The children were all being educated at a residential school for deaf children. Many, but not all, had families who signed. All were native or fluent users of ASL. Some could speak English to an extent, but none would have described themselves as skilled in spoken English. These characteristics, in addition to others, gave rise to a range of social and cultural experiences in which signing was located centrally in their language lives, but English played a vital role as well. The social lives of these children contrasted in a number of ways with those of deaf children who attended schools organized around different guiding principles, such as public schools. Both groups shared the difficulty of access to spoken English and a desire by their parents and teachers that they become competent in written English, but the organization of language and social resources was different in the two groups.

It would be inaccurate to describe the children in our studies as acquiring signed language "first" at home, then acquiring English at school, since for many, their interaction with English began at a very early age. Parents introduced print to children as young as three years old, and by four years of age, the children are actively using systems of English. By systems of English, I refer at least to "fingerspelling" and "written English," although other systems have been identified (Lucas & Valli, 1992; Maxwell, 1980). In the first section I describe Deaf children's early use of a system linked to English orthography, called "fingerspelling," in which they manually represent English words in alphabetic form. The second section looks at examples of their early written creations of English words. The children's use of these two systems, separate but related, reveals much about the early manipulation of English and signed language by young Deaf children. My goal here is to show the complicated language lives of young ASL signers, as represented by the frequency with which they move back and forth between ASL and English within the same activity. In this sense then, bilingualism refers to the way in which language users marshal resources within and across languages, which may turn out to be unevenly distributed between languages.

Early Language Lives of Deaf Children

Thanks to a growing interest in language acquisition, there are now richer accounts of how young Deaf children acquire a signed language. The major result of this work has been to show that first-language acquisition of a signed language follows a pattern comparable to first-language acquisition of a spoken language (see Newport & Meier, 1985; Meier, 1991, for overviews). Studies of ASL acquisition have focused primarily on an aspect of grammatical structure and the way in which the Deaf child masters this structure over the course of development. From this work, there is no reason to believe that acquisition of a signed language should be considered unusual or deviant.

But these studies pointedly avoid discussing how these same children acquire English structures alongside their mastery of a signed language. If during the course of research on ASL morphology, for example, the child produces fingerspelled items or uttered English words, or perhaps interacts with written text while signing, the English language activities are not reported. The result is an incomplete view of the dual language lives of Deaf children, especially their acquisition of English as they are acquiring ASL.

Instead, much of what we know about young signing children's early use of English relates mostly to the difficult task of learning to read and write (Marshall & Quigley, 1970; Trybus & Karchmer, 1977; Karchmer, Milone, & Wolk, 1979; Conrad, 1979; Moores, 1987). This work documents that as a group, Deaf children have difficulty learning to read and write English, although a minority do master these skills. But what we do not know enough about is how young Deaf children encounter and use English in written form at the same time they sign. A notable exception is a detailed description in Maxwell (1980) of the simultaneous acquisition of ASL, fingerspelling, writing, and manually coded English by a Deaf child of Deaf parents. Subsequent studies of emerging literacy (Maxwell, 1984; Ewoldt, 1985; Padden & LeMaster, 1985; Erting, 1992; Padden, 1991; Padden, Chapter 5 of this volume; Ramsey, 1993) have revealed more about practices of reading and writing in signing families, but the quantity of this work has yet to reach a critical mass. How does the children's competence in the different systems emerge? How does competence in ASL interact with competence in other systems of English? In short, we know little about early bilingual abilities of young Deaf children.

English in Signing Environments

There is at least one good reason why the quantity of work on early bilingual English-ASL acquisition in Deaf children is so small: There is a real problem of how to define English in naturally occurring signed language contexts (Lucas & Valli, 1992). "English" in signing has variously been referred to as fingerspelling, reading and writing, mouthing, and speaking, as well as literal translations of English phrases into ASL (called "Sign English," or "Contact Signing"; (Lucas & Valli, 1992). It is vexing to consider the place of English in signed discourse for the reason that English does not appear in its most familiar form, as spoken discourse, yet it is assumed that English is present in signed discourse. Exactly where and how to describe English in such contexts is the basis of the problem.

I will offer here a different angle to this question of defining English in bilingual lives. Instead of asking what constitutes use of English in signing, I ask: How do the children acquire systems of English and how does this acquisition coincide with use of ASL? Both fingerspelling and writing English words involve English, or at the very least, we believe they do. How do deaf children learn to fingerspell and spell English words in written form? Whatever claims we want to make about bilingual acquisition of English and ASL will require that we view language acquisition as the development of interacting systems, each of which has specific social uses. Once we understand how fingerspelling and written spelling skills develop in young Deaf children and we are able to map them alongside

ASL, a picture of their developing competence in English will begin to emerge.

The Acquisition of Fingerspelling

ASL is one of a set of signed languages that use a separate manual system for representing oral language orthography. These manual systems can represent words ideographically, as in Chinese Sign Language for written Chinese characters; syllabically, as in Danish Sign Language's "mouth-hand system"; or alphabetically, as in Swedish Sign Language, British Sign Language, and ASL. These are among the better-known systems, but many sign languages lack a manual system for representing the dominant spoken language. The alphabetic manual system in ASL, popularly called "fingerspelling," is described as executing a single distinct handshape for each letter of the alphabet. Fingerspelling one's name, for example, involves making a handshape for each letter of the name in rapid sequence.

ASL is distinctive among sign languages for its extensive use of fingerspelling. In a limited measure of frequency, fingerspelled words constituted an average of 7% of all lexical items across four different signed narratives (Padden, 1991). Fingerspelled words in ASL include English names of individuals and places, as well as words that are intended to remain foreign, such as representations of titles and scientific names. But not all fingerspelled words are novel; some coexist with signs. For example, R-E-N-T, the fingerspelled word, coexists with RENT, the sign.[2] The sign CAR coexists with C-A-R.

The distribution of fingerspelled words in signed discourse is not equal across all grammatical classes. Over 50% of fingerspelled words identified in a set of signed narratives were nouns; those remaining were distributed as adjectives, verbs, functor words, and pronouns (Padden, 1991). Poplack, Sankoff, & Miller (1988) observed a similar distribution of "Anglicisms" in Canadian French, in which nearly 65% of their sample of words borrowed from English were nouns.

Fingerspelling contrasts with a related set of loan vocabulary in ASL in which fingerspelled words undergo phonological and morphological change and become lexicalized (Battison, 1978). The loan sign #BACK has a reduced number of handshapes, from four to two, and it is two-handed with a path movement. Its distribution is restricted to a verb with the

---

[2] Fingerspelled items are here represented by letters separated by hyphens. ASL signs are represented by capitalized English glosses. Fingerspelled loan signs are represented by capitalized English glosses preceded by a pound sign (#).

meaning "to reconcile, come back together again." In contrast, the fingerspelled word B-A-C-K represents all letters of its written English word, and can be used for nearly any of its meanings in English, for example, "my back hurts" or "the back of my shirt." Because the meaning of a fingerspelled word (as distinguished from a loan sign of fingerspelled origin) more closely resembles its written counterpart, I suggest that fingerspelled words be categorized as "foreign vocabulary." Foreign vocabulary in other languages closely resembles fingerspelled vocabulary in type and category, such as anglicisms in Canadian French (e.g., "mon learner's permit," or "l'halloween").[3] Poplack et al. (1988) argue that in extended contact situations such as in Quebec, borrowed vocabulary plays a variety of functional, aesthetic, and social roles in the language lives of monolingual and bilingual speakers. Canadian French and ASL have much in common; both coexist with a dominant-world language, and both have speakers who cannot avoid living alongside speakers of another language.

The Relationship between Fingerspelling and English

Fingerspelling is a marked manual system (compared to natural signed languages), imported into ASL putatively for representing foreign words.[4] It is popularly referred to as "English," and is said to increase in frequency as the signer attempts to "incorporate more English" in signing. Some have bemoaned the decline of ASL by pointing to the increased frequency of fingerspelled words in younger signers compared to older signers.[5] Others have claimed that the elite members of the Deaf community use more fingerspelling, in so doing marking their affinity with the language of the larger society. Interestingly, Poplack et al. (1988) identify the intellectual elite and the youth subculture among the several subgroups active in borrowing and transmitting English vocabulary into Canadian French. As with any bilingual community, the roles and functions of ASL and English are matters of political signification more than simple personal choice. Insofar as fingerspelling is said to be a representation of English, its use by signers is politically charged.

---

3 These examples were drawn from a longer list gathered by Danielle Ross. I thank her for her help with these data.
4 The American system of fingerspelling can be traced to an alphabetic system invented by a hearing priest in the seventeenth century, Juan Pablo Bonet, who developed it for the purpose of tutoring a young deaf boy.
5 There is good evidence that fingerspelling has coexisted with ASL for at least this century. Films of signed lectures and narratives dating from 1913 feature fingerspelling interspersed with signing (National Association of the Deaf, 1913).

From a structural point of view, however, it is one thing to call fingerspelling borrowed vocabulary and another to call it "English." First, it represents English in alphabetic, not spoken, form. Second, its vocabulary is extremely selective, consisting largely of nouns, with verbs very rarely represented. Furthermore, signers do not fingerspell sentences except in situations where one is attempting to represent extended English text verbatim. For the most part, fingerspelling occurs only as words interspersed in signing. With this kind of distribution, it would be stretching any definition of a human language to call fingerspelling "English." More accurately, fingerspelled words are largely foreign vocabulary used as a resource within the larger resource of ASL.

Early Use of Fingerspelling by Deaf Children

Two studies (Padden & LeMaster, 1985; Padden, 1991) involving six Deaf children ranging in age from two years nine months to four years nine months, examine fingerspelling in a sample of white middle-class Deaf families. The parents used fingerspelling less often with their children than when conversing with adults. Signing adults in a separate study used an average of about 7% fingerspelled words, but in the signing of two adults to their children, an average of about 4% of all lexical items were fingerspelled. Two general observations emerged about early use of fingerspelling. First, fingerspelling appeared early in the child's vocabulary, long before the child could read or write. Its connection to English appeared later, and English was not a condition of its use, at least by young children. Second, the description of fingerspelling as a representation of English alphabetic characters is misleading on one level; it may be more useful and accurate to describe it as a special manual system with its own organizational properties which has links with English alphabetic characters.

With respect to the first observation, videotapes of children as young as two years three months, two years seven months, and three years eleven months feature them attempting to fingerspell their names and the names of siblings. It is a source of great pride to middle-class Deaf American parents if their young children can fingerspell their own names. In one videotape, a child introduces herself by fingerspelling her name into the camera, then turns to introduce others in the room, mimicking the activity of fingerspelling. The children also attempt a small fingerspelled vocabulary of colors, foods, and common objects, such as "blue," "bus," "dog," and "rice." What characterizes this set of early fingerspelled vocabulary is that the fingerspelling of the word is performed almost as a single unit.

One father reported that his daughter used different movement contours for fingerspelling "rice" and "ice." R-I-C-E was fingerspelled with a distinctive semicircle, but I-C-E, with a short opening and closing of the fingers. Another child, recorded on videotape, attempts to spell D-E-L-L, but uses a single L handshape throughout while using the distinctive bounce for doubled letters. The children appear to treat fingerspelled words as a special manual activity in which the internal units are movement units, not units corresponding to alphabetic letters. Akamatsu (1982) has observed similar movement units in her study of the early fingerspelling efforts of young hearing children of Deaf parents. The words' link to English is not yet known to them; indeed, it does not need to be made obvious in order to use fingerspelling.

These early fingerspelling attempts give credence to an alternative analysis of fingerspelling not as sequences of handshapes, but as the execution of sequences of movement units which have one or more handshapes linked to them. Lars-Åke Wïkstrom, a sign language researcher at the University of Stockholm, has analyzed another alphabetic fingerspelling system, coexisting with Swedish Sign Language, as consisting of a set of "core" movement units with other movement units in a dependent relationship to the core units. The core units are made up of a set of movement primes linked to one or two handshapes. A movement prime can consist of a twisting movement, a downward movement, or an upward movement. The combination of these core units and dependent units results in a fingerspelled sequence in which, for example, a sequence is made up of a twisting movement followed by a downward movement. Johnson (1993) has proposed an analysis of fingerspelling as made up of strings of morphemes, one morpheme for each letter of the alphabet, linked together by a set of phonotactic rules.

According to Johnson's approach to fingerspelling, its structure is analyzed not in terms of English alphabetic characters, but in terms of an independent phonological system that may turn out to be more linear, or to consist of more movement units in linear sequence, than ASL. ASL lexemes (the equivalent of a word in spoken languages) have been described as consisting of at least one but no more than two syllables (Coulter, 1988; Perlmutter, 1992). A fingerspelled sequence could well have more sequential units than ASL signs.

At least one consequence of this alternative view of fingerspelling is that the relationship between fingerspelling and English can now be viewed as less direct and less obvious than one might expect. This more subtle and complex view has implications for how we understand bilingual acquisition of ASL and English. Crucially, it is very likely the case that fingerspelling itself is not "English," and Deaf children using fingerspelling at early ages are not necessarily acquiring English. It is possible that the children are acquiring fingerspelling, and the relationship between fingerspelling and English must be consciously constructed by the child at a later time. Up until now, we have assumed that the relationship between English and fingerspelling is an obvious and transparent one. We need to understand the acts by which Deaf children establish that fingerspelling is used to represent English.

How might Deaf children realize associations between fingerspelling and English? Our work suggests that one way associations are formed is by reorganizing links between fingerspelling and other language systems, notably ASL. This seems counterintuitive, that in order to learn fingerspelling's connection to English, the child needs to learn its connection to ASL. But the data show interesting relationships between ASL and fingerspelling. Among the more frequently appearing examples is the use of initialized signs in ASL. Initialized signs are a category of lexemes in ASL in which the handshape of the sign coincides with the first letter of the English word which translates the sign. Many, but not all, color signs are initialized signs, for example, BLUE, PINK, YELLOW. Many name signs are also initialized, as well as other lexical items ranging from verbs, like TRY, to family terms, like UNCLE.

We found several examples of children fingerspelling color words: B-L-U-K-E for "blue," P-I-K for "pink," and Y-P-E-W for "yellow." But what is also notable is how they attempted to extend initialization to signs that are not in this morphological category. In one example, a Deaf child aged four years seven months fingerspelled Y-O-B[6] in response to a picture of an airplane, and began to fingerspell S- for a picture of a racket. The use of Y and S as the initial fingerspelled handshapes repeats the handshapes of the signs AIRPLANE and RACKET, respectively. Ramsey (personal communication) reports from her field notes of children writing in class an example of a child writing n as the first letter of "bacon" and insisting that because the sign uses the handshape N, the written word likewise begins with that

---

[6] It is not clear why the child chose the sequence O-B for the remainder of the word. From observing deaf children trying to spell words, it often seems that they choose from a repertoire of favorite letters, or try to select letters that resemble in some remote way their recollection of the spelling of the word.

letter. Later, Deaf children understand that not all signs fall in this category and not all signs can be linked to the first letter of their English translation. But crucially, in order to discover the relationship between fingerspelled handshapes and English, the child must also learn morphological properties of ASL signs.

At about the time that deaf children realize that there are links between ASL and fingerspelling, they also realize that there are rules to the selection of letters and their order in fingerspelled words, and specifically that fingerspelling is linked to English vocabulary. Deaf children who once enjoyed games of pretend fingerspelling often refuse to invent spelling any longer because they now understand that fingerspelling is linked to a system they do not know enough about (Padden 1991).

Our description of early use of fingerspelling by young Deaf children indicates that fingerspelling exists in an interactive relationship with other language systems, notably ASL as well as English reading and writing. Knowing the alphabetic basis of fingerspelling does not appear to be essential for its acquisition. In fact, many Deaf children make the alphabetic discovery later. When they do make the discovery, they still need to discover which sets of language items can be analyzed in this particular way. The acquisition of fingerspelling does not take place without also learning morphological properties of ASL.

The Acquisition of Written Spelling

The English orthographic system is commonly described as derived from and dependent on the sound system of the spoken language it represents (Venezky, 1970). I have argued elsewhere (Padden, 1993) that this description, while useful, overlooks features of English orthography that are strongly positional-graphemic. For example, the two-letter sequence *ph* is commonly understood as an archaic representation of the phoneme [f]. But this is only true in positional terms. If this same sequence appears straddling two syllables, as in "haphazard," it is not interpreted as a cluster representing one phoneme, but as two separate consonants, [p] and [h]. To use another example, the alternation between short and long vowels in medial position (e.g., "shin" vs. "shine" and "ban" vs. "bane") is signaled by *e* in final position.

Badecker (1988) has proposed that English orthography is accessible by visual means as well as phonemic, and that it can be analyzed as a system involving interaction of two levels – the first of identity, or the selection of alphabetic characters, and the second of position, where the character is located in the word. Orthographic regularities appear at one or the other levels, for example, in the case of doubled letters. In terms of position, except for rare words such as "llama" or "Lloyd," doubled consonants cannot appear in initial position in a word, although some vowels can, as in "ooze" and "aardvark." In terms of identity, some consonants cannot be doubled, e.g., *hh,* or *jj,* while others can, e.g., *tt.* Similar analyses can be made of consonant clusters, i.e., which digrams of consonants can appear in which positions (e.g., *qe* is not a possible combination and *qu* cannot appear in final position).

This multilevel approach allows an analysis that is not solely sequential, an analysis of orthography not solely as a sequence of letters from the first letter of the word to the last, but also as made up of featural characteristics such as positions of doubled letters and consonant clusters. Featural characteristics reveal orthographic rules to be not simply "visual," but based on units larger than the individual letter – rules relating to initial, medial, and final positions. As it turns out, this approach offers an ideal way to analyze early spelling attempts of young Deaf children.

Early Written Spelling in Young Deaf Children

Some have posited that the correct course of acquisition of English orthography in young hearing children is first to analyze the orthography in terms of sound–symbol correspondences, and then later to acquire the special non-phonemic conventions of the system, e.g., that there are spelling regularities across morphological alternations, as in "electric" and "electricity" (Read, 1975; Barron, 1980). The argument is based on the claim that young hearing children need first to establish a correspondence between spoken units and orthographic units. After this connection is successfully made, then the child can learn other kinds of regularities, including morphological regularities that depend more on grammatical knowledge of English. The suggestion is that the system is primarily sound-based, with other regularities derived from, or secondary to, sound.

In a study of spontaneously produced written words in a group of forty young Deaf children ranging in age from four years to ten years old (Padden, 1991),[7] I have found evidence of early use of spelling in which the analysis of English orthography was not by phonemic means, but by

---

[7] Younger children were asked to write all the words they knew in a familiar set, e.g., colors, animals, foods, sports. Some children were prompted with signs for familiar objects, e.g., house, car, tree. Older children were asked to write a paragraph or a short story.

learning positional-graphemic rules. The spelling attempts did not resemble the well-known invented spelling reported by Read (1975) and others (Bissex, 1980; Clay, 1975; Wilde, 1987); indeed, they looked almost disordered. Some of the attempts bore little resemblance to the target words except for certain salient letters. For example, compare the following attempts with targets:

Attempt	Target
hosue	house
bota	boat
umber	umbrella
giffe	giraffe
mokley	monkey
cheale	chair

The attempts involved transpositions of medial letters, as in "hosue," deletions of not only letters but entire syllables, as in "giffe," and substitutions of letters, as in "mokley" (*l* for *n*, with a transposition). The attempts resulted in words that did not "pronounce" similarly to the target words, but what was striking about these attempts was how well they adhered to other types of regularities, notably positional rules. Take for example attempts involving doubled letters:

Attempt	Target
alppe	apple
umbllea	umbrella
ganne	green
frzze	freeze
terre	three
genny	green
gerrn	green

The attempts can be analyzed at two levels, either at the level of letter identity or letter position. In "alppe," the child switched letter position, but retained letter identity, that is, *p* is correctly doubled, but it is after *l* instead of before it. In "ganne," the switch is not in position but identity. The doubled sequence is in the correct, medial position, but the letter *n* is doubled rather than *e*; likewise with "frzze."

Overall, the children's spelling attempts were faithful to the first letter of the word an average of 86% of all attempts in four-year-olds, 95% in six-year-olds, and 100% in eight-to-ten-year-olds. In addition, their attempts were often nearly equal in length to target words, even if letters were transposed or substituted. In older children, transpositions and substitutions occurred more often than deletions, as their awareness of preserving word shape increased.

It may seem that deaf children's spelling attempts are reminiscent of typing errors (Rumelhart & Norman, 1981), in which letters are also transposed, deleted, or substituted. There is at least one important difference between typing errors and the invented spelling of deaf children: In typing, it is possible to create impossible consonant clusters or impossible doubling sequences, but in invented spelling, deaf children are careful to avoid orthographically impossible sequences. While both activities involve print, clearly the cognitive demands are different. In typing, the issue is often speed, creating conditions for confusion at the motor level. In invented spelling, the children write each letter and errors are based on how they believe the word is spelled.

Because the children in this study were mostly four-, five-, and six-year-olds, the spelling attempts showed more of the children's awareness of orthographic structure and less of their awareness of morphological regularities as represented in written form. The next step in a study of written spelling in young children is to follow older children as they begin to spell longer and more morphologically complex words.

Between Fingerspelling and Writing

As deaf children discover the alphabetic principle of fingerspelling, they begin to explore connections between fingerspelling and writing. While trying to write, one child, at age four years eight months, invented iconic representations of the letters *p* and *k* based on features of their fingerspelled handshapes (Padden, 1991). She knew the letters of the alphabet, but appeared to want to represent fingerspelled handshapes on the written page. She used stick marks, one for each extended finger, for the P and K handshapes.

Older children are faced with a different problem. They understand the one-to-one relationship of handshapes and characters, but they need to discover how to watch a fingerspelled sequence and then write the word down. Some children insist on being shown a word one letter at a time. As each letter is fingerspelled, the child looks down to the page and records its written representation. Some children can watch segments of words, but the skill of watching an entire word and then writing it down comes later, when they understand better the orthographic properties of written words. In an example we observed recently, we saw a child, age nine years seven months, ask a teacher how to spell "rubber." The teacher fingerspelled the word quickly, R-U-B-B-E-R. The child copied the word as *r-u-b-b-e* and began to write the word. The teacher waved at the child, and gave one letter, R. The child nodded and wrote down "rubber." This is not a trivial accomplishment. The child understood that the letter R was intended to be the last letter of the word, but the teacher made no explicit reference to this. This is a skill some deaf children struggle to obtain, to be able to appropriate fingerspelled words in whole form and represent them in writing.

Fingerspelling continues to mediate writing throughout the elementary years. In the case of initialized signs, we have often seen children quickly writing down the first letter of the sign and then waiting as they tried to construct the remaining letters of the word. Many children fingerspell a word first before writing it, as though to study the word first-hand, or they may revert to fingerspelling the word if they are struggling to write it. In our observations of children writing extended prose, we have often seen them interrupt writing to fingerspell a word to themselves.

As one might expect, the classroom is an ideal place for studying active connections between ASL and English systems, as the children confront English texts more regularly and more urgently. We hope to describe these examples in more detail as part of a larger study in how young Deaf children use and move between different languages and systems.

Moving Between Languages and Systems

This work suggests that the language lives of Deaf children and adults need to be considered in terms of how ASL and systems of English coexist. I have described here the parallel existence of ASL signing, fingerspelling, and early writing. I argue that what is most significant about young Deaf children's early use of fingerspelling and written spelling is not only the uniqueness of the tokens they produce and how they match up (or do not match up) to English, but how the children actively seek to form correspondences between these systems and other categories of symbols, notably ASL. In our new work, we have noted that as English figures more prominently and powerfully in the lives of young deaf children, the children begin to experiment with moving between languages and systems, which include but are not limited to fingerspelling and written English. We have seen much use of the systems of mouthing, forms of speaking, and the much-used but little-understood activity of "Sign English" or contact signing. We have found it useful to inquire about how children learn the properties of these systems within activities involving the learning of reading and writing skills (see also Ramsey, 1993).

Analysis of the tokens themselves reveals that Deaf children attach different types of signification to fingerspelling and writing. In the case of fingerspelling, the younger children showed that it was possible to use the system without understanding its alphabetic principle, suggesting that the system may have properties unrelated to print. In the case of early spelling, the children produced spelling attempts which reflected positional and graphemic regularities in English orthography, not its phonemic-graphemic associations. Their persistence in discovering these principles indicates to us that this approach is a useful and productive strategy for learning about English words, as different as it is from the more widely described early spelling attempts of hearing children. This work suggests that deaf children take a different route to acquiring command of English, one by way of systems that have no parallel in hearing American children's acquisition of English. Before we can ask whether the different routes are fruitful ones, we have to understand what these routes are. Then we can ask how these routes influence their subsequent command of English.

When questions are raised about deaf children's competence in a language or languages, the competence is often thought about in abstract terms. But it may be useful in the case of deaf children to understand their competence in language in terms of the unusual ways in which they acquire the language. Deaf children seem to acquire competence in English via the routes of fingerspelling, writing, even signing, mouthing, and speech. These different routes may well shape the nature of their competence in English.

Ultimately, the key to understanding bilingual acquisition in Deaf children is to track their manipulation of these different systems through their early years, and the ways in which they call upon the systems in different contexts. If we can watch acts of correspondence, of fingerspelling while writing or signing while writing, it is our hope we will be able to observe how Deaf children manage to learn English.

Acknowledgments

Preparation of this chapter was supported by a grant from the Spencer Foundation and the U.S. Department of Education, H023T30006.

References

Akamatsu, C. T. (1982). *The acquisition of fingerspelling in preschool children*. Unpublished doctoral dissertation, Department of Psychology, University of Rochester.

Badecker, W. (1988). *Representational properties common to phonological and orthographic output systems*. Unpublished manuscript, Johns Hopkins University, Baltimore.

Barron, R. (1980). Visual and phonological strategies in reading and spelling. In U. Frith (Ed.). *Cognitive processes in spelling* (pp. 195–213). London: Academic Press.

Battison, R. (1978). *Lexical borrowing in American Sign Language*. Silver Spring, MD: Linstok Press.

Bissex, G. (1980). *Gnys at work: A child learns to read and write*. Cambridge, MA: Harvard University Press.

Clay, M. (1975). *What did I write?* London: Heinemann.

Conrad, R. (1979). *The deaf schoolchild*. London: Harper & Row.

Coulter, G. (1988). *On the nature of ASL as a monosyllabic language*. Unpublished manuscript, University of Illinois.

Erting, C. (1992). Deafness and literacy: Why can't Sam read? *Sign Language Studies, 75*, 97–112.

Ewoldt, C. (1985). A descriptive study of the developing literacy of young hearing-impaired children. *The Volta Review, 85* (5), 109–126.

Grosjean, F. (1982). *Life with two languages: An introduction to bilingualism*. Cambridge, MA: Harvard University Press.

(1992). Another view of bilingualism. In R. Harris (Ed.), *Cognitive processing in bilinguals* (pp. 51–62). New York: Elsevier Science Pub.

Johnson, R. (1992). *Possible influences on bilingualism in early ASL acquisition*. Paper presented at the Fourth International Conference on Theoretical Issues in Sign Language Research, San Diego.

(1993). *Lexical movement segments: Evidence from lexicalized fingerspelling in ASL*. Unpublished manuscript, Gallaudet University, Washington, DC.

Karchmer, M. A., Milone, M. N., Jr., & Wolk, S. (1979). Educational significance of hearing loss at three levels of severity. *American Annals of the Deaf, 124*, 97–109.

Lucas, C., & Valli, C. (1992). *Language contact in the American Deaf community*. New York: Academic Press.

Marshall, W., & Quigley, S. (1970). *Quantitative and qualitative analysis of syntactic structure in the written language of deaf students*. Urbana: University of Illinois, Institute for Research on Exceptional Children.

Maxwell, M. (1980). *Language acquisition in a deaf child: The interaction of sign variations, speech and print variations*. Unpublished dissertation, University of Arizona.

(1984). A deaf child's natural development of literacy. *Sign Language Studies, 44*, 191–224.

Meier, R. (1991, January–February). Language acquisition by deaf children. *American Scientist, 79*, 60–70.

Moores, D. (1987). *Educating the Deaf*. Boston: Houghton Mifflin.

National Association of the Deaf. (1913). *The preservation of the sign language by George W. Veditz.* [Film].

Newport, E., & Meier, R. (1985). The acquisition of American Sign Language. In D. Slobin (Ed.), *The crosslinguistic study of language acquisition, 1* (pp. 881–938). New York: Lawrence Erlbaum.

Padden, C. (1991). The acquisition of fingerspelling by deaf children. In P. Siple & S. Fischer (Eds.), *Theoretical issues in sign language research, 2* (pp. 191–210). Chicago: University of Chicago Press.

——— (1993). Lessons to be learned from young deaf orthographers. *Linguistics and Education, 5* (1), 71–86.

Padden, C., & LeMaster, B. (1985). An alphabet on hand: The acquisition of fingerspelling in deaf children. *Sign Language Studies, 47,* 161–172.

Perlmutter, D. (1992). Sonority and syllable structure in American Sign Language. *Linguistic Inquiry, 23* (3), 407–442.

Poplack, S., Sankoff, D., & Miller, C. (1988). The social correlates and linguistic processes of lexical borrowing and assimilation. *Linguistics, 26,* 47–104.

Ramsey, C. (1993). *A description of classroom language and literacy learning among deaf children in a mainstreaming program.* Unpublished dissertation, University of California, Berkeley.

Read, C. (1975). Lessons to be learned from the preschool orthographer. In E. Lenneberg & E. Lenneberg (Eds.), *Foundations of language development.* (Vol. 2, pp. 329–345). New York: Academic Press.

Rumelhart, D., & Norman, D. (1981). *Simulating a skilled typist: A study of skilled cognitive-motor performance.* Center for Human Information Processing, University of California, San Diego. Series title: CHIP report; 102.

Trybus, R., & Karchmer, M. (1977). School achievement scores of hearing impaired children: National data on achievement status and growth patterns. *American Annals of the Deaf: Directory of Programs and Services, 122,* 62–69.

Venezky, R. (1970). *The structure of English orthography.* The Hague: Mouton.

Wilde, S. (1987). *Spelling and punctuation development in selected third and fourth grade children.* (Research Report 17). Charlotte: University of North Carolina.

CHAPTER SEVEN

Communication Experiences of Deaf People: An Ethnographic Account

SUSAN B. FOSTER

Introduction

As Grosjean (1982) has pointed out, definitions of individuals who are called "bilingual" range from minimal to nativelike control of two or more languages, and everything in between. Certainly this range of definitions can be applied to deaf people who use American Sign Language (ASL) and English. Deaf people may demonstrate high proficiency in both ASL and English, or they may have greater skill in one language (ASL or English). There are also deaf people who, for a variety of reasons, have never developed high levels of proficiency in either ASL or English.

Barriers to communication between deaf and hearing people often are associated with differences in language – for example, when the deaf person is using sign language and the hearing person is using English. However, deaf people who demonstrate high levels of competence in English grammar, syntax, and vocabulary may still experience difficulties in the mode most often used by hearing people for informal and spontaneous communication – the mode of speaking and listening. Even with

Susan B. Foster (Ph.D., Special Education, Syracuse University), Associate Professor, National Technical Institute for the Deaf, conducts and publishes research employing an ethnographic approach to the study of educational policy and practice for deaf students and the performance and attainments of deaf adults in the workplace. She is the author of *Working with Deaf People: Accessibility and Accommodation in the Workplace* (1992, Charles C. Thomas), and has coedited, with Gerard Walter, *Deaf Students in Postsecondary Education* (1992, Routledge). Her address is: Department of Educational and Career Research, National Technical Institute for the Deaf, Rochester Institute of Technology, 52 Lomb Memorial Drive, Rochester, NY 14623.

superb speech and speechreading skills, the inability to hear often inter-feres with expression and reception in a speaking and listening mode: cues go unnoticed, subtle meanings associated with voice tone are not properly conveyed, comments made while a back is turned or the television is on are missed completely. In this chapter, barriers to interaction associated with communication differences (of both language and mode) between deaf and hearing people are explored. The chapter concludes with a discussion of the implications of these barriers for deaf people.

The Use of Ethnographic Methods in Research on Deafness and Communication

Over the past eight years, the author has conducted eleven studies in the field of deafness, using one or more ethnographic, or qualitative, re-search methods.[1] The ethnographer's approach to research is quite different from that of more quantitative-minded researchers. Grounded in symbolic interactionist theory (Becker, 1970; Blumer, 1969; Mead, 1934, 1938; Park, 1915; Thomas, 1951), ethnographic research is built upon the premise that human behavior is a product of how people interpret their world. Instead of surveys or controlled experiments, the ethnographer's research tools are observation and open-ended or semi-structured, in-depth interviews (Bogdan & Taylor, 1975; Bogdan & Biklen, 1992). Instead of "respondents" or "subjects," she thinks of the people she observes and interviews as "informants," in the sense that they teach and inform her about their experience (Spradley, 1979). Detailed field notes and interview transcripts are the ethnographer's data, and quotations from interviews and field notes are used to illustrate points in written reports, instead of tables and charts. While some questions cannot be answered through ethnographic research, this approach is ideally suited to studies in which the goal is to describe the experiences of people in *their* words, from *their* perspective.

Ethnographic research methods have been used to explore the experi-ences of deaf people in a variety of areas. For example, the work of Higgins (1980) and Becker (1980) has described different aspects of the community life of deaf people. Bateman (1990) has used in-depth interviews to learn the perspectives of deaf people who are political leaders within their own

---

[1] Each of these studies focuses on the experiences of deaf persons in the areas of family, school, employment, and/or community. The eleven studies have been published in a variety of formats and professional journals. For further details please refer to the list of publications under the author's name in the References section at the end of this chapter.

deaf communities. Using open-ended interviews with two deaf adults, Seidel (1982) studied "the points at which deaf and hearing worlds intersect," with particular attention to the tensions which sometimes infuse these interactions. Saur et al. (1986) and Evans and Falk (1986) identified issues in the education of deaf people through ethnographic methods, the first focusing on mainstream classes and the second taking a look at residential schools for deaf pupils. Mertens (1986) and Stinson et al. (1990) included qualitative components in their research on educational experiences of deaf students, as did Crammatte (1968) in his study of the employment experiences of deaf adults. In each case, the goal has been to learn about the experiences of deaf people from their perspectives, and to reflect these experiences through analysis of recorded field notes and interviews in which informants describe and interpret their lives.

Barriers to Communication between Deaf and Hearing People

More than 150 deaf people were interviewed over the course of the eleven studies conducted by the author of this chapter.[2] Topics addressed in these interviews included the experiences of informants within the settings of family, school, work, and community. Not surprisingly, differences of language and mode, and the barriers to communication between deaf and hearing people posed by these differences, emerged as a significant, if not central, theme in every study. In the following pages, persistent and central themes from these eleven studies regarding informants' experiences with communication barriers are presented, organized within the broad categories of family, school, and work. Interview excerpts from the published papers are included as examples of informants' experiences and ideas.

Experiences with Hearing Family Members

Most deaf people have hearing parents (Schein & Delk, 1974). While the trend today is to encourage family members to learn sign language, in the

---

[2] These interviews have lasted between forty-five minutes and two hours. Communication took place in sign language or spoken English, according to the preference of the informant. Interpreters holding the Comprehensive Skills Certification of the Registry of Interpreters for the Deaf facilitated communication as needed for interviews conducted in sign language. With the permission of the informants, interviews were recorded on audiotape and transcribed verbatim. Transcripts were then coded for recurring themes.

past the opposite advice was given. As a result, many deaf adults recall growing up in homes in which sign language was never used. Those who could speechread and speak were able to follow some of the conversations around them, under specific conditions (i.e., if people faced them, were in well-lit locations, and took turns speaking). For those who were unable to speechread or speak clearly, however, communication with family members was more limited.

It was a general experience of the deaf people interviewed that, even when family members of deaf people made an effort to learn sign language, high levels of fluency were seldom attained, and it was the rare family that conversed in sign language all the time or extended skill development beyond parents and siblings to aunts, uncles, cousins, or grandparents. If hearing family members do not learn and consistently use sign language, the deaf person is often left out of casual banter as well as more formal or directed conversations. Many of the deaf people interviewed said their worst memories were of conversations around the dinner table, when family members would share the events of their day and discuss local news. The fast-paced and often overlapping nature of these spoken exchanges made them almost impossible to follow through speechreading. As a result, the deaf person was usually excluded. In the following quotation, a deaf informant recounted his experience at these times:

> They were pretty much limited and talked to themselves . . . like, when we sit down and eat supper, I'd eat and I'd say, "What did you say?" And they'd say, "Wait a minute." And I'd wait and wait and wait. I'd say, "Hey, what are you guys talking about?" They'd say, "Wait a minute." And [then] they'd say, "Well, what do you want?" You know, they should at least come back and finish the conversation, but they do that over and over . . . so I give up . . . I just ignored it and eat. And I'd leave, I'd go out . . . Yeah, that's how it's been ever since I was a kid . . . they always left me out of everything. (Foster, 1989c, p. 229)

Relationships with extended family members are often particularly strained as a result of communication barriers. In the following excerpt, an informant recalls her frustration with the lack of communication with her grandparents, and the negative impact of this frustration on their relationship:

> I don't have any communication with my grandparents . . . I know they want to talk to me and I want to talk to them, but I can't. They use my mother as an interpreter all the time and I'm so pissed off . . . I'm glad I

came here [to college] so I won't see them much. I do like my grandparents, yes, but sometimes it bothers me with no communication, especially my grandmother. (Foster, Barefoot, & DeCaro, 1989, p. 562)

Ironically, events traditionally associated with family camaraderie and closeness are frequently the most difficult for deaf people. Speechreading and use of residual hearing are made much more difficult when several people are conversing in a group, or when there is background noise. One informant recalled that "when the family all gets together during the holidays to have a celebration or a family reunion I experience a lot of isolation. My parents try to include me . . . but my experience is still that, for me, I am sort of a loner" (Foster, 1989c, p. 229).

Experiences in Mainstream School Environments

In the field of education, Public Law 94–142 (also known as the Education for All Handicapped Children Act of 1975) has made mainstreaming the norm for many children with disabilities. Deaf children, routinely identified by educational policymakers and administrators as disabled (as opposed to members of a linguistic or bilingual minority), are frequently sent to mainstream schools rather than separate programs. Often a deaf student is the only deaf person in an entire school.

It is a serious problem that in school, where communication is essential for learning, language barriers often persist. Students who use ASL but do not have interpreters in the classroom are naturally at a great disadvantage. Speechreading under ordinary classroom conditions, however, is also fraught with problems. The classic situation is one in which the teacher continues talking while turning away from the class to write on the board – effectively cutting the deaf student off completely from the lecture. Difficulties are compounded when deaf students do not have notetakers, since they must make the "no-win" choice of what to do without – the opportunity to follow the lecture by watching the teacher or the opportunity to take notes:

It wasn't easy in school, especially from the sixth grade, because the notes were written on the blackboard and I was really frustrated because I wasn't able to sit in the front. It was really hard for me to catch up, especially the notes, cause they were talking and talking and I'd try to do the notes and it was real difficult. My grades were starting to go down. (Foster, 1989b, p. 43)

Even when interpreters and notetakers are provided for classroom instruction, communication is still frequently limited. Lag time (the time between the completion of the teacher's spoken message and the interpreter's translation of the message into sign language) insures that deaf students are always a few seconds behind their classmates in getting information, a condition which hampers participation in group discussion and response to the teacher's questions. Moreover, not all interpreters are similarly skilled. In relating his experience as a doctoral student at a major university, a deaf colleague explained the importance of having an interpreter who could accurately convey his ideas to the class. As he put it, "in order for me to appear intelligent and present myself as a capable student, the interpreter must articulate my comments accurately, that is, use appropriate vocabulary along with inflections that match the intent of my message. Otherwise, my comments might appear choppy, unintelligent, or downright inappropriate" (Foster & Holcomb, 1990, p. 161). Not surprisingly, a poor interpreter can dampen a deaf student's motivation to participate in classroom discussion. In the following excerpt, a deaf college student recounts his experience with an interpreter who is unable to translate his signs into spoken English:

> INTERVIEWER: Is it difficult for you to ask questions in class?
> INFORMANT: Yes, because I'm not very happy with the interpreter. For example, I raise my hand to ask a question and I'm talking to the interpreter, then the interpreter reverses to the teacher. Sometimes the interpreter doesn't understand me and I spell it again, and I spell it again . . . it's very embarrassing, the people all listening to this repetition. I get really frustrated. (Foster & Brown, 1989, p. 84)

Furthermore, students are unable to access the tremendous amount of knowledge – both academic and social – that is acquired through informal conversations among students both within and outside the classroom. Group work and lab situations are particularly troublesome, since interactions within these settings tend to be more spontaneous and open, circumstances which make conversations more difficult both for the deaf student to follow and for the interpreter to translate. An example:

> INTERVIEWER: You said that sometimes you will interrupt and ask people what they were saying [during lab].
> INFORMANT: A little bit. I try not to do it too much. Like, during an experiment, I wanna know what's going on. I'll see people talking and I might say, "Can you tell me what you just said?" Sometimes they give me just a short, limited synopsis and not the whole story. Sometimes they say, "It's not important." And often, I'll ask the interpreter to interpret for me what's going on.

INTERVIEWER: How do people react when you do that?

INFORMANT: Well, they don't like to repeat it. They show a willingness, but they're put out a little bit . . . It depends on the situation . . . In one hearing class, the hearing people will get all excited about some news that goes around and there'll be all this chatter from one person or another, and I'm depending on the interpreter. Sometimes the interpreter will allow me to join their conversation by interpreting it, but sometimes I feel left out during class. (Foster & Brown, 1989, p. 563)

Academic performance is not the only area in which deaf students suffer when they are unable to access informal conversations and information exchange. In the following excerpt, a deaf colleague describes the impact of communication barriers on his ability to play what he calls "the university game":

Because I cannot always play the "university game" right, I have found myself subject to scorn or missing an opportunity. For example, there were times when I needed information or assistance with paperwork (registration, parking stickers, receipts, and so forth). It took me longer than most to discover that some secretaries are more helpful than others; apparently, the university game includes access to information about which secretaries are the most cheerful, understanding and resourceful . . . Similarly, in past courses I often did not have the slightest clue of what the teacher's expectations really were other than what was documented in the handouts or articulated in the class. In a few classes where I was fortunate enough to have a hearing classmate who could communicate in sign language . . . I was frequently amazed at the amount of knowledge students share with each other about teachers. (Foster & Holcomb, 1990, pp. 165–166)

Extracurricular school activities are generally recognized as vehicles for student development in a variety of areas, including those associated with physical, emotional, social, and intellectual growth. Often, deaf students' participation in these activities is severely limited by communication barriers among students and between deaf students and hearing coaches/club advisors. For example:

In the seventh and eighth grade, I was a member of . . . a sports athletics association . . . [We went] bowling in the fall, and winter I think it was basketball, in spring volleyball . . . It was very hard to communicate. . . . Then, ninth grade and tenth, [I was in] home economics club. I enjoyed that, but there wasn't much activity there, so I stopped after tenth grade. Eleventh and twelfth grades, nothing. . . . At that time, I had just given up. Just did things at home . . . because hearing people weren't interested in me. No one would talk to me, so I just gave up . . . I just had to sit there and watch. . . . They'd just tell me what to do, and that's all. I know why – [it's] because we had a hard time . . . when we were talking. (Foster, 1989a, p. 73)

Difficulties with communication also reduce deaf students' opportunities to develop friendships with hearing peers. They often miss the jokes, the "messing around," and the informal banter that are prerequisite to the formation of friendships among young people. One person who was able to succeed academically in a mainstream classroom with the support of a notetaker and her mother (who reviewed material with her) added that, still, "I miss the fun. I mean, the kids shared laughter. I didn't know what they were laughing about" (Foster, 1989b, p. 43). Conversations with hearing peers are often limited to what one student described as "hi and bye."

Most informants were aware of what they were missing, and some expressed regret over the lack of close friends. In responding to a question about the quality of her social life in high school, one person said, "like at lunch or something, I never know what the conversation was about. I got frustrated and cried a lot. . . . I could not understand the people and it was hard to talk to them. . . . I didn't really care for high school that much. . . . I had a hard time trying to make friends and . . . that made it hard" (Foster, 1988). Another person explained that "being deaf was hard on me because I wanted more friends. I wanted someone really close to me, you know, who I could share a lot of things [with]. So I was very lonely" (Foster, 1989b, p. 44). Often, deaf students experienced the rejection of hearing peers who were unwilling to find ways around communication difficulties, as in the case of a woman who said that boys wouldn't accept her when they discovered that she "couldn't hear on the phone" (Foster, 1989b, p. 45).

The overall impression of many informants was that hearing people simply didn't have the patience or motivation to work through difficult communication situations, especially when they could turn instead to other hearing people for conversation and companionship. In the words of one woman, "it's so easy to just sit back and gab with your [hearing] friends; but with me they have to really pour more effort to communicate if they want to be friends. And a lot of times, a lot of people don't want to be bothered" (Foster,1989b, p. 45). As a result, many informants frequently described their experience in mainstream schools in terms of academic and social isolation.

Experiences with Hearing People in the Workplace

Unless they seek employment in special services organizations or educational institutions, deaf people generally find themselves in the monolingual, speaking and listening world of hearing English users when they enter the work force. Once again, they are cut off from much of the communication going on around them.

Most informants said that interpreters were seldom provided except in large meetings or workshops. The same difficulties associated with a lack of access to information in mainstream classrooms emerges at department meetings and small group training sessions in the workplace. In the following examples, two informants recall their frustration at meetings when interpreters were not provided:

> I would sit there and would try to catch on [to] whatever I could and then, after a while, everybody started to talk at once. And then I just sit there like a fool. People laugh and they joke and I sit there with a smile on my face and fire in my chest. (Emerton, Foster, & Royer, 1987, p. 10)

> They [meetings] were a big problem, because when I first went there, they never bothered to call me for any meetings, and then I asked the employer, "What are they talking about?" [And he said] "Oh, nothing important." I'd say, "Why are you leaving me out? I have a right to know what's happening." And I walked up to the supervisor and said, "I would appreciate that you [notify] me by doing some writing as to what you're talking about." So they did that. And I didn't want to hear any excuses any more because no matter what they're talking about, it's still important to me. (Foster, 1987, p. 11)

Even when supervisors make efforts to keep deaf employees up to date on information disseminated through meetings, there are limitations. Written or verbal summaries do not convey the more subtle messages transmitted through the tone of participants; the richness of the dialogue is lost to deaf workers, as are the banter and side conversations through which much of the information presented at meetings is filtered and interpreted. In the following example, a woman recalls her lack of satisfaction with the post-meeting updates provided by her supervisor:

> She [my supervisor] would talk with me after the meeting. We get together a few minutes. She said a lot at the meeting, and in the office we talked about ten minutes! And then I say, "We had a meeting for one hour, and now you talk to me for ten minutes! This is it? Ten minutes! I want to know what people said, what people were laughing about!" (Foster, 1987, p. 5)

Perhaps most important, deaf people may be left out of social and professional networks, informal gatherings, and casual conversations among workers. As one person put it, "they [co-workers] like to talk. I couldn't hear their talking. I'd love to hear what they're talking about. . . . It's sad because I can't hear what they're saying, to share the fun, the jokes" (Foster, 1987, p. 3).

This is not the only consequence of being outside the employee grapevine. Information about the informal rules and organizational culture is often transmitted through such networks and conversations. In these situations, deaf people are at a disadvantage both professionally and personally. The feeling that one is always "the last to know" was expressed by more than one person:

> It's not fair . . . there are some things that everyone knows except me. . . . That's why some of the people are ahead of me in some ways, because they know about the change or whatever, and I don't know anything about it. When I ask about it, they say, "We done away with that a long time ago," and I'll say, "Well, why didn't you tell me?" (Foster, 1987, p. 3)

As the story cited above suggests, sometimes informal on-the-job training occurs through casual conversations among co-workers, in which case deaf employees may find their job performance affected by the inability to access informal communication. In recounting her experience in a computer programming company, a deaf woman recalls a similar experience:

> We had cubicle offices. I'm sitting there typing, learning out of books and from the people who teach me. But the hearing people yell out, "Hey, why isn't this working?" And somebody else over in another cubicle hears and starts to work on it. That's really not fair. It was frustrating. (Foster, 1992, p. 96)

Inability to access informal communication networks may also reduce deaf employees' opportunities to develop relationships with co-workers. Many informants expressed a persistent sense of isolation at work, a feeling of being "alone in a crowded room." As one person put it, "it's lonely . . . I always want another person who knows sign language, who understands deaf people. Then I would be fine. But I hate working alone, even though there's a lot of hearing people around" (Foster, 1987, p. 7). In the experience of many informants, the best one can hope for is to be included in routine matters having to do with day-to-day operations. As illustrated by the following quotation, often this is not enough to make one feel a part of the group:

They're not interested in being friends. . . . Forget it. They only would talk to me for business things, you know, say, "We have a meeting," or just small [things] . . . nothing really like a conversation. Or they might say, "How're you doing?" But they don't go into real conversation at all. It is lonely there. (Foster, 1987, p. 3)

Finally, communication barriers can affect a deaf person's career development. For example, in explaining their lack of interest in pursuing managerial roles within their companies, the informants quoted below focus not on job skills, but on their inability to access the routine communications which they see as central to fulfilling management responsibilities:

INFORMANT: I don't have that ability as the management. I don't have it. . . . I don't want to . . . be a manager or anything.
INTERVIEWER: Why not?
INFORMANT: I don't want responsibility. I don't want any problems with communication with hearing people. If I become a boss, it's gonna be a problem. I think it's better if you're hearing, and you hear what's going on before you fall off the top. I don't know. I'm afraid of losing power. . . . If you want to get up to the top, you have to stay in power, defend yourself from falling off. You have to hear what's going on or you have some trusty persons by your side. Hearing people can hear what's going on. I'm deaf. I can't hear. Even somebody talking behind my back, I can't hear. And so the chance is you can be beat out easily. (Foster, 1987, p. 9)

INFORMANT: My project manager is trying to boost me up.
INTERVIEWER: Really, promotion?
INFORMANT: Yes, I'm trying to hold it down.
INTERVIEWER: Why?
INFORMANT: The load of responsibilities . . . more work, more depth, more engineering level. I am qualified, yes, but you can develop a high stress to it. It's a lot of pressure and I don't like pressure.
INTERVIEWER: Pressure from what?
INFORMANT: Communication between one person and another person, become a middle man . . . suppose I misunderstood them. . . . It would be totally my fault because I'm vulnerable when it comes to hearing impaired. . . . [Later] The supervisor uses the phone so much. Thirty or 40 times a day, she's on the phone . . . and . . . she has to go to a lot of meetings . . . going to all those different places and trying to interact, that would be too difficult. (Foster, 1987, p. 9)

The concern of these informants was shared by some supervisors. Analysis of data collected through interviews with twenty hearing supervisors of deaf employees revealed that barriers to communication and resistance to a deaf manager on the part of hearing employees were viewed as constraints on promotion of deaf employees to positions of management (Foster, 1992). For example, one supervisor wondered whether the deaf person in his department "would be able to train people . . . [or] explain things in enough detail for them to understand" (Foster, 1992, p. 151). Another supervisor responded to the question of whether he felt the deaf person in his group could be promoted to manager:

> I think that would be . . . difficult because [if you are deaf] you are going to be writing [instead of speaking]. I've got people pulling me in every direction, sometimes asking me this and . . . I am giving them directions and . . . I am walking over here and I am giving this guy directions on what to do. It would be a little slower process [if the manager were deaf and had to rely on written communication]. (Foster, 1992, p. 151)

In summary, informants' discussions of barriers to communication in the workplace were very similar to their descriptions of communication within families and at school. Failure to access the conversations of those around them can result in social as well as professional separation from hearing colleagues. Additionally, deaf employees may find their career advancement limited as a result of communication barriers at work.

Impact of Communication Barriers

Failure to access communication networks impacts a variety of areas within the settings of family, school, and employment, including those associated with formal or professional interactions as well as those characterized by intimacy and close relationships. Central to informants' experiences in all areas was a loss of "real conversation," defined here as meaningful, rich, and sustained dialogue through which complex, sensitive and subtle information can be exchanged. The loss is experienced by both deaf and hearing people. However, since the dominant form of communication in our society is spoken English, hearing users of English are far less disadvantaged as a result of these communication barriers than are deaf people. In this section, ways in which barriers to communication between deaf and hearing people negatively affect the experience of deaf persons are discussed, as well as ways in which these barriers have contributed to the development of positive interactions and relations among deaf persons.

Negative Consequences of Communication Barriers

Barriers to communication between hearing and deaf people have several negative consequences. First, deaf people sometimes find it difficult to establish close relationships with hearing people. For example, they may find it difficult to experience fully the closeness, acceptance, and shared identity traditionally associated with family. Many deaf people experience some level of frustration in interactions with hearing family members, even in those situations when interactions are the most relaxed and intimate, such as during mealtimes and holiday gatherings. At school and work the separation persists, reflected in descriptions of difficulties in establishing friendships with hearing students and colleagues, and stories of sitting alone in the school cafeteria or bringing a book to read during coffee break.

The most obvious result of this experience is the feeling of loneliness and social isolation expressed by many informants in their recollections of interactions with hearing people. But beyond this, given the role of relationships and social networks in personal development as well as professional advancement, the consequences of limited relationships with hearing people may have far-reaching effects on the attainments of deaf people over a lifetime of social interaction. The old adage, "It's not what you know, but who you know," has more than a grain of truth to it. Communication barriers may limit the ability of deaf people to get to know who could make a difference in their lives.

Second, deaf people often miss important information. For example, in mainstream school and employment settings where there are no support services, academic and technical information may be partly or even totally inaccessible. When hearing students and co-workers are learning new procedures through direct instruction and team meetings, the deaf person must rely on speechreading (generally under difficult circumstances) or written and verbal summaries. Perhaps even more damaging, deaf people rarely enjoy access to information that is transmitted indirectly or through informal means, including the subtle information which children pick up by overhearing casual conversations between parents and other adults as well as the wealth of incidental information transmitted through casual conversations among peers (e.g., classmates, co-workers, and neighbors).

Most people acquire knowledge about the norms and values of their culture as part of their natural development, beginning in infancy and continuing over a lifetime. As children, they learn by observing their parents and listening to conversations between other adults. As young adults, they observe friends, learning and adopting the values and accepted behaviors of the group in order to fit in. As adults, they use the same skills to access social and professional networks.

The communication barriers many deaf people face over a lifetime of interactions with hearing people make it difficult for them to acquire the wealth of social and cultural knowledge which hearing people learn incidentally, through observation and overhearing the conversations of others. They are often cut off from these learning experiences as children, especially if they grow up in homes in which they are the only deaf person and attend mainstream school programs, since peers and adults in these settings rarely use sign language for communication with the deaf person and almost never for communication with another hearing person which might be observed (i.e., "overheard") by a deaf person. Failure to access technical, social, and cultural information has many negative consequences, ranging from inaccurate perceptions of social protocols to missed information about procedures to be followed in completing school and work tasks. While interpreters and notetakers are helpful in providing deaf people access to direct or formal instruction, they are much less helpful in facilitating access to incidental or informal learning experiences.

A Positive Consequence of Communication Barriers: Communication and Community among Deaf Persons

The deaf community may be, in part, a natural outgrowth of and reaction to the communication barriers which deaf people encounter over a lifetime of interactions with hearing people. Deaf people often find in a community of deaf peers the real conversation, family, information, and friendships which they do not get from interactions with hearing people. It is therefore not surprising to learn that deaf youth whose hearing family members do not use sign language often prefer interactions with deaf peers to those with family members. The person quoted at the beginning of this chapter, who described himself as left out of dinner conversations at home, concludes his remarks by saying, "I needed that communication. I needed to find out a little bit more of what was happening, and I learned from other deaf people" (Foster, 1989c, p. 229). Another informant made the same point: "my Mom and Dad didn't teach me, so the heck with them. . . . I get my information from others, from my [deaf] friends" (Foster, 1989c, p. 229).

Similarly, in contrast to the experience of informants who attended mainstream programs, informants who attended schools for deaf pupils often described a rich linguistic community in which access to communication – and by extension to information and relationships – was complete. While some informants said there were drawbacks to separate programs, communication in these environments was rarely a problem.[3] In most of these schools, teachers used sign language, a practice greatly appreciated by most deaf students. In the words of one person, "at the [school for the deaf], I understood everything. I know what to do all the time because the teachers could sign and explain things more deeply. [A] lot of information" (Foster, 1989a, p. 65).

Informants who attended schools for the deaf frequently described these settings as places where they had opportunities to develop strong relationships and a sense of identity and belonging. The ability to communicate with teachers and peers, and the sense of connectedness this engendered, was central to their positive experiences. In some cases, informants described the influence of the school for the deaf in relationship – or even contrast – to their experiences at home. The following examples are illustrative:

> I went to the [residential school]. I was home four times a year. I didn't see my family much, but I felt that I belonged to the family at the institution. And still, in my heart, I belong to the family at home, too. (Foster, 1989c, p. 230)

> My family, there wasn't a lot of opportunity to talk, really not much. They would talk, talk, talk. My family would be talking away and I would just sit there. . . . I would have to say, "What did they say?" And [they would tell me, but] in real simple sentences, not fully, just a simple explanation. I am not interested in that. I am interested in the specifics of what you're saying, I am curious, what did they say. At my school, it is much better there. Any time anybody said anything, it was always in sign. Then you knew what they said, to be fair with the deaf. That was nice. I appreciate that. (Foster, 1989a, p. 65)

> I started to learn sign [when I] was sent to school, you see. Mother was so worried because it was four hours away. The school was a four hour drive. I

---

[3] Some informants noted that separate programs might be less academically challenging than mainstream programs. Others said that residential programs required students to live away from home, creating distance between the deaf student and his or her family and neighborhood. A third criticism was that separate schools failed to provide sufficient opportunities for students to interact with hearing people (Foster, 1989a, 1989b).

was only seven years old. But then I learned and learned. I was so enthusi-
astic and I just talked and talked in school. I learned so much. Many children, always have great influence. We learn so much from each other. I was
so happy. I would come home and realize that I didn't fit in my family, in
some way. I preferred school. (Foster, 1989a, p. 67)

Fluent communication with deaf peers also made possible opportunities for friendships that had not been available in mainstream settings.
In the following quotation a student who had been mainstreamed during
her primary and secondary school years described the change she experienced when she went to a college for deaf students:

> I became so popular and I couldn't understand it. It was . . . . amazing, it was
> just from darkness to light in . . . a flash of lamp, and all of a sudden I was
> well recognized. I was well liked. I had a lot of friends, and I fit into almost
> any social situation. I was beginning to learn sign language. I was on a
> dormitory floor with all hearing-impaired. It was an amazing experience
> and [I thought] "Wow, this isn't so bad!" (Foster, 1986, p. 15)

As adults, most of the informants continued their pursuit of contact
with other deaf people. Almost all of those who were married had a deaf
spouse. Many said they belonged to deaf clubs or regularly participated in
informal social activities with deaf friends. Others attended deaf churches
or were members of deaf professional or political organizations. Their
discussions of these activities centered on the common theme of shared
experience and the need for social interaction. For many, deafness was a
crucial bond. As one man put it, "you're deaf, I'm deaf – we're family."
Running through their comments was the sense of distance from hearing
people and isolation within the hearing world. Two examples:

> The deaf find a meeting place for social[izing]. You know, when we are in
> the hearing world, we cannot fit in, and we become very lonely. So we need
> a place to social[ize] . . . you know, I think it's like unity . . . for our own
> benefit 'cause, like, you know, there's some . . . that might be a lot worse
> than me . . . even though I'm frustrated myself in the hearing world. But
> I'm sure there's much worse, people much worse frustrated than I am,
> because where does it leave them? They're so lonely always. So deaf people,
> they really need one another. (Foster, 1989c, p. 233)

> I married my wife and she's deaf. We are both deaf and we go to . . . the
> deaf clubs. If I married [a] hearing wife, what would happen to her? I'd
> leave her flat. Why? Would she visit the deaf club? I'd say maybe one
> sixteenth would say "Yes" and fifteen sixteenths "No." They [would] go to
> the hearing club – they go to the clubs and dance. Am I going to be able to

interact with the hearing? No way. They don't know me . . . I'd be just sitting back doing nothing. I'd say, "I don't want to go to a hearing club," and my wife would say, "I don't want to go to the deaf club." We become opposites. Opposite cultures and opposite lives. (Foster, 1989c, p. 233)

In summary, through interactions with other deaf people, informants found many of the experiences they missed with hearing people: friendship, real conversations, information, community, even another kind of family. In this sense, the persistent experience of rejection and difficult interactions with hearing people, combined with more accepting and fluid interactions among deaf persons, may contribute to the development of separate communities and, some might argue, separate cultures.

Concluding Remarks

In her study of deafness on Martha's Vineyard, Nora Groce (1985) found that when everyone on the island used sign language, deaf islanders were full and equal participants in a genuinely bilingual and multimodal society. They held important posts, married hearing people, and in general were respected and active members of their community. There was no reason or need for them to form a separate subgroup. Nash (1987) suggests that the power of ASL in defining and maintaining the social identity of the deaf community derives in part from the fact that it has historically been repressed through official language policies that favor English (and, relatedly, the speaking and listening modes).

In combination with the work of Groce and Nash, the experiences of the deaf people cited throughout this chapter lead to the question, To what degree does our monolingual and monomodal culture of hearing English users create as well as sustain the need for a separate community and culture of Deaf people? Perhaps this chapter will encourage deaf and hearing people to explore this question together, and discuss ways to develop a truly multilingual and multimodal society in which everyone has equal access to communication.

Acknowledgments

The research reported in this chapter was produced at the National Technical Institute for the Deaf in the course of an agreement between the Rochester Institute of Technology and the U.S. Office of Education.

References

Bateman, G. (1990). *The Political activity of adult deaf leaders and their constituents in Rochester, New York.* Unpublished doctoral dissertation, Graduate School of Education and Human Development, University of Rochester, Rochester, NY.

Becker, G. (1980). *Growing old in silence.* Berkeley: University of California Press.

Becker, H. (1970). *Sociological work: Method and substance.* Chicago: Aldine.

Blumer, H. (1969). *Symbolic interactionism: Perspective and method.* Englewood Cliffs, NJ: Prentice-Hall.

Bogdan, R., & Biklen, S. (1992). *Qualitative research for education: An introduction to theory and methods* (2nd ed.). Boston: Allyn & Bacon.

Bogdan , R., & Taylor, S. (1975). *Introduction to qualitative research methods: A phenomenological approach to the social sciences.* New York: Wiley.

Crammatte, A. B. (1968). *Deaf persons in professional employment.* Springfield, IL: Charles C. Thomas.

Emerton, R. G., Foster, S., & Royer, H. (1987). The impact of changing technology on the employment of a group of older deaf workers. *Journal of Rehabilitation of the Deaf, 21* (2), 6–18.

Evans, A., & Falk, W. (1986). *Learning to be deaf.* Berlin: Mouton de Gruyter.

Foster, S. (1986). *Perspectives of selected NTID graduates on their college experience.* Technical Report, National Technical Institute for the Deaf at Rochester Institute of Technology, Rochester, NY.

(1987). Employment experiences of deaf RIT graduates: An interview study. *Journal of Rehabilitation of the Deaf, 21* (1), 1–15.

(1988). Life in the mainstream: Reflections of deaf college freshmen on their experiences in the mainstreamed high school. *Journal of Rehabilitation of the Deaf, 22* (2), 27–35.

(1989a). Educational programs for deaf students: An insider perspective on policy and practice. In L. Barton (Ed), *Integration; Myth or reality?* (pp. 57–82). London: Falmer Press.

(1989b). Reflections of deaf adults on their experiences in residential and mainstream school programs. *Disability, Handicap and Society, 4* (1), 37–56.

(1989c). Social alienation and peer identification: A study of the social construction of deafness. *Human Organization, 48* (3), 226–235.

(1992). *Working with deaf people: Accessibility and accommodation in the workplace.* Springfield, IL: Charles C. Thomas.

Foster, S., Barefoot, S., & DeCaro, P. (1989). The meaning of communication to a group of deaf college students: A multi-dimensional perspective. *Journal of Speech and Hearing Disorders, 54,* 558–569.

Foster, S., & Brown, P. (1989). Factors influencing the academic and social integration of hearing-impaired college students. *Journal of Postsecondary Education and Disability, 7* (3 & 4), 78–96.

Foster, S., & Holcomb, T. (1990). Hearing-impaired students: A student-teacher-class partnership. In N. Jones (Ed.), *Special educational needs review* (Vol. 3, pp. 152–171). London: Falmer Press.

Groce, N. (1985). *Everyone here spoke sign language: Hereditary deafness on Martha's Vineyard.* Cambridge, MA: Harvard University Press.

Grosjean, F. (1982). *Life with two languages: An introduction to bilingualism.* Cambridge, MA: Harvard University Press.

Higgins, P. (1980). *Outsiders in a hearing world: A society of deafness.* Beverly Hills, CA: Sage Press.

Mead, G. H. (1934). *Mind, self, and society.* Chicago: University of Chicago Press.

(1938). *The philosophy of the act.* Chicago: University of Chicago Press.

Mertens, D. (1989). Social experiences of hearing-impaired high school youth. *American Annals of the Deaf, 134*(1), 15–19.

Nash, J. (1987). Who signs to whom? The American Sign Language community. In P. Higgins & J. Nash (Eds.), *Understanding deafness socially* (pp. 81–100). Springfield, IL: Charles C. Thomas.

Park, R. (1915). *Principles of human behavior.* Chicago: The Zalaz Corporation.

Saur, E., Layne, C., Hurley, E., & Opton, K. (1986). Dimensions of mainstreaming. *American Annals of the Deaf, 131,* 325–329.

Schein, J., & Delk, M. (1974). *The deaf population of the United States.* Silver Spring, MD: National Association of the Deaf.

Seidel, J. (1982). The points at which deaf and hearing worlds intersect: A dialectical analysis. In P. Higgins & J. Nash (Eds.), *Social aspects of deafness,* Vol. 3: *The deaf community and the deaf population. Proceedings of the 1982 conference: Sociology of deafness* (pp. 131-137). Washington, DC: Gallaudet University.

Spradley, J. (1979). *The ethnographic interview.* New York: Holt, Rinehart, & Winston.

Stinson, M., Chase, K., & Kluwin, T. (1990). *Self-perceptions of social relationships in hearing-impaired adolescents.* Paper presented at the Annual meeting of the American Educational Research Association, Boston, MA.

Thomas, W. I. (1951). *Social behavior and personality.* New York: Social Science Research Council.

CHAPTER EIGHT

Marginality, Biculturalism, and Social Identity of Deaf People

R. GREG EMERTON

The term "marginality," is often misunderstood. It is commonly seen as a negative used to describe a person with little status and few choices who is located on the border of a group or community (e.g., Napier & Gershenfeld, 1987). With the heightened awareness of Deaf pride in recent years, attempts to discuss this concept as it might apply to deaf people is frequently enough to irritate, if not anger, members of an audience interested in deafness.[1] Such a reaction is understandable in terms of the values and norms of the Deaf community, which will be discussed below. Yet the issues associated with marginality will not go away. During the past two years more than 40% of the essays contributed to the annual monograph of the *Deaf American* have contained references to or discussions of issues related to marginality (Garretson, 1992, 1993). This chapter will attempt to extricate this concept from the realm of emotions and rhetoric and to show

R. Greg Emerton (Ph.D., Sociology, Western Michigan University), Associate Professor, National Technical Institute for the Deaf, conducts and publishes research on the impact of hearing loss and socialization across the life span. He is also a professional mediator working to resolve group and individual conflicts in community, family, and educational disputes. He grew up in the days before mainstreaming and learned first hand the difficulties of being marginalized as a deaf or hard-of-hearing person in a hearing world. As a deaf faculty member at NTID for more than twenty years, he presently enjoys the benefits of being bicultural. His address is: Liberal Arts Support Department, National Technical Institute for the Deaf, Rochester Institute of Technology, 52 Lomb Memorial Drive, Rochester, NY 14623.
[1] In acceptance with a convention used by Padden and others, the capitalized form "Deaf" will be used to refer to the cultural aspects of Deaf people such as the Deaf community, while the lowercase form will refer to noncultural aspects such as the audiological condition of deafness.

its relationship to the seemingly more popular concept of biculturalism. In turn, these ideas will be linked to issues of personal and social identity – questions such as Who am I and Where do I belong? Following this will be a discussion of "normalization and equality" as sources of social change for the Deaf community and the potential effects of these changes on the social identity of Deaf people.

Marginality and Biculturalism

As previously indicated, "marginality" is perceived by many to be a negative term used to describe someone who is not accepted and resides on the fringe of the group. Biculturalism, on the other hand, is currently viewed favorably in many circles. A person who is bicultural is often said to have the best of two or more social environments – the ability to participate in two cultures and the freedom to choose the best combination. Correctly defined, "marginality" can also reference a person who is highly involved in two or more culturally distinct groups (Hoult, 1969). Either way, however, this participation can lead an individual to experience a "divided conscious" as to what is right or wrong in any given situation and to display inconsistent behavior (Rose, 1965). Socially mobile people are frequently marginal and such individuals may be rejected by the group to which they aspire and no longer accepted by the group from which they came. They may become individualistic and have a dual orientation to the social reality of any given social situation. As a consequence, marginal people often have unorthodox views and are frequently found in the vanguard of social change (Shibutani, 1986). Strikingly similar descriptions are offered by Grosjean (1982) of the bilingual/bicultural person trying to live within two or more languages and cultures. The fact that "biculturalism" is a favorable term while "marginality" is not may be simply due to misunderstandings about what these terms mean. In this chapter it is suggested that "biculturalism" and "marginality" can often be used interchangeably without affecting the underlying message.

Personal and Social Identity: Who Am I and Where Do I Belong?

Among the fundamental notions of social science is the assumption that all people are social beings. They begin within a group and cannot long exist without a group. Lacking major instincts or innate knowledge for survival, most people learn what they "know about" from other people.

This knowledge represents the accumulated experience of the group members in solving the problems of daily living. Such solutions are frequently institutionalized as expectations of how things are and ought to be for both the success of the individual and the maintenance of the group. A person born into the group is usually socialized by parents, friends, teachers, and others. Individuals progressively learn about the ideas, norms, and values of the family, the community, and the society in which they live, and about the objects and technologies that make up their social world. They learn about themselves and how they fit into the world around them. This process has traditionally been called enculturation (Herskovits, 1949), for culture is the link between the individual and the group or society. It is a complex process requiring complex communication. To become a full member, one is expected to learn and internalize the culture of the group.

This general notion of how enculturation should occur poses certain critical problems to be solved usually by the parents. To begin with, the complex communication needed for socialization usually takes the form of a language wherein speaking and listening are the norm. But face-to-face spoken communication is often found to be incompatible with deafness. This is compounded by the fact that more than 90% of the parents of deaf children are themselves hearing (Schein & Delk, 1974). Few of these parents have ever known anyone who grew up deaf and rarely have they had close relatives who were deaf from birth.[2] Most people tend to parent their children by drawing upon their own experiences growing up, but these parents seldom have any experience in using alternate modes of communication or any knowledge of what it takes to be a successful deaf adult. Thus the communication and content so vital to the socialization process is often severely restricted.

Many hearing parents of deaf children are grief-stricken when first told that their child cannot hear. Their response is understandable. The child that they had anticipated with such joy is found to be unlike themselves. They search for the "right thing to do" (Spradley & Spradley, 1985). But whatever their feelings about the situation, most hearing parents of deaf children, like parents everywhere, want their children to grow up to be educated and to become successful adults. Traditionally, deaf children were sent at an early age to a school for the deaf. Although varied in their educational philosophies, these schools served to bring children together

---

[2] The incidence of profound prelingual and pre-educational deafness is estimated to be between one and two per thousand. Other deaf people generally experienced their hearing loss after they acquired the use of spoken language (Schein & Delk, 1974).

on the basis of this relatively rare physical characteristic. In schools for the deaf, the children met many others who shared their deafness. Some of the children in school were from families where parents and even grandparents were deaf. They also frequently met other deaf adults working at the school in a variety of capacities (Van Cleve & Crouch, 1989). A latent function of this specialized academic setting was exposure to deaf culture – that is, the accumulated experience of group members solving the problems of daily living as a deaf person. The schools thus provided a viable milieu for enculturation.

In a recent article for the general public, Dolnick (1993) refers to deaf people as "a new 'ethnic' group." Although deaf people follow most of the prescriptions and proscriptions of society, it is clear that the most ordinary means of communication, speech, often does not satisfy their needs. Deaf people have developed sign language within their own subculture to address this.[3] It is a wonderful cultural invention that solves their major problems with complex communication. It is not expensive and requires no technology. But it has a major drawback: most of the general population including most parents of deaf children, use speaking and listening as their primary mode of communication. Use of sign language is therefore restricted to those who have learned to sign; usually other enculturated members of the Deaf Community. Furthermore, communicating in sign disrupts the expected behavior of everyday life in the larger society. It sets the user off as someone who is not following the rules and is not behaving as one ought to. Moreover, this inability to listen and/or to speak disrupts what are perhaps the most fundamental assumptions of what should happen in face-to-face conversations. Differences of this sort are devalued by the larger group as an undesired characteristic, that is, they are stigmatized (Goffman, 1963).

Another term for these "ethnic groups" is "minority groups." Minority groups are often stigmatized. There are four characteristics associated with this status: (1) observable ascribed traits by which most minority group members can be recognized; (2) differential treatment of individuals by society on the basis of possessing these traits; (3) organization of self-image around this identification; and (4) an awareness of shared identity with others in the same group (Hess, Markson, & Stein, 1991). As we shall see, these apply very clearly to Deaf people in the Deaf community.

---

[3] "Subculture" does not imply inferiority. It simply means that while most features of the larger culture are followed by the group, there are a few significant differences.

To begin with, sign language is obviously an observable trait by which deaf people can be recognized. Even more critical in everyday life is the inability to follow the norms for speaking and listening. This quickly results in noticeably different treatment by others in the hearing society. In fact, the history of deaf people is largely recorded in the efforts of deaf people to overcome such discrimination and the prejudices that accompany it (Gannon, 1981; Lane, 1984; Van Cleve & Crouch, 1989).

Unlike most minority groups, new members of the Deaf community are seldom born into the culture. Most deaf children, having hearing parents, tend to enter the community in another manner, usually through the educational system. Deaf children have the opportunity at school to develop an awareness of a Deaf identity shared with others and can begin to organize their self-image around this, at least in part. Participation in such a group does three things for the individual. First, it provides a sense of belonging needed for self-definition. Since the self is dependent to a large extent upon an interpretation of how others see one, a healthy self-concept is engendered by the acceptance of a group that values one (Gordon & Gergen, 1968). Second, such a group maintains patterns of primary group relationships.[4] School relationships within the Deaf community are known to be especially strong. For example, the protocol for meeting a new person in the Deaf community is to ask whether the person is hearing or deaf (or hard of hearing) and to ask where they are from, which generally means where they went to school. Such things are often perceived to be far more salient than a person's name. Indeed, one's acceptance in a deaf group in another locale is frequently dependent upon school affiliation and previous relationships with others in the community (Hall, 1989). Third, the larger society is interpreted through the traditions of the minority group. Within the Deaf community this means "Deaf Pride." Profound deafness, growing up in a deaf family, and signing fluently are seen as virtues, while "hearing activities" such as use of the telephone or one's voice in conversation are suspect (Higgins, 1980; Padden & Humphries, 1988). In these sorts of ways, people construct a subculture and develop a community that protects and nurtures those who remain within its network of primary and secondary social ties. In addition to giving meaning to how the larger society should be viewed, the Deaf community expects a member to participate fully in the activities of the group. Failure to do so is said to be denial of one's deafness, that is, one's social identity. Thus in the

---

[4] Primary groups are groups in which members are known in more than one role and are valued by others as individuals rather than for any specific function they might perform.

process of "normalizing" deafness, the community becomes very ethno-centric: the assumption is made that the values and norms of the in-group (the Deaf) are superior to those of the out-group (the hearing), and the community actively maintains group boundaries through preservation of its heritage. Except perhaps for work, it is entirely possible for an individual to construct his or her social world within the boundaries of this subsociety, and the individual who does so is likely to be rewarded richly in terms of recognition and acceptance by the group.

Normalization and Equality: Sources of Change

The Deaf community and the associated subculture are results of an effort by a minority subgroup to normalize the readily observable ascribed traits and subcultural characteristics that stigmatize the group in the view of the dominant society. There is a strong sense of group pride. Instead of viewing deafness as a handicap, Deaf people are fond of quoting Dr. I. King Jordan, the first deaf president of Gallaudet University, as saying that the only thing that deaf people cannot do is hear. For many deaf people, the idea of a cochlear implant to provide some semblance of hearing is an atrocity because it implies that there is something wrong with being deaf or even that some hearing is better than no hearing. Indeed, advocates in the Deaf Community now proclaim that deafness is not a disability in need of repair but rather a linguistic minority group (Bahan, 1989; Dolnick, 1993). The values of the Deaf world are in this sense a counterculture to the hearing world.

Attempts to "normalize" deafness have not been confined to advocates of the Deaf community. Often the parents' fondest hope is that somehow their child will learn to communicate just like everyone else. Their child will then be "normal." The oral approach (lip-reading and speech training) is historically an attempt to follow the conventional norms for communication in the larger society.[5] Few deaf people have mastered it and many have failed. No matter how skilled an orally trained person is, the social danger is always that communication will break down. If the deaf individual is trying to pass for hearing in the larger society, he or she may be discredited or stigmatized.[6] It is a common problem for many minorities trying to conceal ascribed traits.

---

[5] Traditional oralism is discounted or devalued by the Deaf community in much the same way that sign language is devalued by the larger society.

[6] If an oral person is not "acting as if" he or she were hearing but trying instead to facilitate the communication, such a breakdown is likely to be less stigmatizing.

Mainstreaming represents yet another attempt to "normalize" children with disabilities including deafness. The Education for All Handicapped Children Act (Public Law 94–142), passed in 1975, was not aimed specifically at deaf children. Rather it spelled out the rights of handicapped children and their families to secure a "free and appropriate public education" in the "least restrictive environment." Schools were mandated to provide necessary services to deaf children such as tutoring and/or notetaking in a regular classroom if at all possible (DuBow et al., 1984). A majority of deaf students today are educated in their local school system and live at home with their parents. The manifest intent of the law was to integrate all children classified under the act with their peers in the local community. The indirect effect was to isolate deaf children from large numbers of their deaf peers and from the milieu in which the culture of the Deaf community is traditionally learned. As a result many are not enculturated in the Deaf community until after they leave the public school system. This attempt to "normalize" is seen by many Deaf advocates as contrary to the interests of developing a strong self-image or shared group identity as a member of the Deaf community.

Another set of laws, Section 504 of the Rehabilitation Act of 1973 and the Americans with Disabilities Act of 1990, further attempt to ensure the civil rights of "disabled" people. Discrimination in the workplace, public transportation, public accommodations, and public communications is largely prohibited. Although displeased with the label of "disability," Deaf advocates have been largely supportive of these initiatives because the laws and recent technological innovations such as telecommunication devices and closed-captioning for television and movies have helped to eliminate impediments to the equality and advancement of deaf people in society. The demand for qualified interpreters and the laws which require them have led to a larger number of people knowing sign language. The "Deaf Prez Now" movement which played out in the national media and led to the first deaf president of Gallaudet University in 1988, heightened societal awareness of deaf people as competent individuals, and undermined the stereotypes of "deaf and dumb"(Gannon, 1989). These social and technological advances have opened opportunities to deaf people in the United States that never existed before.

Change Affects the Future and the Future Is Now

Social change is not always progress. Progress implies that things have improved. It is a value judgment. Social change means that there has been a fundamental alteration in the patterns of the culture, social structure, and social behavior over time. Things are different than they were before. So it is for deaf people in the United States. Today, deaf people are no longer dominated by hearing people who want them to speak and listen as they were for close to a hundred years following triumph of the oral perspective set out in the Treaty of Milan in 1880. But they are also no longer insulated in small groups that cluster around the schools for the deaf where they grew up. Laws and technology have presented deaf people with new challenges and opportunities. They can be prouder than ever of who they are as Deaf people, not only within their own community but also in the eyes of society at large. At the same time, they are far more heterogeneous than they have ever been before. No longer can one categorize people as hearing or deaf, oral or manual. People who grew up in the "oral tradition" now sign openly without embarrassment. Hard-of-hearing people no longer have to pretend that they are either hearing or deaf. American Sign Language (ASL) is rapidly evolving to incorporate more and more signed English. With the increased demand for interpreters, larger numbers of hearing people are becoming proficient in the use of sign language. Today, most young deaf people grow up in a mainstreamed school setting. Some of these individuals are exposed to Deaf culture through summer camps and other programs, others discover the "world of deafness" after they leave high school, often when they enter college. For better or worse, the past twenty years have seen fundamental alterations in social structure and behavior for deaf people.

Effects on the Development of Social Identity

Deaf people in American society today are similar to traditional immigrants becoming acculturated and assimilated into the larger society. While Deaf people may choose to speak for the benefit of hearing people, they are not trying to pass for hearing. Nor are they are isolated in a small, separate community. They are a diverse group with varied interests. Deaf people today are proud of their social heritage and at the same time they are comfortable pursuing their interests as individuals in the larger society. The social changes that we have experienced during the past twenty-five years have contributed to the social development of a group of young people who want to be part of more than one group, to use more than one language, and to function in more than one culture. While it is true that one may often feel torn as a marginal person in the midst of social change when the norms of two groups conflict, the fact remains that many deaf people today are, as a result of their upbringing, a blend of two cultures and they choose to participate in both worlds. They are bicultural. The new social identity of Deaf people is now or will soon be a bicultural identity. For better or worse, both the Deaf community and the larger society need to recognize and accept as fact that the social conditions that previously separated these groups so effectively no longer do so. The bicultural deaf (or hearing) needs to be able to move back and forth between these groups with a minimum of interference and without the concomitant discomforts of marginality.

References

Bahan, B. (1989). A night of living terror. In S. Wilcox (Ed.), *American deaf culture: An anthology*, pp. 17–20. Silver Spring, MD: Linstok Press.

Dolnick, E. (1993, September). Deafness as culture. *The Atlantic*, pp. 37–53.

DuBow, S., Goldberg, L., Geer, S., Gardner, E., Penn, A., Conlon, S., & Charmatz, M. (1984). *Legal rights of hearing impaired people*, 2nd. ed. Washington, DC: Gallaudet Press.

Gannon, J. R. (1981). *Deaf heritage: A narrative history of deaf America*. Silver Spring, MD: National Association of the Deaf.

(1989). *The week the world heard Gallaudet*. Washington, DC: Gallaudet Press.

Garretson, M. D. (Ed.). 1992. *Viewpoints on deafness*. A Deaf American Monograph. Vol. 42. Silver Spring, MD: National Association of the Deaf.

(Ed.). (1993). *Deafness: 1993–2013*. A Deaf American Monograph. Vol. 43. Silver Spring, MD: National Association of the Deaf.

Goffman, E. (1963). *Stigma: Notes on the management of spoiled identity*. Englewood Cliffs, NJ: Prentice-Hall.

Gordon, C., & Gergen, K. J. (1968). *The self in social interaction*. New York: John Wiley and Sons.

Grosjean, F. (1982). *Life with two languages: An introduction to bilingualism*. Cambridge, MA: Harvard University Press.

Hall, S. (1989). Train-gone-sorry: The etiquette of social conversations in American Sign Language. In S. Wilcox (Ed.), *American deaf culture: An anthology*. Silver Spring, MD: Linstok Press.

Herskovits, M. J. (1949). *Man and his works: The science of cultural anthropology*. New York: Knopf.

Hess, B. B., Markson, E. W., & Stein, P. J. (1991). *Sociology*, 4th ed. New York: Macmillan.

Higgins, P. C. (1980). *Outsiders in a hearing world: A sociology of deafness*. Newbury Park, CA: Sage Press.

Hoult, T. F. (1969). *Dictionary of modern sociology*. Totowa, NJ: Littlefield, Adams.

Lane, H. (1984). *When the mind hears: A history of the deaf*. New York: Random House.

Napier, R. W., & Gershenfeld, M. K. (1987). *Groups: Theory and experience*, 4th ed. Boston: Houghton Mifflin.

Padden, C. (1988). The deaf community and the culture of deaf people. In S. Wilcox (Ed.), *American deaf culture: An anthology.* Silver Spring, MD: Linstok Press.

Padden, C., & Humphries, T. (1988). *Deaf in America. Voices from a culture.* Cambridge, MA: Harvard University Press.

Rose, A. (1965). *Sociology: The study of human relations,* 2nd ed. New York: Knopf.

Schein, J. D., & Delk, M. T. (1974). *The deaf population of the United States.* Silver Spring, MD: National Association of the Deaf.

Shibutani, T. (1986). *Social processes.* Berkeley: University of California Press.

Spradley, T. S., & Spradley, J. P. (1985). *Deaf like me,* 2nd. ed. Washington, DC: Gallaudet Press.

Van Cleve, J. V., & Crouch, B. C. (1989). *A place of their own: Creating the deaf community in America.* Washington, DC: Gallaudet Press.

CHAPTER NINE

Attitudes of the Deaf Community Toward Political Activism

GERALD C. BATEMAN

Introduction

We live in a democratic society in which all of us should have the right to be politically active in various ways. But is this really true? Historically, it has been demonstrated that not all Americans have had equal opportunities to participate in the political process. Deaf people are one of the several minority groups who have experienced a sense of oppression and feeling of futility in changing their lives. In other words, many deaf people feel a sense of "civic disenfranchisement" (Verlinde, 1987, p. 97). They feel that they have little voice in the decision-making processes that would determine their political, social, and economic futures. Some feel victimized by the larger hearing society. As Higgins (1980) states in his study, many deaf adults feel that they are "outsiders in the hearing world."

It is a widely accepted view that an important way for people to feel a part of the decision-making process of the government is by voting. As Gaventa (1980) has noted, in a democracy, voting in elections is a principal means by which the deprived public may act upon its concerns, since candidates chosen as representatives are mandated by the electorate to act

Gerald C. Bateman (Ed.D., University of Rochester), Associate Professor and Interim Director of the Master of Science in Secondary Education of Students who are Deaf or Hard of Hearing at the National Technical Institute for the Deaf, has been involved in the field of deaf education for many years and has published research on political activism in the Deaf community. He is a member of the Deaf Professional Group at NTID. His address is: Center for Baccalaureate and Graduate Studies, National Technical Institute for the Deaf, Rochester Institute of Technology, 52 Lomb Memorial Drive, Rochester, NY 14623.

upon their interests. However, minority groups often do not fully participate in the voting process. In his extensive study of political participation among the poor in central Appalachia, Graventa observes that

> the rural poor in America are unorganized, dispersed and less visible.
> The pattern is not unique to the Appalachias; it is found in the country more generally. It is a fundamental problem for American democracy, for it calls into question the relationship of political participation and social and economic equality. Social and economic deprivations – lower levels of education, lower status occupations, inadequate income – that political participation is supposed to be used to overcome, impede political participation. . . . (pp. 39–40)

In other words, he found that the most disadvantaged people participated in the political process the least. The most privileged people had the most influence on the political or decision-making process of our government. This raises some very important and researchable questions which warrant further investigation. Does the Deaf community understand its political rights and does it actively participate in the political process?

This chapter will address these two questions. It will provide (1) an overview of the literature of other studies and writings on barriers to the political participation process as well as barriers to the development of political leadership; and (2) a summary of the four major barriers to political participation that Deaf leaders discussed in the study I conducted in the Rochester area (Bateman, 1990). In addition, there will be a discussion of the political activism in the hearing Hispanic community and the Deaf community which will focus on the parallels that exist between these two minority groups.

In the attempt to find out about political participation by members of the Deaf community, this investigator used an ethnographic research approach by conducting an interview study of twenty Deaf leaders from the Rochester area. These people were presidents, chairs, or board members in the twenty-plus organizations of the deaf in the community. The major focus of this study was to determine factors that have helped or hindered these Deaf leaders to become politically active as well as obtain their perceptions of the forces that have shaped the sense of political activism of other deaf people in the Rochester area. During the one-hour interview, each leader discussed his or her experience and perceptions on the meaning and levels of political activism in the community and the influences, such as schooling, families, and communication, on their becoming politically active. Through this research methodology, the investigator was able to describe the facilitators and barriers to political activism among deaf people through the personal experiences and perceptions of the leaders.

Barriers to Participation in the Political Process

All too often, it is assumed that communication is the primary barrier to Deaf people becoming politically active because they rely on and prefer the use of American Sign Language. It is a significant barrier, but this assumption overlooks other barriers that have hindered their ability to become politically involved in community affairs. In this section, I will describe some of the barriers that the Deaf community faces in its effort to become politically active.

Low Socioeconomic Status

Lower levels of education and poorer social/occupational status are common among deaf adults when compared to their hearing counterparts. These may very well be barriers that influence deaf people's participation in the political process, as they seem to be for other minority groups in America.

Perceived Powerlessness

In my study (Bateman, 1990), Deaf leaders in the Rochester, New York, area reported that the proportion of Deaf people who were registered voters and actually voted was quite small. A primary reason cited by these leaders was that Deaf people knew that they were outnumbered by hearing people and felt that they had to live with the will of the majority. In other words, Deaf people perceived themselves to be powerless to make changes because of their small number. Thus, another barrier for political participation is the perceived powerlessness to change the system.

Limited Access to Information

The feelings Deaf people have that voting would not make a difference and that they are outnumbered by the hearing community have led to their perception that they are second-class citizens and not part of the political mainstream. These perceptions were also expressed in an earlier study that was conducted in the Rochester area by Verlinde (1987). In addition, she found that many Deaf people never voted in national elections. The primary reason cited was that Deaf people lacked access to information on political issues: Many Deaf people perceived that limited technology, especially captioning, made it difficult for them to inform themselves. Although this has been changing during the last few years with more and more captioned television news programs available for deaf people, limited access to information continues to be a barrier for Deaf people to full participation in the political process.

A related finding by Hostin (1988) is that deaf people also feel that they lack an understanding of methods of political action and thus do not have the confidence needed to become actively involved in the political process.

Schooling

In discussing the lack of political participation among Deaf people, several Deaf leaders in my study (Bateman, 1990) mentioned how school experiences have impeded many Deaf people from becoming part of the political mainstream. These leaders believed that critical thinking was a crucial element in becoming politically active. They believed that few Deaf people had been taught or encouraged to be critical thinkers in school and few deaf students had been given enough opportunities to evaluate information, analyze problems and solutions, identify values, and so forth. The leaders acknowledged that deaf adults in the Rochester area now had the benefits of captioned local news and a variety of newspapers and magazines written by and for deaf people. But having access to those sources of information, the leaders said, does not necessarily mean that the deaf viewers fully comprehend or can analyze what they have seen and read.

Political Literacy

What has been implied in these discussions is that many deaf people are not politically literate. For example, Brookfield (1987), a renowned researcher and author in the area of adult learning and education, believes that "political literacy is a cluster of knowledge, skills, and attitudes that allow someone to act, change his mind, appreciate other points of view, weigh evidence and arguments fairly and recognize the difference between truth and ideology" (p. 172). What several Deaf leaders have often found is that their peers cannot identify or address the different points of views while issues are being discussed; therefore, they are not yet politically literate.

Lacking sound critical thinking or political literacy skills is a hindrance to political activism for all adults, but especially for deaf adults because of their minority status. "Political learning is evident whenever people notice, and begin to ponder, the discrepancies and inequities among groups in their societies" (Brookfield, 1987, p. 1). Educators of the deaf need to create an environment in which deaf students feel comfortable and competent to reflect upon and take action in making changes in their lives, through open dialogues in the classroom, exercises in critical thinking, and involvement in student government where students are encouraged to identify and analyze problems and possible solutions and implement them. The bottom line is that students have to be allowed to become active participants in the educational process.

Barriers to the Development of Political Leadership

"Historically, the success or failure of any minority group has rested primarily upon whether or not successful leaders arise from among the minority itself" (Vernon & Estes, 1975, p. 3). In this section, I will describe some of the factors that impede the development of political leadership among deaf people.

Family Life

One important factor is the family life of deaf children, especially those who grow up as the single deaf member of hearing families. In that situation, too often decisions are made for the child, who then becomes a passive and sometimes resistant follower. This kind of family history discourages the development of leadership and a sense of responsibility for what happens to one. It encourages naiveté about influencing the community and helping oneself and other deaf people (Vernon & Estes, 1975, p. 4). Vernon & Estes added that those who were involved in family discussions and decisions developed feelings of influence and control over their lives.

Passivity in School

Passivity caused by a deaf child's home life is often compounded by his school life as well. Deaf leaders have found that both residential and mainstreamed schools have posed barriers to the development of leadership skills among their students. They found that residential schools tend to be paternalistic and do not always foster a sense of autonomy among their students. But at the same time, these leaders acknowledged that being with other deaf students is a tremendous benefit to their sense of belonging to a community. They felt that students who are isolated from other deaf students in mainstreamed programs do not have this critical benefit, which has a long-range impact on their becoming politically active within the Deaf community.

Communication

According to Vernon & Estes (1975), the communication problems of deaf people pose barriers to effective leadership. On one hand, problems with reading and writing caused by deafness put deaf people "at a unique disadvantage. . . . as a group, deaf people hate to write letters. Many have language limitations that make it difficult, embarrassing and in some cases impossible to write letters to legislators." On the other hand, "part of the communication problem is the lack of a more aggressive public information policy on the part of deaf people" (p. 5).

Type of Education

There is another feature of our students' passivity which Paulo Freire (1970) calls the "narrative characteristic" (p. 57) of education: The teacher is the primary conduit of information and the students are the passive listeners. Freire also calls this the "banking" concept of education because the students are only receiving and storing away the information they see and hear from the teacher. Dialogue between teacher and students as well as among students, activities that foster creativity and problem-solving, rarely occurs. This highlights the experience many deaf people encountered during their elementary and secondary education which had long-range negative impact on developing leadership.

Lack of Community Support

The "continual backbiting and criticism" deaf leaders often face is another reason many capable deaf persons avoid leadership roles (Vernon & Estes, 1975). Because the Deaf community is small and everyone knows everyone else, it seems that everyone is aware of private aspects of their leaders' personal lives. This public knowledge makes most leaders vulnerable and hesitant "to expose themselves to such attacks for rewards that often seem small for the price which must be paid" (p. 5).

Visibility of the Deaf Community

Vernon and Estes (1975) have pointed out that successful minorities control many of their own institutions; for example, Jews and Mormons dominate their places of worship, hospitals, and schools. They are also involved in the public institutions of their communities by running for political offices or supporting those who do. This raises the issue of how successful the Deaf community has been as a minority group. Historically, deaf people have not controlled their own institutions, especially educational programs for the deaf, although in the last few years, several schools for the deaf have hired deaf superintendents. Very few deaf people have run for public office. A notable exception is Kevin Nolan, who was elected to a seat on the city council in Northhampton, Massachusetts. It appears that historically the Deaf community has been invisible or unsuccessful in the political field for a variety of reasons, the primary one being their lack of access to political or socioeconomic power because of the society's treatment of them as disabled people. Although it is a difficult task to change the society's perception, the "invisibility" of the Deaf community as a minority group has become a barrier for deaf people in their pursuit of political leadership.

In summary, many factors are involved in the development of leadership in the Deaf community, as in other minority groups. When leadership is lacking in a community, several factors could be at work.

The Ethnographic Study

Are the aforementioned barriers pervasive problems in the deaf community? From the interviews with the Deaf leaders (see Bateman, 1990), several major themes emerged from their perceptions on the barriers that have impeded deaf people from participating in the political process. Specifically, these barriers are: (1) lack of understanding of political activism and the political process; (2) a sense of social and political isolation; (3) dependency, powerlessness, and lack of interest; and (4) complacency and resistance to change. These barriers act and build upon each other. For example, the lack of understanding and sense of isolation lead to increased loss of interest, dependency, and powerlessness, which in turn promote complacency and further resistance to change.

Lack of Understanding of Political Activism

In their attempts to be politically active and to make changes within the Deaf community, the leaders have encountered misunderstandings among their peers about the full significance of being politically active. In this vein, several respondents said that many deaf people do not fully understand what politics or political activism is or how they can make it work for them, as in the following example:

> When Deaf people try to explain the meaning of the term "politics," they tend to explain it in a simplistic manner. . . . [For example,] they may say that means writing bills and having them passed by Congress. They do not understand their [own] role in the political process.

Another example of this misunderstanding is the attitude that prevails among Deaf people that they are not capable of being politically active. To them, political activism is for "upper-crust, well-educated" deaf people. One of the respondents stated that most of his deaf peers do not believe that they have had the academic training to understand the political process. As a result of this misunderstanding, many members of the Deaf community do not become involved in political activities, leaving the work of political activism up to the leaders or well-educated deaf people.

The Sense of Social and Political Isolation

Several respondents commented that many Deaf people feel politically and socially isolated from the larger hearing community. They further suggested that this experience has, in turn, caused them to have a narrow perspective or scope on the issues that affect everyone – deaf and hearing – in the community.

From the leaders' experience, the majority of people in the Deaf community think about political activism in terms of issues related to deafness, such as telephone relay service, television captioning, and interpreting services. They seldom express interest in more general issues such as pollution, the environment, and health concerns. Unless the issue is directly deaf-related, they are not interested. This narrow perspective contradicts the beliefs of most of the leaders who have much interest in community-wide issues. As one respondent remarked while discussing this concern, "[Deaf people] tend to put blinders on and only concentrate on [the deaf-related] issues. . . . I'm involved with a lot more general things. Most Deaf people don't see the big picture."

Some respondents perceived that the lack of interest in world issues results from a general sense of isolation from the larger hearing world experienced by many members of the Deaf community. Interaction among Deaf and hearing people is often stressful and frustrating; as a result, a "Deaf ghetto" has evolved. And so in the words of one respondent, "in the Deaf ghetto, there's a tendency to isolate. . . . just stay within that world and [not] be drawn out of that world and cross over those boundaries."

The feeling of isolation has had a significant impact on Deaf people's willingness to become politically involved in community affairs. It has also led to the feeling of dependency, powerlessness, and lack of interest.

Dependency, Powerlessness, and Lack of Interest

The leaders believed it is common for deaf people to experience a sense of dependency, powerlessness, and lack of interest relative to change in their lives. These feelings relate to their lack of understanding of the political process and of the roles of their leaders. In addition, Deaf people perceive a sense of isolation from the hearing community.

Some of the leaders had encountered an attitude of "it is not my problem" or "let [the leaders] do it for me" from their peers. Many Deaf people do not believe that they have the knowledge or skills to achieve any changes, so "they tend to sit back and wait for others to do [the work] for them." Receiving support from the majority of Deaf people in an organization has been rare because of their negative attitudes toward political activities. Several of the leaders had learned to be more self-reliant and do the work on their own and not depend on their members for support. One of the respondents reached a conclusion common to several of the leaders: "[a political activity is usually not] the work of a full organization or an established group; it is only the work of a few concerned individuals."

In addition, Deaf people have become dependent upon their leaders to educate them about the current political and social issues. Some of the respondents believed that many of their peers were aware of the issues but did not take the initiative to discuss and resolve them. As one respondent said:

I feel maybe they have a feeling that it's not their responsibility. Let somebody else take care of it. They don't understand what's going on or maybe they haven't been encouraged by their families or the schools. Maybe they just plain don't care.

These negative attitudes made it very difficult for the leaders to initiate political activities. Several leaders noted that many deaf people believe they are powerless to change the feeling of dependency. This powerlessness is a result of their lack of understanding of politics or political activism and an accompanying lack of interest and confidence to access the process. One respondent described this sense of dependency and powerlessness among his peers as a feeling that the issue is not their responsibility or has nothing to do with them or there is nothing they can do about it. With this sense of powerlessness, deaf people have felt helpless to change conditions or to develop services that are needed in their communities. Either they depend too much on their leaders to be their advocates to initiate the changes, or they leave the decisions to the larger hearing community.

Complacency and Resistance

The experiences of the respondents suggested that the feelings of dependency, powerlessness, and lack of interest have led to complacency. For example, they often found that deaf people in their communities are content with their lot in life and do not want to see changes made.

This complacent attitude has been a major area of concern for several of the respondents. One explained it as due to a feeling that Deaf people have had enough frustration and they don't want any more. Complacency has also led to resistance to change. Several leaders had met resistance from the members of their communities when suggestions were made for bringing new ideas or changes into the community.

They offered several explanations for this resistance. First, some said that people resist political involvement out of fear that if they challenge the government, they might lose the economic support they already have (such as the Supplementary Security Income that many receive monthly). Second, there was an attitude that being politically active might cost people their jobs. In this vein, one leader reported that some members of his organization said things like "Don't create a stir!" or "Don't rock the boat!"

> They're afraid it will [affect] their jobs. They don't want to lose that job. It's very precious to them, and they say to themselves, "Well, if I become politically active, if I complain, maybe I'm going to lose my job."

Another leader remarked,

In the Deaf community you can't get your ideas across because they don't want to hear [them]. They're afraid of change. They like things the way they are now . . . [and do not want anything changed].

It was the opinion of many respondents that many Deaf people do not understand what political activism is. Because of their relationship with the hearing community, they also feel socially and politically isolated. As a result, these deaf people have lost interest in the process and become dependent upon the leaders to be their advocates. They believe they are powerless to make changes needed in their communities. Rather than "fight the system," they have become complacent and have resisted any suggestions that they believe might cause them to lose the services or privileges they already have.

Political Activism in the Deaf Community and the Hearing Hispanic Community

A few of the Deaf leaders compared the political struggles of their community to those of the hearing Hispanic community. The two communities share a common trait: English is the second language of many of their members, and that fact has caused serious communication barriers. To investigate this further, the researcher conducted an additional interview with a hearing Hispanic leader to find out if similarities between the two minority communities indeed exist.

Several similarities surfaced from the interview with the Hispanic leader. As with deaf people, having to learn English to blend in with the Rochester community has been a significant barrier for many Hispanic people. There are also similar attitudinal barriers between each community and the majority community. As in the Deaf community, members of the Hispanic community also question the value of being politically active. The leader pointed out that "being politically active is not necessarily their priority because they are still dealing with the bread-and-butter, day-to-day issues." She added that "until the government tries to create better housing conditions, better educational services, and better employment opportunities, the people's attitude is not going to change very much." At the same time, there is an attitude of indifference to the political process as Hispanics believe that the government has not been responsive to their needs. In addition, this leader found that Hispanics can be resistant to change and "become complacent and protect the status quo."

Again, as in the Deaf community, there is a shortage of role models in the Hispanic community, and this shortage has had an impact on the services the members of the community have received. As the leader said,

We found some large gaps . . . very few members of the Hispanic community serving on the Board of Directors, advisory committees, planning committees; therefore, there was an absence in the development of programs and policies and understanding of the needs of the Hispanic community.

This Hispanic leader criticized the non-Hispanic community for the lack of appropriate human services to meet the needs of the Hispanic community. Language has been an obvious barrier, as few people who work in these service agencies are bilingual. These agencies have not tried to "reach out and bring people in." Because "Hispanics have not traditionally used agency services as effectively as they could . . . [the agencies] take the attitude, 'well they don't come, that means they don't need the service.'" Hispanic role models are needed to set the examples for the members of the community and show them how to access the system and receive the services they need and are entitled to.

As ways of raising the issues in the Hispanic community, their leaders have

coordinated a variety of conferences and seminars or activities for Hispanics for them to become much more aware of the issues affecting them and how they could become involved. . . . [People] can't wait and assume that the establishment is going to be sensitive and that they're going out to meet their concerns, that's not necessarily the case. In many cases, they may be ignorant of the needs and the problems, and they have to be educated. They have to attend awareness sessions and seminars. They need to understand the factors and how different an experience that is.

There are other parallels between the Deaf and Hispanic communities. One is the communication barrier that exists between each of these communities and the dominant English-speaking community. Another example is the common belief in the Deaf and Hispanic communities that the political system, in general, has not been responsive to their needs. This has resulted in their sense of political disenfranchisement and uninterest in politics. They believe they are oppressed by the dominant society. Many of the Deaf leaders and the Hispanic leader pointed out the need for more role models in their communities to set examples for how to be more politically involved and get needed services from government agencies.

Maybe the time has come for an alliance among bilingual groups or among groups for whom English is not the primary language.

Conclusion

The divergent views on the meaning of political activism and the extent of attitudinal barriers among many Deaf people to becoming politically active in community affairs are significant concerns. It is apparent that many politically active Deaf people, including some of the leaders, tend to focus their energies on deaf-related issues only (e.g., relay services and interpreting services) and not on the broader issues that affect all people in a community (such as taxes, crime control, and pollution). This supports the belief among many deaf people that political activism is a process of making changes to improve the lives of deaf and hard-of-hearing people by overcoming the inequities caused by the hearing community. The lack of emphasis on broader issues may be an indication that the immediate wants and needs of deaf people have been unmet or ignored by the hearing community. It may also mean that members of the Deaf community cannot begin to relate to broader issues until they have a sense of equality or parity with the hearing community. The same could be true for other minority groups that are experiencing a sense of civic disenfranchisement.

The common goals among the leaders have been to improve the educational, economic, social, and civic lives of everyone in the Deaf community. They have worked diligently to bring standards and services up to par with those of the hearing community. When full equality and respect for Deaf culture are achieved, there is a good chance that more Deaf people will become politically active on issues relevant to the larger community.

References

Bateman, G. C. (1990). *The political activity of adult deaf leaders and their constituents in Rochester, New York*. Unpublished doctoral dissertation, University of Rochester, Rochester, NY.

Brookfield, S. D.(1984). *Learning democracy: Eduard Lindeman on adult education and social change*. Wolfboro, NH: Croom Helm.

    (1987). *Developing critical thinkers*. San Francisco: Jossey-Bass.

Erickson, J. G. (1984). Hispanic deaf children: A bilingual and special education challenge. In G. L. Delgado (Ed.), *The Hispanic deaf* (pp. 4–11). Washington, DC: Gallaudet University Press.

Freire, P. (1970). *Pedagogy of the oppressed*. New York: Continuum.

Gaventa, J. (1980). *Power and powerlessness: Quiescence and rebellion in an Appalachian valley.* Urbana: University of Illinois Press.

Higgins, P. C. (1980). *Outsiders in a hearing world.* Beverly Hills: Sage Publications.

Hostin, T. D. (1988). The political involvement of a select deaf adult population. *The Deaf American, 38* (2), 13–16.

Jacobs, L. M. (1980). *A deaf adult speaks out.* Washington, DC: Gallaudet University Press.

Padden, C. (1980). The deaf community and the culture of deaf people. In C. Baker & R. Battison (Eds.), *Sign language and the deaf community* (pp. 89–103). Washington, DC.: National Association of the Deaf.

Verlinde, R. A. (1987). *Deaf adults' use of social network to overcome barriers to learning: An exploratory study.* Unpublished dissertation, Teachers College, Columbia University, New York.

Vernon, M., & Estes, C. C. (1975). Deaf leadership and political activism. *The Deaf American, 28*(3) 3–6.

CHAPTER TEN

Cultural and Language Diversity in the Curriculum: Toward Reflective Practice

BONNIE MEATH-LANG

In considering issues of cultural and linguistic diversity in the curriculum, I would like to begin by borrowing the image from the title of Kenji Hakuta's well-known book, *Mirror of Language* (1986). I would like to take that mirror in hand, and move it off to the side a bit. In this way, we can look over our shoulders into the history which has brought us educators of deaf persons here, in a much-abbreviated parallel to Dr. Hakuta's act of reconstructing the history of bilingual education. Then, I would like to move that mirror back to the center, where it belongs. For the image of the language teacher is the reflection of a language learner, and we are well advised to gaze long and hard into that looking glass before we run to class or confront the next batch of essays or videotapes.

For those of us involved in the cultural and language education of young deaf adults, it is wise to be mindful of the larger forces which have underscored our students' schooling. These forces have revealed themselves over the years in a variety of forms, and left their mark on the social, personal, and political lives of students. At the same time, the historical accounts which we have studied in the hope of illumination have become

Bonnie Meath-Lang (Ed.D., University of Rochester), Professor, National Technical Institute for the Deaf, has taught writing, literature, and drama since 1972 to deaf, non-native-English-speaking, adult students and has done research on the relationship of journal and biographical writing to curriculum and teaching. A hearing professor married to a deaf professor, Harry Lang, she spent a semester teaching and consulting with her husband in a new bilingual deaf education program at the University of Leeds, West Yorkshire, England. Her address is: Department of Performing Arts, National Technical Institute for the Deaf, Rochester Institute of Technology, 52 Lomb Memorial Drive, Rochester, NY 14623.

suspect, as current scholarship reveals them to be almost exclusively hearing persons' versions of the educational progress of people who are deaf (Van Cleve, 1993; Lang, 1994). Accounts of the key roles that deaf individuals and deaf communities played have been overlooked or excluded, and are only now beginning to emerge. Nonetheless, it is important to understand, reexamine, and perhaps deconstruct the standard "canon" of literature on the education of deaf persons, and the core concepts represented by its dramatis personae; for these are the stories told to students in the curriculum of programs and schools for deaf children. The vigorous resurgence of inquiry and text analysis focusing on literature of the *deaf* community and school archives promises not only to correct a limited view, but also to explain more fully how this view came to be. Thus I come, for the first time, to a key assumption of this chapter: *We can do more than one thing at a time.* We can study more than one perspective on the past with our students. Moreover, we can view the past, present, and future both historically and personally, and chart the intersections of our social-cultural, linguistic, and personal experiences. As Richard Rorty (1982) would assert, human existence is essentially linguistic (hence, cultural) and historical; and the educator's task is to present these in the curriculum, not as certainties, but as opportunities for dialogue and the work of reinterpretation.

Teaching and learning, living in the culture of the school and addressing the various cultures brought to the school, involve a continuous cycle of interpreting and being interpreted, of clarifying through backward glances what has brought each of us to this point. This includes the autobiographical dimension. Personal history, the relationship of one's own story to one's knowledge, thus transcends self-indulgence and becomes an object of inquiry. This study of experience, or phenomenological view, becomes particularly important to the study of culture and language in schools. The grounding of teaching in acknowledgment of the participants' struggles and assumptions provides a backdrop for a study of culture and language that is, in the best sense, critical – not given to easy generalities, stereotypes, and superficial assessments of "in-ness" and "out-ness," right and wrong. Such reflective teaching also resists the tendency observed by some educational theorists that students – and colleagues – still want to be Platonists, existing in a deceptively simple, dualistic, "either/or" universe (Rorty, 1982; Warehime, 1993). The teachers of persons who are deaf, both deaf and hearing, did not arrive in their classrooms without experience. The question becomes: How best can we use that experience, and work with students to access their own linguistic strength? How best can we use the experience of living in multiple "worlds" – as most modern adults inevitably do – to encourage both thoughtful, multicultural perspectives and positive community or cultural identity?

As Hakuta has pointed out, the bilingual person works with two languages in "a delicate pattern of coexistence, cooperation, and competition" (1986, p. 3). These shifting states in the individual can be said to characterize interacting with multiple cultures as well, as teacher and student alike work to live their individual lives on many different levels, in many different groups. A Deaf colleague recently reported his morning to me:

> I took Chad on his paper route, because of a blinding snowstorm. He missed his school bus; so I had to drop him off at the school for the deaf, where I was cornered to help with the Deaf Club fundraiser. Then I had to race to Marianne's school, the public school, where I volunteer for two hours a week, because we feel that being with the hearing parents, teachers, and kids is important. The interpreter was snowed in this morning, but everyone was working hard to communicate. Right after the curriculum committee meeting, I launch into my lecture on Gandhi for the college study group. I have no time to meet with the voice interpreter in advance on all the names of the places – and I was just informed that Jane is bringing two friends from the local India Society!

These events were reported as hectic and humorous, but not at all remarkable, the price of living in a world where we have choices and the capacity to use a variety of languages and registers within those choices.

Hakuta (1986) has also pointed out the current view that one's native and second languages can work in a complementary manner, without one language subtracting from and diminishing the other. The attractiveness of bilingualism and multilingualism is acknowledged in many European, African, and Asian cultures. Unfortunately, these views did not and do not characterize the U.S. society's notions of bilingualism and biculturalism; and they have not prevailed in the field of deaf education. The opportunity to do more than one thing at a time – and expand a world view – was denied to many of us second- and third-generation American children of immigrants, as well as to deaf children.

Education of Deaf Persons: Dualistic Visions

In the "canonical" text of the history of deaf education noted above, we see all too clearly the scholars' penchant for creating dichotomies. The story of the well-known hearing educators reveals a mastery of dualism, notably beginning in the 1700s when battle lines were drawn between the oralists Heinicke, Pereire, and Braidwood and the signing educators de l'Epee, Sicard, and Stark. These battles were enacted by larger-than-life men whose goals included nothing less than unlocking the spirituality of their pupils and debating – at the French Academy and Royal Society, among other places – the separability of language and thought. In the later nineteenth century, a similar battle of the Titans was played out by Alexander Graham Bell and Edward Miner Gallaudet, for whom the "manual versus oral" controversy represented not only beliefs about appropriate pedagogy, but, for Bell, the advancement of science and human perfectibility, and, for Gallaudet, the legal, moral, and political responsibilities of educators to communities. While these versions of history are, as has been stated, incomplete; they are important and illustrative. The tendency toward dualism continues in the very way the field expresses itself: children are taught language by natural *or* analytical methods (see discussion in Moores, 1987); they are mainstreamed *or* placed in schools for deaf children; ASL *or* English is the language of instruction. Exclusionary strategies and forced choices are the norm in the rhetoric of the field.

The problems with these forced choices rest, in large part, on the notions of life, culture, and language that underlie the demand for these decisions. The first assumption of forced choices with regard to life suggests that life is predictable and linear, and that varieties of approaches result in inconsistency and chaos. In a world where children might expect to attend one school throughout their educational careers, this idea may have been understandable. In the highly mobile postmodern world, this is an impracticable and unrealistic assumption (one reason, in fact, for the dearth of longitudinal research in education). A second assumption, identified in the broader field of education by feminist scholars (see, e.g., Spender, 1980), is that life is meaningful only when one possesses a consistent and unshakable philosophy, and can state one's position in thundering certainties. Whether or not this is the "masculinist" view identified by feminist educators is the subject of other studies, but the history of the desire for certainty by powerful men is an interesting counterpoint to the exploratory nature of the educational inquiry in which they were so much engaged.

The demand to "choose" a culture also may be reflective of the relative complexities of the times. As mentioned above, the preparation of students for the majority culture, a preoccupation in the United States at the height of its immigrations, was echoed for years in the education of people who are deaf.

This preoccupation was expressed most explicitly in the teaching of the majority language. Learning the majority language was viewed as an act of commitment to one's adopted country, and, in the minds of many, required a throwing off of the old language and customs. To become truly American was to repudiate the mother tongue and culture, and to become like everyone else. That "becoming like everyone else" made its way, inevitably, into many programs for deaf students.

A limited view of the purpose of language may have been at work in this historical period. If language is defined in highly instrumental ways – with a purely "ends-means" orientation – we should not be surprised if competition overtakes complementarity and cooperation. In the case of Gallaudet and Bell, who initially were cooperative, and, in earlier times, for de l'Epee (Heinicke appears never to have cared to cooperate; he and the Braidwoods repeatedly demonstrated secrecy and a profit motive in communicating their methods – Harmon, 1987; Lysons, 1987), the impulse to view language not only as utilitarian but also as creative, intimate, and spiritual was strong, as evidenced in their personal letters and journals. The political and social forces that demanded from one or the other proof that *his* way was the better one dominated their later years, however. These nineteenth-century forces are similar in many ways to those manifested in attitudes toward bilingualism at the same time in history. Such forces viewed language as a means to show intelligence, assess genetic stock, and integrate. The presence of a "foreign" element (in the case of deaf persons, American Sign Language) was seen not as an addition, but as a subtraction. Any deviation from the norm was viewed as a threat to the end of creating a unified society. This version of social Darwinism persists in many places in the United States even today.

Rethinking Educational Goals: Current Curriculum Theory

In keeping with Rorty's notion that human existence is essentially historical and linguistic, in both the personal and cultural sense, I would like to shift now to the present, and connect the larger historical context of deaf education to the use of personal context and experience. The bridge between these is built using a brief examination of the field of curriculum in education. It is in the curriculum, after all, where cultural and language diversity is expressed, elicited, and addressed most directly; and the way in which this occurs is of vital concern to current curriculum scholars.

Like linguistics and psychology, education – in particular, the area of curriculum theory – shifted from a view of the student as a passive or machinelike absorber of knowledge to a highly contextualized view of human development in the 1970s. This movement was largely influenced by the Dutch phenomenologists of the Utrecht School and their North American proponent, the Japanese-Canadian curriculum scholar Ted Tetsuo Aoki (e.g., Aoki, 1987). Having tried and rejected semiotics and general systems theory as ways of conceptualizing the curriculum (Werner, 1987; Aoki, 1971), Aoki turned to the philosophical work of phenomenologists and critical theorists, such as Habermas, Gadamer, and Ricoeur, with particular attention to their concerns for reflection and interpretation. He put into practice the Utrecht educators' work of using autobiography and biography, analyzing teachers' and students' stories within the deeper structures of context and culture and reflecting on the patterns and differences that emerged. He encouraged and supported such approaches, not only in the classroom, but in the areas of administration and program evaluation as well. Aoki wrote and lectured often about *situation,* and of the "irreducible situational unit," a set of relationships among teacher, students, and texts that was subject to constant and critical reinterpretation (Aoki, 1978, 1980, 1983). In so doing, he was pointing out the need for understanding that any text (I use the term "text" here in the broadest sense, to refer not only to written and sign literary texts, but also to the text of classroom discourse itself) must be analyzed from the biographical situation and understandings of the reader and multiple readers, as well as from its content and stated purposes. The goals of such work include the understanding of multiple perspectives, realities, and ways of knowing, the conceptualizing, tolerance, and embrace of pluralism, and critical reflection in the context of community. Aoki did not, and does not, assume that these goals happen as a side-effect, co-curricular activity, but that they constitute the basis for *competence* and for the curriculum itself (1984). In his call for attentiveness to relationships and individual and cultural self-examination, as well as to the content of classroom texts, Aoki, too, believes that we can do more than one thing at a time.

Professor Aoki's students have observed that he often distinguished in his lectures between "language as culture" and "language as a tool of communication" (Martel, 1987). He did so not to dismiss the latter notion, with its relational usefulness, but to use the former as a direct link between experience and expression. In so doing, he has echoed, as a curriculum theorist, the concerns currently studied by language theorists such as Bakhtin (1990). Language as defined here is the social meeting ground between individuals. Using two languages is a dwelling in two cultural expressions. Thus, language becomes a "dwelling," in Aoki's terms, in a world of in-betweenness. While challenging, this notion evokes an opportunity for both teacher and student. Our language variations, whether in the effort to master English or the effort to master ASL or British Sign Language, emphasize that each individual is different, yet the same; because we can learn to make sense together.

Clearly, this is a shift from some of the loftier aims of the nineteenth century. These ideas also stand in contrast to both the purely pragmatic and the exclusionarily formal views of language that have dominated thinking in fields such as the education of deaf persons. They are the views and research of a scholar who himself experienced the in-betweenness of second-language learning, ethnicity, and marginalization. The students with whom he worked and conversed – often native and Francophone Canadians – lived in an in-betweenness that was both similar and different from his. They simply worked together, from a phenomenological stance, to make sense of experience. For a generation of curriculum theorists and for me, this has been a model.

The Use of Journals and Writing for Reflection

In concluding this chapter, I would like to describe one of many ways that we can begin to bring multiple, culturally diverse perspectives to curriculum and to our pedagogy, even in the act of teaching the majority language.

In 1980, I did a research study asking students to describe in writing their English language learning experiences (Meath-Lang, Caccamise, & Albertini, 1982). People told me at that time that college-age deaf students would be incapable of doing this. Fortunately, they were wrong (I did do some validation in American Sign Language; the responses were consistent between the English and Sign texts, if varied in metaphors and examples chosen). The students told stories of highly formalistic methods, little dialogue or conversation in class, teachers who could not communicate, and personal motivation despite frustration. They also wrote beyond the purely personal, expressing wonder at how hearing persons learn language and how languages are taught in the larger world. Since that time, I have been interested, as a writing teacher, in types of research that would bring deaf people's narratives, their voices and experiences, into both professional discourse and into a culturally diverse curriculum. While this is certainly being done in the fields of American Sign Language and other sign languages, anthropology, and history, and in certain bilingual programs in schools for deaf students, there is a need to view ways in which the Deaf experience of critical literacy in English can be expressed. To focus purely on the mere collection of such information, however, now seems one-sided to me. It is time to borrow Hakuta's mirror and Aoki's definition of situation once again.

Educational involvement, in the best sense, demands dialogue and engagement with one another's texts. If we view cultural and language diversity in education as a set of single-voiced texts, listing stock characteristics and uncritically touting the virtues of one or the other culture or language without examining the dark sides and the surprising intersections and borrowings, a promising perspective will become moribund. The cultural perspective will merely become another expression of "either/or." The teaching of American Sign Language, English, and bicultural and multicultural education must be informed, in the end, by classroom communities engaged on the careful and vigorous analysis of relationships. While personal and cultural identity may, indeed, be established by asserting *la différence*, the relationships that undergird communities and cultures are supported by exploration of both similarities and differences.

This has not been the traditional view in English language teaching, where literary texts have been seen as objective and universally interpretable, and student texts have been valued only when they imitate or model other texts. Poststructuralism and modern hermeneutics, with their current emphasis on multiple interpretations, have recently served as critical tools of multiculturalism, however. These theoretical positions support a view of educational experience – including the experience of reading and writing – that values transformation and creativity over reproduction (Gallagher, 1992). While these theories have not always spoken in a useful or transparent way to educators, the underlying principles mediated by writers such as Aoki have; and there are numerous ways that teachers concerned for the relationships and knowledge that diversity offers are acting on those principles.

Dialogue journals, dramatic script writing, computer networking, process writing, and other strategies for producing double-voiced texts have been written about extensively in teaching research (Albertini & Meath-Lang, 1986; Peyton & Batson, 1986; Peyton & Staton, 1993; Miller, 1993). I am also interested in other ways to capture both the student's and teacher's interactive language on the page. We need to understand more fully, I believe, our in-betweenness, our intersubjectivity, captured in both

American Sign Language and English. Much of the literature now reads of the different worlds deaf students and hearing teachers inhabit. True enough. But there are times we share the same space and similarities of experience, and I want to know about those as well as the differences. How do deaf students and hearing teachers write together (for that matter, and the literature on writing is deeply concerned with this, how do *any* two people write together)? How do forty-year-old Deaf teachers and eighteen-year-old Deaf students find a common ground? How may I learn about Asian cultures more systematically from my Asian students, given my thoroughly Western education? How do we all make sense together?

The respectful use of intersubjective writing in the classroom, both among students and between teacher and student, allows us to know one another better and allows a more mutual "control" of the conversation. In this way, we construct an experience through expression, bringing our histories, languages, and cultures to text. We hold the mirror to one another and to ourselves. At the same time, I can attend to other matters of the English curriculum, and still have a basis for understanding students. For it would be dualistic again to elevate the cultural and creative aspects of language and to deny flatly that language, indeed, is a tool – to get a job, make a speech, order a sandwich. The field of deaf education has simply devoted an unbalanced share of its attention to the instrumental uses of language and far less to the expressive possibilities of language as culture. Where language is seen only as a tool, ASL is reduced to a means of learning English; English is reduced to an achievement score that will result in a fully mainstreamed class schedule; and the multiple cultures and worlds in which students and teachers dwell will be ignored. As Gallagher (1992) has stated,

> Educational experience depends on our involvement. . . . However, this cannot be equated with instrumental attempts to control the educational process as a means to a certain end. . . . Educational involvement means that the student and teacher are in a hermeneutical situation, rather than what Dewey would call a "problematic situation." The hermeneutical situation is more of a mystery in which we are essentially involved than a problem which we simply confront. . . . [Involvement] can be positively characterized in terms of self-transcendence. In self-transcendence, subjectivity is not maintained within itself and opposed to its object. Rather, subjectivity is drawn out of itself toward its possibilities. (p. 187)

Gallagher, Aoki, Hakuta, and others have put the mirror, and the task, before us. The creation of a truly culturally diverse curriculum demands a sense of history – both collective and individual; a willingness to engage with multiple perspectives and texts; a commitment to learning and respecting the languages of students; and an enthusiasm for grappling with the mysteries of one's own and other people's cultures. Most importantly, teachers committed to cultural diversity should be prepared for a journey of learning and the intense work of making sense of the world together.

References

Albertini, J. A., & Meath-Lang, B. (1986). An analysis of student–teacher exchanges in dialogue journal writing. *Journal of Curriculum Theorizing, 7*(1), 153–201.

Aoki, T. T. (1971). Controlled change: *A crucial curriculum component in social education*. Paper presented at the Conference of the National Council for Social Studies, Denver.

(1978). Toward curriculum inquiry in a new key. In J. Victoria & E. Sacca (Eds.), *Phenomenological description: Potential for research in art education* (pp. 39–58). Montreal: Concordia University.

(1980). *Competence as instrumental action and as practical action*. Paper presented at the Conference on Competence, Pennsylvania State University.

(1983). Toward a dialectic between the conceptual world and the lived world: Transcending instrumentalism in curriculum orientation. *Journal of Curriculum Theorizing, 5* (4), 4–21.

(1984). Whose culture? Whose heritage? In J. Mallea & J. Young (Eds.), *Cultural diversity and Canadian education* (pp. 265–289). Ottawa: Carleton University Press.

(1987). In receiving, a giving. *Journal of Curriculum Theorizing, 7*(3), 67–88.

Bakhtin, M. M. (1990). *Art and answerability*. M. Holquist & V. Liapunov (Eds.), V. Liapunov (trans). Austin: University of Texas Press.

Gallagher, Q. (1992). *Hermeneutics and education*. Albany: State University of New York Press.

Hakuta, K. (1986). *Mirror of language: The debate on bilingualism*. New York: Basic Books.

Harmon, R. (1987). Samuel Heinecke. In J. V. Van Cleve (Ed.), *Gallaudet encyclopedia of deaf people and deafness* (Vol. 2, pp. 35–38). New York: McGraw-Hill.

Lang, H. G. (1994). *Silence of the spheres: The deaf experience in the history of science*. Westport, CT: Begin & Harvey.

Lysons, K. (1987). Thomas Braidwood. In J. V. Van Cleve (Ed.), *Gallaudet encyclopedia of deaf people and deafness* (Vol. 1, pp. 147–148). New York: McGraw Hill.

Martel, A. (1987). Ethnicity, language, and culture in the teachings of Professor Ted Aoki: Or, the celebration of double-vision. *Journal of Curriculum Theorizing, 7*(3), 43–50.

Meath-Lang, B., Caccamise, F., & Albertini, J. A. (1982). Deaf persons' views of their English language learning. In H. Hoemann & R. Wilbur (Eds.), *Interpersonal communication and deaf people* (pp. 295–327). Washington, DC: Gallaudet College.

Miller, J. D. (1993). Script writing on a computer network: Quenching the flames or feeding the fire? In B. Bruce, J. K. Peyton, & T. Batson (Eds.), *Network-based classrooms: Promises and realities* (pp. 124–137). New York: Cambridge University Press.

Moores, D. (1987). *Educating the deaf: Psychology, principles and practices.* Boston: Houghton Mifflin.

Peyton, J. K., & Batson, T. (1986). Computer networking: Making connections between speech and writing. *ERIC/CLL News Bulletin, 10* (1), 1–6.

Peyton, J. K., & Staton, J. (1993). *Dialogue journals in the multilingual classroom: Building language fluency and writing skills through written interaction.* Norwood, NJ: Ablex.

Rorty, R. (1982). Hermeneutics, general studies and teaching. In V. Gras (Ed.), *Synergos Seminars, 2,* 1–16.

Spender, D. (1980). *Man-made language.* London: Routledge & Kegan Paul.

Van Cleve, J. V. (Ed.). (1993). *Deaf history unveiled: Interpretations from the new scholarship.* Washington, DC: Gallaudet University Press.

Warehime, N. (1993). *To be one of us: Cultural conflict, creative democracy, and education.* Albany: State University of New York Press.

Werner, W. (1987). The text and tradition of an interpretive pedagogy. *Journal of Curriculum Theorizing, 7*(3), 22–33.

CHAPTER ELEVEN

Minority Empowerment and the Education of Deaf People

JOAN B. STONE

Without special arrangements, students who are deaf constitute an oppressed minority similar to a variety of language minority groups for whom standard education is inaccessible. That I begin this chapter with such an explicit statement of ideology, informed by the work of Brazilian educator Paulo Freire, is testimony to the progress made by educational and political leaders who are deaf. I intend to do three things in this chapter. First, I will give a brief description of Freire's work and its relationship to contemporary thought about minority education. Second, I will attempt to show the connections between minority education and the education of students who are deaf. Finally, I will relate some of the concepts from Freire's philosophy to the specific process of the mathematics education of students who are deaf.

Freire has said that education is never neutral. Whether or not we acknowledge it, we always work from a philosophical perspective about the world when we teach. It would be a mistake to ignore the ideology inherent in Freire's work. His best-known book is entitled *Pedagogy of the Oppressed* (1970), and he does not use the concept of oppression metaphorically. He is referring to specific instances of power and domination of one group of people over another. As difficult as it may be for many of us

Joan B. Stone (Ed.D., University of Rochester), Professor, National Technical Institute for the Deaf, teaches mathematics courses to college-level deaf students. She conducts and publishes research on mathematics curriculum, learning and instruction. Her address is: Department of Physics and Technical Mathematics, National Technical Institute for the Deaf, Rochester Institute of Technology, 52 Lomb Memorial Drive, Rochester, NY 14623.

to imagine, Freire dreams of a world in which no group of people would be under the control of another. He sees education as holding the possibility for obliterating oppression. Freire's notion of education is not the ordinary teacher-centered process that is designed to perpetuate the status quo in a society. He speaks not of problem solving, which assumes that a problem has already been stated, but of problem posing, which requires investigation and analysis of the situation in which students and teachers find themselves. Teachers and students together, as co-investigators, confront their shared world, discover its limits and contradictions, and attempt to change that world through their own labor within it. Those who hear echoes of Marx in that description are correct. Freire and his followers have taken from Marx, not grand schemes of a new world economic order, but rather concepts of equality, humanity, and liberation among groups of people who know each other well, in particular among students and teachers.

Freire's early work was with Brazilian peasants after an agrarian revolution broke up large, single-owner estates and turned them into small farms to be owned and operated by many who had originally been tenants. Before the revolution, the farmers who were now the new landowners had been cared for by the estate owners. They had no need to interact with the larger, outside world of commerce. There were few decisions for the peasants to make. Silent in the face of domination, they had always done what they were told to do. Following the revolution, they faced complex issues related to productive farming. Processes such as irrigation, fertilization, even planting, had been managed by the estate owners. There had never been a need, for example, for the workers to communicate with the Brazilian equivalent of the Army Corps of Engineers, who regulated the dams, in order to irrigate their fields downstream. Negotiations for selling crops had always been done by another. Following the revolution, these complex tasks which connected the small farms to the larger world outside needed to be understood and done by people who were unable to read and write the language of the dominant culture. The liberation anticipated through revolution could be only partial without education. Freire and his colleagues understood well that traditional "school" methods and curricula would not succeed. They established a literacy program in which the words that were studied emerged from the interactions of the farmers with each other and with the problems that were part of their everyday tasks. Such words Freire called "generative words," for they led to the development of reading and writing other words and because their source was the language of the farmers themselves. The curriculum of Freire's literacy program in Brazil was derived from the daily experience of the students and teachers, from their encounter with reality and the inevitable contradictions within it. It was not a curriculum designed to perpetuate old patterns of paternalism, no matter how benevolent those might have been in the past. It was not a curriculum designed to "transmit an ideology of accommodation" (Freire, 1985, p. 9). It was, instead, a curriculum designed for transforming the real world of the farmers through their work and that of their teachers.

Freire's ideas of problem posing, literacy, and liberation through education have been brought to contemporary American problems by scholars such as Henry Giroux (1992), Madeleine Grumet (1988), Donaldo Macedo (Freire & Macedo, 1987), and Ira Shor (1987), each of whose work in one way or another explores existing forms of domination. Among the first to realize the significance of Freire's work were people involved with teaching English as a second language. Students in such programs are often adults who are recent immigrants. It is not unusual for these programs to exist outside of the mainstream educational systems and, thus, not be bound to curricula and teaching methods designed to perpetuate the status quo. In some instances, the task may be quite the opposite. People in the United States who do not speak and use English are powerless almost by definition.

Historically, power was achieved frequently through physical force, particularly when power meant how much land or property one owned. Over time, power through property ownership gave way to power associated with productivity. The more factories and workers one owned and controlled, the more powerful one was. Power continues to exist in that form today. Recently, however, it is becoming more and more clear that power is associated with having and controlling information. The so-called information superhighway will give those who have access to it extraordinary influence over those who are excluded from it. In the same way that the interstate highway system created inner city ghettos in the 1950s and 1960s, the information superhighway is creating "information ghettos." At the same time that many of us celebrate the easy access to such resources as the Library of Congress, there are many more who celebrate easy access to the "catalog channel." Manipulated by consumerism, the possibilities inherent in telecommunications are as likely to be profitmaking as they are to be enlightening. In the past, power relations shifted when oppressed people revolted and took by force the land that had been owned by the privileged classes. More recently, the emergence of labor unions forced factory owners to negotiate with employees over compensation and working conditions. Contemporary power relations are even more complex, for they bear the traces of history at the same time they are rooted in rapidly evolving technological possibilities. While historically the power associated with land ownership was attained through physical force, the power of today which is associated with information control requires literacy as a necessary if not sufficient force. At the present time, not all of us are residents of the "global village," that romantic notion of a world made smaller and borderless through networks of telecommunication. Such residency requires literacy, and for many language minority groups literacy has been an elusive dream.

Why this might be so is suggested by J. U. Ogbu (1990) in his description of the difference between "voluntary" and "involuntary" minority groups. Voluntary or immigrant minorities are "those who have more or less chosen to move [to a culture] . . . in the belief that this change will lead to an improvement in their economic well-being or to greater political freedom" (p. 145). On the other hand, involuntary or castelike minorities are "people initially brought into [a country] through slavery, conquest, or colonization. Resenting the loss of their former freedom and perceiving the social, political, and economic barriers against them as part of an undeserved oppression, American Indians, black Americans, Mexican Americans, and native Hawaiians are characteristic American examples" (Ogbu, 1990, p. 145). Learning to read and write the language of the dominant culture is clearly a different social and psychological experience for these two groups of minorities. The dominant educational system which perpetuates the existing power relations serves members of voluntary minority groups very well. It is, in fact, the reason they came. For members of involuntary minority groups, an educational experience which ensures that they will remain disenfranchised is hardly something they should feel motivated to participate in. In fact, the resistance of members of involuntary minority groups to the dominant educational system might be understood as a sign of ego strength.

Psychiatrist Hilde Schlesinger (1987) has proposed that psychoanalytic principles underlie an earlier version of Ogbu's (1978) description of the difference between voluntary and involuntary minority groups. In particular, she describes how those principles might inform our understanding of the dynamics in families with children who are deaf and how the interactions between parents and their children who are deaf can unwittingly perpetuate involuntary minority status of these deaf children generation after generation. For Schlesinger, the birth of a child who is deaf creates an involuntary minority status for parents and child alike, regardless of their previous status in society. Without direct reference to Freire, Schlesinger uses psychoanalytic theory to explain the underlying mechanism in his notion of the internalization of the oppressor by those who are themselves oppressed.

> The parents of disabled children feel powerless because usual parenting practices do not result in expected behaviors by the child. Parents who feel powerful are more likely to act permissively toward impulse expression in oral, sphincter, sexual, and aggressive behavior. They are more likely to grant and expect autonomy and to behave in egalitarian terms. They describe desirable qualities of the child as happiness, consideration, curiosity, and self control. Less powerful parents tend to have excessive contact, to be controlling, intrusive, punitive, and irritable, and to consider neatness, cleanliness, and obedience as desirable qualities. . . . (Schlesinger, 1987, p. 9)

Schlesinger contends that feelings of powerlessness affect the ways in which parents communicate with their children. She suggests that "Parents who feel powerless are more likely to use *words* with the intent to 'control.' Parents who communicate with the intent to control use fewer *real* questions, more imperatives, more attention getting devices, more negative actions and verbalizations, more rapid topic changes, more monologue, and less dialogue" (Schlesinger, 1987, p. 11).

What Schlesinger has described as characteristic of powerless parents helps us to understand some of the interactions we find between students and teachers. Her research helps us to understand, from a psychoanalytic perspective, the phenomenon that Freire calls "banking education," where the learner is understood to be an "empty vessel" into which knowledge is "deposited." According to Freire, banking education is designed to perpetuate the status quo. The outcome of banking education is not a change in power relations. Ogbu and others (e.g., Giroux, 1992; Grumet, 1988; Shor, 1987) have demonstrated that much of what happens in schools, especially schools for students who are involuntary minorities, is banking education. Schlesinger's psychoanalytic explanation of power relations helps us to understand why that is the case. Teachers, as well as parents, frequently feel powerless in the face of economic, social, and political realities. Understanding the limited horizons of their students in contemporary society, they seek to protect them in the same way that parents have sought to protect them – through control.

Schlesinger (1987, pp. 9–10) is correct when she notes that people who are deaf have a great deal in common with the involuntary minority groups described by Ogbu. People who are deaf did not choose their status. It is not unreasonable to say that people who are deaf have been effectively "colonized" by the dominant culture which never consciously questions its capacity to hear. The use of the word "conscious" is important here. Much of what Ogbu refers to when he discusses the fate of involuntary minorities is not part of the conscious awareness of members of the dominant culture. And this is what Freire means when he says that the oppressed will free the oppressor at the same time he frees himself (1970, p. 28).

Those of us who work in special settings, such as the National Technical Institute for the Deaf (NTID) in Rochester, New York, which is supported by the U.S. government for the purpose of offering degrees only to students who are deaf, can frequently be accused of paternalism, benevolent though it may be. Even though our expressed mission at the NTID is to provide programs which lead to improved career opportunities – that is, to challenge the status quo regarding educational possibilities for people who are deaf – our methods do not always match our mission. Part of this, I suspect, originates in our own insecurity.

We, too, wonder about the society our deaf graduates will enter. Frequently, we catch ourselves worrying about our students' understanding of the American work culture and about the ability to use English well enough to communicate on the job. Too often, we let our curriculum reflect the status quo rather than challenge it. Our students are sometimes more bold than we. Since the Gallaudet "Deaf President Now" protest of 1988, students at NTID have been increasingly aware of their ability to challenge standard practice. They understand the power of symbols in our culture. In 1992, several students, in a meeting with administrators, challenged the fact that their diplomas are different from those of students who can hear and who are graduating from other colleges of Rochester Institute of Technology, the university of which the NTID is one college. Those students challenged the conflation of their education with the fact that they were deaf. While the students' activism is encouraging, things change slowly. Although it was pointed out several years ago, a sign at the entrance to the university campus still shows "NTID" with an arrow pointing one way and "Academic Buildings" with an arrow in the other direction.

At NTID, we are all aware of the extraordinary complexity of the political, social, and linguistic issues in our college. All of the categories of bilingualism apply and more so. We have students whose dominant language is ASL, we have students whose dominant language is English, and we have students who know both languages equally well and who are highly fluent in both. And we have students who have limited access to either ASL or English. When we consider also that our college is a technical institute in which each area of study has its own highly specific "language," the language that many of us are most competent to teach, it is easy to see why we, too, experience some of the insecurity that parents and teachers of disadvantaged students feel.

In my own case, I teach mathematics. Bertrand Russell (1901) once said that "mathematics may be defined as the subject in which we never know what we are talking about, nor whether what we are saying is true" (p. 84). Understood this way, mathematics must be the most decontextualized form of language possible. Yet this most decontextualized language is itself the very context within which my daily conversations with students occur. Essentially what we are doing together, my students and I in my classroom, is trying to make sense of the mathematics Bertrand Russell has described by using a variety of different systems of symbolic representation. Some of what we say is recognizable as pure English, some as ASL, some as technical mathematics signs, some as mathematics inscribed in English, some as pure mathematical symbolization, and some as graphic representation of mathematical concepts. Our task together is to create a common meaning. Mathematics is a fairly arbitrary system of signs and symbols which have been developed through the interactions of many people over the years. To learn mathematics, one has to learn what has been agreed upon by those who have gone before.

Given the preceding description, it is fair to wonder what mathematics has to do with issues of power and literacy today. Mathematics is far more than a lesson in the history of agreed-upon systems of signs and symbols. Although mathematics and the language of technology are not identical, there is significant overlap. It is through mathematics that we understand how to represent and manipulate data or information. Technological advances in computing, for example, have made it possible to control and manipulate large amounts of information almost instantaneously. Consider what a small part currency actually plays in our lives anymore. Many of us have our salary checks directly deposited from our employer's account into our personal accounts. We can use credit cards in almost any store, gas station, or restaurant, so no actual cash need ever change hands. Within fifteen minutes, we can send money to our children anywhere in the United States by calling Western Union and giving a credit card number. Admittedly, sending amounts of $10,000 or more takes a little longer, but the system is not quite perfect yet. In each case, the only thing that is exchanged is information. Whether or not we ever actually participate in the processes associated with exchanging such information, it is essential that we understand how those processes are happening. Without some sense of that, we are dominated by the technology.

Many of my students are preparing to enter the field of visual communication, and many others will be consumers of visual, graphic information. Understanding how to shift the vertical axis on a graph to better show a profit or a loss, a huge tax increase by the Republicans if you are a Democrat, a small tax increase by the Democrats if you are Democrat, all require a basic form of mathematical literacy. Freire would suggest that this mathematical literacy develops out of a process of problematizing the everyday world. That is not such a difficult thing to do in a college environment. The automatic teller machine in the hall of our classroom building will give at least one student in my class the "insufficient funds" message at least once a quarter. The relationship between earnings and information exchange is never clearer. Political accusations in newspapers and on television of one party or the other increasing taxes are made on an almost daily basis. The complicated part, particularly for teachers who are themselves members of the dominant culture, is to find ways to ensure that the knowledge of that culture emerges and is accessible through the problem-posing pedagogy suggested by Freire. Not to do that is to romanticize oppression and ensure that it will be inescapable. Finally, I have arrived at the nagging question that anyone who teaches students who come from involuntary minority groups must face. Is it possible to disregard the status quo curriculum entirely?

The answer is no. I had an opportunity in 1991 to meet with Paulo Freire when he visited the United States and to ask him directly about my work teaching mathematics to students who are deaf. Would all they needed to know in order to be empowered in today's technological society emerge through the investigation of their everyday experience? He responded that the existence of the knowledge of the dominant culture, whether that is knowledge of language and literature or mathematical knowledge, cannot be kept from the oppressed, because the effects of such knowledge are, in fact, part of the everyday reality of people who are oppressed. When such knowledge is absent, that absence becomes a problem in the everyday reality of people. It is the teacher's task to find the ways in which that knowledge can develop through the problems that emerge from an investigation of everyday experience. The Brazilian peasants with whom Freire and his colleagues worked needed to understand botany and soil mechanics, but it was the experts in those areas on Freire's team that recognized how to create a curriculum that included principles of biology and engineering as responses to the problems posed by the peasants themselves. Similarly, as I teach mathematics, I need to find ways that algebra, geometry, statistics, and trigonometry, which have been part of the status quo curriculum, emerge as responses to the problems that are identified through the students' investigation of their own everyday experiences. This is not an easy task, and it requires that my students and I become co-investigators of experience. It is also a process that I know will one day have a bittersweet outcome. I have never forgotten a story I read several years ago about a white teacher who had spent her life teaching in a black school in the south (Chesnutt, 1981). One September, late in her career, a young man whom she had taught and who had gone on to become a teacher himself applied for her job and was given it. The irony for those of us from the dominant culture who work in the field of minority education is that one day we will succeed, and our work will be over.

Freire's pedagogy addresses the automatic privileged status associated with race, gender, class, and physical ability. His educational project is about ways to work alongside those who are not privileged as they liberate themselves. It is important to understand that no one can liberate another. Freedom cannot be bestowed; it must be taken. Once taken by those who were formerly oppressed, the world will be a different place. Is it large enough for us all to coexist peacefully? One would certainly hope so, but that will depend. If one form of oppression is simply replaced by another, we will have gained nothing. This is why Freire's pedagogy is so important. It is designed to create a world in which all people are empowered and no group controls the destiny of another. For those who currently enjoy control over others, no matter how benevolent that control might be, the world will indeed be a different place.

Times have changed, perhaps. Some of us may be invited to write chapters such as this, but we need to be alert. There are those who will accuse us, pejoratively, of insisting on a "politically correct" position. People who are deaf, and those of us who work alongside them, should not flinch from the accusations of those who are invested in maintaining conditions of oppression among language minorities in the name of preserving a very narrow and unenlightened view of culture and tradition.

References

Bartolome, L. I. (1994). Beyond the method fetish: Toward a humanizing pedagogy. *Harvard Educational Review, 64*(2), 173–194.
Chesnutt, C. W. (1981). The march of progress. In N. Hoffman (Ed.), *Woman's "true"*

profession: Voices from the history of teaching (pp. 189–199). Old Westbury: Feminist Press.

Fleming, J. E. (1976). The lengthening shadow of slavery. Washington, DC: Howard University Press.

Freire, P. (1970). Pedagogy of the oppressed. New York: Seabury Press.

——— (1985). The politics of education: Culture, power and liberation. South Hadley, MA: Bergin & Garvey.

Freire, P., & Macedo, D. (1987). Literacy: Reading the word and the world. South Hadley, MA: Bergin & Garvey.

Giroux, H. A. (1992). Border crossings: Cultural workers and the politics of education. New York: Routledge.

Grumet, M. R. (1988). Bitter milk: Women and teaching. Amherst: University of Massachusetts Press.

Ogbu, J. U. (1978). Minority education and caste. New York: Academic Press.

——— (1974). The next generation: An ethnography of education in an urban neighborhood. New York: Academic Press.

——— (1988). Class stratification, racial stratification, and schooling. In L. Weis (Ed.), Class, race, & gender in American education (pp. 163–182). Albany, NY: State University of New York Press.

——— (1990). Minority status and literacy in comparative perspective. Daedalus, 119(2), 141–168.

Reyes, M. (1992). Challenging venerable assumptions: Literacy instruction for linguistically different students. Harvard Education Review, 62(4), 427–446.

Russell, B. (1901). Recent work on the principles of mathematics. International Monthly, 4, 84.

Schlesinger, H. S. (1987). Effects of powerlessness on dialogue and development: Disability, poverty, and the human condition. In B.W. Heller, L. M. Flohr, and L. S. Zegans (Eds.), Psychosocial intervention with sensorially disabled persons (pp. 1–27). Orlando: Grune & Stratton.

Shor, I. (1987). Critical teaching and everyday life. Chicago: University of Chicago Press.

Solomon, R. P. (1992). Black resistance in high school: Forging a separatist culture. Albany: State University of New York Press.

CHAPTER TWELVE

Social Assimilation of Deaf High School Students: The Role of School Environment

THOMAS K. HOLCOMB

Introduction

A study of the social assimilation experiences of deaf students was conducted on the campus of the Rochester Institute of Technology (RIT). As a part of this study, freshmen were instructed to reflect back on their high school careers and report on the extent of their involvement in school-sponsored activities. In addition, they were asked to provide reasons for their involvement or lack of involvement. Findings of hearing students were compared with those of students from schools for the deaf as well as those coming from mainstream environments.

The organization of this chapter is as follows: An overview of the literature related to the topic of social assimilation and social development of both deaf and hearing adolescents is presented. Empirical findings related to this topic are outlined. Data illustrating the differences between the high school experiences of three populations (hearing students, mainstreamed deaf students, and students from schools for the deaf) are also presented. A discussion of the findings concludes the chapter.

Thomas K. Holcomb (Ph.D., Education, University of Rochester), Associate Professor at Ohlone College, conducts and publishes research on social assimilation of deaf students, attitudes toward deafness, and accessibility of mainstream environments. He is co-author with Sam Holcomb and Roy Holcomb of *Deaf Culture, Our Way* (1994, Dawn Sign Press). He is a Deaf native ASL user and comes from a family of deaf people. His address is: Ohlone College Deaf Center, 43600 Mission Blvd., Fremont, CA 94539.

The Role of Schools in Social Development

Two of the primary tasks for students during the adolescent years, regardless of their hearing status, are developing social competence and gaining acceptance by their peers (Hunter, 1985; Mergendoller, 1982; Oetting & Beauvais, 1987). Among the most important functions of schools are providing opportunities for social development, creating an arena for social interactions and consequently for peer affiliations (Mergendoller, 1982; Leslie, Larson, & Gorman, 1976; Popenoe, 1974). Through these regular contacts at school, students seek to be accepted, and relationships are formed (Berscheild & Walster, 1983; Lewis & Rosenblum, 1975; Oetting & Beauvais, 1987).

Peer affiliations are often achieved through classroom and informal interactions with other students at school but are more likely accomplished through involvement in school-sponsored activities such as athletics, social and academic clubs, and/or student government (Clark, 1985; Grinder, 1973; Leslie, Larson, & Gorman, 1976). This involvement, or social assimilation, is crucial to the development of social competence for adolescents, which in turn contributes to the development of a healthy and positive self-identity. This identity is necessary for the successful transition from adolescence to adulthood, both in the community and in the world of work (Garbe & Rodda, 1988; Grotevant, Thorbecke & Meyer, 1982; Mergendoller, 1982).

The importance of peer acceptance in schools has been discussed by various authors (e.g., Johnson & Johnson, 1980; Mergendoller, 1982; Rice, 1978). A network of friends and participation in co-curricular activities have been found to have a positive influence not only on academic achievement but also on professional and personal aspirations (Rice, 1978; Weatherford & Horrocks, 1967). In addition, research has indicated that involvement in school activities contributes to various positive attributes, including higher self-esteem, increased positive peer interaction, and a stronger sense of belonging (Marks & Cohen, 1978; Mergendoller, 1982; Tripp & Turner, 1986). Often, the most popular students in school are those who are "joiners" and who play an active role in many different school activities (Rice, 1978). Conversely, for those who are unsuccessful in becoming affiliated with a group at school, there is a higher incidence of poor academic performance and attrition (Havighurst, 1962; Rice, 1978).

Deaf Students and School Involvement

There is a limited amount of research that focuses specifically on socialization patterns of deaf adolescents. However, there is ample literature focusing on social experiences of mainstreamed deaf students. For example, there are articles written from the perspectives of deaf students (e.g., Shettle, 1987; J. Thomas, 1988; Whitney, 1989); of parents (e.g., Carver, 1966; Greaves, 1989; Siegel, 1989; R. Thomas, 1987); of concerned deaf adults (e.g., Andersson, 1987; Bahan, 1989; Garretson, 1977; Mutti, 1989; Wixtrom, 1988); and of professionals in the field (e.g., Brill, 1975; Kindred, 1980; Moores, 1987; Roman & Tucker, 1987; Tripp & Turner, 1986).

The following work was done from a research base. Mertens (1989) did a survey on deaf students' perspectives of their high school experience. Foster (1988, 1989) interviewed deaf students regarding their experiences during high school. Gregory, Shanahan, and Wahlberg (1984) examined a national survey on high school seniors to identify characteristics of deaf students. Reich, Hambleton, and Houldin (1977) measured variables to determine characteristics for successful mainstreaming experiences.

In Mertens's study (1989), 49 deaf undergraduate students were asked to report on their high school experience using an eighteen-item questionnaire. Students from schools for the deaf were almost unanimous (21 out of 22) in their positive feelings about their social experiences at the school. In contrast, only 9 out of 15 students who attended a mainstream program without support services expressed satisfaction with the quality of social experiences at their high school. Those who had support services while attending the public school were equally divided (6 out of 12) in reporting positive feelings about social experiences in high school. In addition, those who participated in co-curricular activities were generally more satisfied with their high school experience. The students who reported negative experiences indicated unsuccessful attempts to become involved in school activities. Mertens also found that the presence of deaf peers at the school improved the quality of the high school experience as a whole. Deaf peers are a plus when many deaf students are congregated in a school setting. Unfortunately, the majority of schools that serve deaf children generally had fewer than three deaf students per program (Siegel, 1989).

Foster (1988, 1989) reported extensive qualitative findings supporting Merten's research (1989). At RIT, deaf students attending the National Technical Institute for the Deaf (NTID) were asked to reflect on their high school experiences. A large portion of these studies focused on the students' social experiences. Overall, the respondents indicated a desire to participate actively in social events at their school. This desire stemmed from wanting to belong and wanting to be accepted by their peers. Several students who attended a public school had active, rich co-curricular experiences. However, many reported school as a place of social isolation and loneliness with little or no opportunity for friendships. Foster (1988) noted that because social integration outside the classroom environment required more verbal, casual, and often spontaneous interactions, mainstreamed deaf students had difficulties developing friendships at school.

Foster's (1988, 1989) and Mertens's (1989) research illustrated a major dilemma surrounding the practice of mainstreaming. A quality educational experience was seen as a compromise between attending a public school and a school for deaf children. By attending a public school, deaf students sacrificed social development opportunities for what was perceived as a more appropriately challenging academic curriculum. In the studies cited above, deaf students in the mainstream frequently reported not being invited to parties and other social events attended by their hearing peers. Conversations and friendships were often limited and superficial. Loneliness was a major part of their scholastic experience. Foster questioned whether the price for mainstream placement (i.e., social isolation) was too great for deaf students. She recommended further studies in the area of social interactions between deaf and hearing students to identify strategies for effective mainstreaming practices.

In another study, Gregory et al. (1984) analyzed data from a national survey on high school seniors ($n = 26,146$) and identified 574 of those seniors as having some form of hearing impairment. The majority of the identified hearing-impaired students were reported as active in their schools' co-curricular programs. Gregory et al. found that the primary reason for their involvement might have stemmed from dependence on the school's organized activities for their social experience rather than from a personal interest or desire to participate.

Another study relating to socialization of mainstreamed deaf students was done by Reich, Hambleton, and Houldin (1977). They measured several variables to determine the necessary characteristics for successful integration. One hundred ninety-five students from three different academic placements (fully integrated, partially integrated, and itinerant support) were assessed with respect to their hearing loss, oral communication skills, intelligence, achievement scores, self-concept, and social adjustment. The findings indicated that while academic and language development may be enhanced in the integrated settings, personal (i.e., self-concept) and social problems may become more severe.

Thus, empirical findings to date have indicated that deaf students in the mainstream are isolated, rejected by their hearing peers, and afforded little opportunity to participate actively in school activities. Recognizing the importance of school activities, this study examined the social assimilation patterns of high school deaf students. A model illustrating the importance of school-sponsored activities was developed by Kaufman, Goettlieb, Agard, and Kukic (1975) and is discussed below.

Kaufman et al.'s (1975) Model of Social Acceptance

Kaufman's model consists of four components: physical proximity, social interactive behavior, social assimilation, and social acceptance. Physical proximity is the primary requirement for social interaction to take place. Physical proximity increases the probability that social contacts between students will occur. The second step toward social acceptance is social interactive behavior (or social contacts) and involves both verbal and non-verbal communication among students sharing physical space. Through social interactions, students become assimilated into school functions and are actively involved in school activities (social assimilation). As a result of this involvement, students become an integral member of their peer group (social acceptance).

This model is helpful in understanding the various dynamics involved with social interactions among students. It identifies a primary motive for participation in school activities (social assimilation) and demonstrates that relationships are built on proximity and casual interactions. As a result of these interactions, students are drawn into co-curricular school activities and are eventually accepted as full members of the group.

In the literature, the potential benefits of mainstreaming experiences for deaf children seem to emphasize socialization as a positive outcome. For example, several authors have offered goals for mainstreaming that include access to social integration (Antia, 1985; Mertens, 1989; Roman & Tucker, 1987); enhanced social development opportunities (Asher, 1978; Furman, Rahe, & Hartup, 1979); a higher level of social skills (Bitter & Johnston, 1974; Dale, 1984; Kindred, 1980); improved perspective and attitude toward one another (Kindred, 1980; Vernon & Athey, 1977); and improved communication skills (Brackett & Henniges, 1976; Kindred, 1980). However, studies to date have pointed out that a major challenge for deaf students in mainstreamed schools is social interaction.

For deaf students, the main difficulty is gaining access to what Garretson (1977) refers to as "the unwritten curriculum" of the school. The importance of interactions and the exchange of information during recess, athletic competition, and student meetings is often overlooked in the process of mainstreaming deaf students in favor of academic considerations. Because of these documented problems, mainstreaming has often been identified as one of the most important and controversial issues in the field of education of deaf children (e.g., Lane, 1987; Lippa, 1988; Meadow, 1980).

The Study

The purpose of this study was to examine and compare the extent of the mainstreamed deaf high school students' involvement in school activities and their reasons for participation or nonparticipation with deaf students from schools for the deaf and hearing students. A questionnaire was developed, based on Kaufman et al.'s (1975) model described above, to assess selected students' level of social assimilation.

Method of Data Collection

A fifteen-item questionnaire was developed to elicit feedback from students regarding their involvement in school activities to determine the social assimilation patterns of deaf students. Hearing students were included in this study as a comparison group in order to provide a better understanding of the high school experiences of the majority group.

The questionnaire included six sections:

1. Personal Information. Data such as gender, age, and hearing status were collected. These were used initially to separate deaf and hearing students as well as to collect demographic information.
2. School Background. General information about the high school environment was elicited. This permitted an analysis of the relationship between school setting and level of participation.
3. Experience at High School. Students reported on their participation in their high school co-curricular activities. This included both participation in and attendance at school-sponsored programs.
4. Access and Barriers for Deaf Students. Deaf students were asked to respond to questions regarding access and barriers to participation in school activities due to their deafness.
5. Reflections. The students were asked to reflect back on their high school experience and express their personal thoughts about co-curricular activities.
6. Additional Information. The students' social security numbers were recorded.

The data were quantitatively analyzed, utilizing cross-tabulations, t-tests, and correlations to determine whether the differences in experiences among deaf students from special school settings, mainstreamed deaf students, and hearing students were significant. In addition, the written responses to Section 5 regarding their personal thoughts about their participation in school activities were coded and sorted into categories. These categories were then analyzed for recurring patterns and themes. This chapter primarily focuses on the qualitative analyses of the data from Section 5 of the questionnaire and discusses selected findings from other sections which supported such analyses. A full account of this study can be found in Holcomb (1990).

A total of 170 hearing students and 124 deaf students completed the questionnaire for the study. Of the 124 deaf students, 81 (65%) were from mainstreamed high school programs while the remaining 43 students (35%) graduated from a school for the deaf. Of the 81 previously mainstreamed participants in the study, 45 students came from a program where there were fewer than ten other deaf students in the school, and 6 students reported being the only deaf individual at the school.

Findings

Although the focus of this chapter is to discuss the findings of the qualitative data analyses, relevant findings from other parts of the study are presented here in order to create a clearer description of the experiences of the participants in the study. More specifically, the baseline participation rates and leadership opportunities are discussed below.

The data indicated that while the rate of participation of mainstreamed deaf students in co-curricular activities (3.14 activities) was similar to that of their hearing peers (3.5 activities), students from schools for the deaf (5.1 activities) were found to be involved at a rate that was significantly higher than those two groups. This might be due to the relatively small size of many schools for the deaf, which necessitates student participation in more activities in order to maintain the organizations' active statuses. For example, in many schools for the deaf, practically every high school boy is expected to play on the football team; otherwise, the school would risk having to drop the sport for lack of players. Conversely, the options that are available to students for participation are often limited, again due to the size of these schools.

For mainstreamed deaf students, the opportunities for involvement in school activities were as broad and varied as those for their hearing peers.

The mainstreamed deaf students reported having been successful in becoming involved in school activities with only a few exceptions. Instrumental music was one activity that was cited as being inaccessible to them. In addition, activities requiring a high degree of verbal intercourse, such as student government and academic clubs, appeared to have posed considerable barriers.

Communication obstacles may have limited the opportunities for leadership experience among mainstreamed deaf students. Twenty-two percent of the mainstreamed deaf students who were involved in school activities reported having had positions of authority at school, a rate significantly lower than that of their peers from schools for the deaf (55%) and of those who are hearing (49%). In addition, it appears from their responses that limited peer support might have prevented them from assuming leadership positions within the organizations in which they were involved. This was discussed by many students and this information is presented below.

Students' Reflections on Their Social Experiences

In this section, the data are presented from the students' responses to the question, "As you reflect back on your high school experience, do you wish (A) you had participated more in school activities?; (B) you had participated less in school activities?; (C) things were exactly the same as they were?" In follow-up, the subjects were asked to provide reasons why they responded the way they did.

The responses to the question assessing the participants' desire to change the level of participation in school activities were analyzed. It was found there was no significant difference between the responses of deaf students from special schools and those of hearing students. However, the responses from mainstreamed deaf students differed significantly from hearing students and special school students. Many of the mainstreamed deaf students expressed a desire for greater involvement in school activities and were dissatisfied with their level of participation in school. More specifically, 60% of the students from schools for the deaf and 52% of hearing students indicated that they were satisfied with their level of involvement in high school. Only 26% of mainstreamed deaf students had similar feelings. Conversely, 63% of mainstreamed deaf students expressed a desire to have been more involved in school activities while only 30% of students from schools for the deaf and 44% of hearing students responded this way.

In examining the participants' individual reasons for their satisfaction or dissatisfaction with their levels of participation, it was found that only one out of five mainstreamed deaf students made positive statements about the experiences they had in high school. In contrast, more than half of the deaf school students' and hearing students' responses reflected a pleasant and positive high school experience.

Hearing Students. Many hearing students were quite content with their high school experience. Approximately half of the written entries by hearing respondents indicated a glowing memory of their high school career. They described how wonderful those days were. These feelings are reflected in selected quotations from the students taken from the questionnaire:

My four years at high school were some of the best years of my life!

It was awesome.

High school was fun and fulfilling.
I did not participate in everything but I got to hang out with the crowds I wanted and since I was popular, I also got invited to parties. . . .

I was pleased with what I did in my high school and how my years went.

I had a great time and wanted to do more. . . .

Several hearing students discussed how their high school activities matched their goals and how they were able to accomplish everything they had wanted and could accommodate in their schedules:

I feel that the number of activities I chose and spend time in were adequate to give me a balanced high school life. I had just the right schedule for work and play.

I achieved everything I had set in my mind. I was pleased with the experience I got.

Any or all of the activities I did not participate in were done consciously, and most likely I could have attended if I had wanted to. However I didn't have the desire and therefore had no regrets.

I had everything planned out to my time table.

These comments represent decision making from a position of power and choice. The students indicated that their level of participation met their needs or that they could have participated more if they had wanted to.

A total of seventy-four hearing students indicated a desire to have participated more in high school activities. Reasons provided typically reflected the desire to have had an even better high school experience:

I had a great time and wanted to do more.

. . . it was fun to participate.

. . . wished to become involved in more sports[,] the more, the better.

. . . the more things you can experience, more interesting and fulfilled your life becomes.

Other reasons for low participation referred to factors unrelated to the school. For instance, five students reported having a job after school which prevented them from becoming more involved in school activities. Other students expressed dissatisfaction in hindsight regarding their own levels of participation by explaining that their college application would have been more impressive with a longer list of co-curricular activities. A few students felt that they should have contributed more to the school by, for example, being better representatives of black students. Yet other students felt they would have turned out to be a better adult if they had developed various skills through activities in high school.

Students from Schools for the Deaf. The majority of students from schools for the deaf also reported positive experiences in school activities. Like hearing students, it was evident that they, too, had the luxury of making choices from a position of power:

I have participated enough in high school.

I was satisfied of what I achieved and accomplished during my high school year which most of them were set as my goals.

I participated in all the sports I liked that my school offered me.

I participated so many activities yet I wanted to learn more but unfortunately time didn't permit very much. . . .

It was clear that these students were able to participate in any activities they desired at school. In fact, several previously mainstreamed students gave lack of opportunity to participate in school activities as their reason for transferring to a school for the deaf:

During my first two years of high school I attended a public school and I [was] afraid to join sports.

I have not joined sports when I went to public school and finally went [to a] deaf school to join sports.

Not every student from schools for the deaf reported a positive experience associated with school-sponsored activities at the school. Five students expressed frustration with their inability to benefit from school activities. Poor communication skills among the staff members and transportation problems were some of the barriers identified by the students.

There are more hearing people which they learned little sign language.

All deaf students lost their interesting in any activity. Also, they [the staff] had hard [time] communicate with deaf children. If, staff in school use sign language very expert, then it can influence deaf students more activity. Also influence about education future.

Because I had a transportation problem and my parents were too tired to pick me up very late so I went home about 6 or 7 o'clock.

An additional obstacle to participation in schools for the deaf seemed to be the limited number of activities offered by the school. This is not surprising as many of these schools have fewer than 200 students in their student body, making it difficult for them to offer a wide array of activities.

Because the school has small students . . . about 120 students. Almost not have little activities.

They do not have enough girls participate in volleyball and basketball team!

Mainstreamed Deaf Students. Relatively few deaf students from schools for the deaf, and hearing students, cited the lack of friends or a need for more friends as a reason for their responses. This reason was far more common among mainstreamed deaf students. Seventy-three percent of the written responses from mainstreamed deaf students were related to the frustrations they had with their efforts to participate in activities or to the need for more opportunities to make friends. The following quotations from respondents represent these feelings.

I was feeling lonely because no one seems to ask me to participate.

I was not accepted. I was very shy. I had no friends and I was embarrassed because of being the only deaf student.

I would have participated, but due to lack of encouragement, I was unable to participate.

I had no one to be with.

I had no friends (hearing nor deaf). I never experienced boys. I was unaccepted.

I feel that they reject me because of my hearing disabilities. And also I did not feel comfortable in some kind of activities which they don't give some kind of encouragement.

I was the only deaf person in high school. It was difficult to do things.

Being alone and/or lonely was cited by nineteen mainstreamed deaf students. This reason was frequently given to explain their desire to have participated more in school activities as a way of making friends. In addition, some students reported feeling insecure when people treated them differently because of their hearing impairment. Lack of encouragement by people at the school or not having confidence to participate was also reported. In addition, communication barriers appeared to be a major obstacle.

I wish I had participated more in school activities but they are all hearing people who did not know how to communicate deaf people well enough. So if I were hearing, I probably participated more than I do right now. But the main thing – problem – is communication.

I was treated different because of my hearing impairment. Teachers and students felt I couldn't do anything. I was afraid I would be made fun of.

I did not feel comfortable a lot of the time because I don't have good communication skills with the hearing.

Unlike the case with hearing students and deaf students from schools for the deaf, mainstreamed deaf students' motives for participating or not participating were based on their exclusion, not on a position of power. Lack of support services was also a major consideration for some students. As noted by several respondents, there is a clear relationship between communication barriers, confidence, and participation.

School would not provide interpreters to help the hearing-impaired.

Students made fun of me so I lost my self-confidence.

I felt that the hassle of getting an interpreter wasn't worth it for participating in my high school activities.

In three responses mainstreamed deaf students reported positive feelings about their participation in high school. Two were:

I enjoyed the activities I did in high school.

I seem to be happy with my life and about what I did.

The third response was from a student who described how successful she was in the public school because of her active involvement in school activities and because hearing students had been taught sign language:

I don't know really [how] I have lived in the hearing world so far, but anyway, being the deaf person in school [who is] the most popular to the hearing students cuz, I am the photographer for the yearbook. So, most students likes to learn sign language . . .

Most of the mainstreamed students who indicated a positive and active involvement in school activities were involved in organizations that were formed specifically for deaf students, such as the local chapter of the Junior National Association of the Deaf (Jr.NAD).

Finally, a few mainstreamed deaf students said that they felt cheated out of a positive high school experience. One student wrote

High school was supposed to be the best time of my life but it was not!

Summary and Conclusions

This study confirmed the general findings in the literature regarding the experience of many deaf students in the mainstream: social isolation and loneliness. Although the students in the study appeared to have available a wide range of activities in which they could choose to participate, they seemed to find it a challenge to become fully assimilated with their hearing peers.

An exception to this experience was a situation where a large number of mainstreamed deaf students were congregated in a public school. In addition, activities designed specifically for deaf students, such as a Jr.NAD chapter, were available to them, increasing the opportunity for them to participate in a school activity. For these reasons, they were less likely to cite the lack of friends or loneliness as reasons for wishing they had participated more in school activities.

For students from schools for the deaf, the positive influences came in the areas of social interactive behavior (including a barrier-free communication environment), which led to social assimilation. Like hearing students, they had power and the ability to make choices regarding their involvement in school activities. In addition, the data confirmed that these students had enjoyed a wealth of leadership experiences. The major drawback reported by the students was the lack of options available within a school due to the small size of its student body.

It follows, therefore, that to ensure optimal opportunities for social development for deaf students from both settings, some intervention strategies must be taken. For deaf students in schools for the deaf, one major change is recommended. Increased options need to be made available for these students. This can be accomplished establishing joint programs with local public schools with interpreting support available so that deaf students can participate in activities unavailable at the school for the deaf.

For mainstreamed deaf students, the recommendations are more complex. It appears important for the number of deaf students to reach a critical mass. Consolidated programs would encourage deaf students to develop friendships among one another, thus increasing the opportunities for confidence-building as well as increasing comfort in participating in school activities. In addition, activities targeted specifically to deaf students such as a Jr.NAD chapter would provide deaf students with an organization within the public school in which they could actively participate. These strategies would give deaf students the opportunity to assume a position of power and choice when it comes to participating in school activities. Finally, the provision of support services must be expanded to include extracurricular functions so that deaf students can participate and benefit fully from these activities.

Considering the disparity between the experiences of mainstreamed deaf students, deaf students who attend schools for the deaf, and hearing students, it is clear that teachers and administrators in mainstream programs must design adequate opportunities for deaf students to enjoy a positive social experience in school. The findings of this study suggest that participation in school activities does not appear to be the problem. Students participated when given the opportunity. But more needs to be done to enhance the quality of social assimilation opportunities for mainstreamed deaf students. Practitioners in public schools need to devote greater effort to enhance the opportunities for co-curricular activities for these students. Strategies might include those that would minimize communication barriers, such as the establishment of sign language classes for hearing students, increased provision of support services for after-school activities, sensitivity training for school personnel, and assertiveness training for deaf students. To minimize communication obstacles among students, information that encourages the development of effective communication with deaf people needs to be shared with hearing people.

In addition, involvement of mainstreamed deaf students in school activities should be made more purposeful so that social interactive behavior can occur more frequently, more completely, and more positively. Close monitoring of group dynamics within activities can assist school personnel in designing and implementing intervention strategies to enhance positive interaction patterns between groups. Often minor changes in the way activities are conducted can significantly reduce communication difficulties between deaf and hearing students. Tips for such modifications are available in a variety of publications (e.g., Foster & Holcomb, 1990; Higgins, 1990). Suggestions include such behaviors as waiting to be recognized before speaking (enabling deaf participants to follow the discussion), making leaders responsible for recognizing speakers (enabling deaf members an equal chance to participate), and arranging seating in a circular pattern (allowing a clear line of vision for all deaf members).

Mainstreamed deaf students need to be encouraged and perhaps given special training to enable them to participate more fully in leadership capacities. Personal satisfaction is often a result of a successful and/or rewarding leadership experience. If barriers continue to exist for mainstreamed deaf students, their potentially devastating effects on the formation of a healthy identity will continue to be prevalent among deaf students attending public schools.

Since deaf students constitute a relatively small proportion of individuals needing special education services, certain needs and challenges of this population may tend to be neglected in pursuit of generic policies and practices. This study revealed the unique needs and experiences of deaf students and indicated how important it is for practitioners and policymakers to devote special consideration to these students. On a policymaking level, a better understanding of and increased sensitivity toward the dynamics of integrating deaf students are needed. The implications of placing a deaf student in an isolated setting – one where she or he is the only deaf person – need to be carefully considered. Policymakers must not be satisfied with mere academic results of mainstreaming practices, but must seek advancements in social growth for deaf students as well. Deaf students need a social support system. This might be provided by consolidating programs serving deaf students to increase the number of deaf students at one site. A community-wide organization might also be established which would allow mainstreamed deaf students to congregate on a regular basis for social interaction. Joint efforts with schools for the deaf would provide mainstreamed deaf students with additional opportunities for socialization.

References

Andersson, Y. (1987, February). Mainstreaming to be topic #1. *World Around You.*

Antia, S. D. (1985). Social integration of hearing-impaired children: Fact or fiction? *Volta Review, 87,* 279–289.

Asher, S. R. (1978). Children's peer relations. In M.E. Lamb (Ed.), *Sociopersonality development.* New York: Holt, Rinehart, & Winston.

Bahan, B. (1989). Who's itching to get into mainstreaming? In S. Wilcox (Ed.), *American deaf culture: An anthology* (pp. 173–177). Burtonsville, MD: Linstok Press.

Berscheild, E., & Walster, E. (1983). *Independent attraction.* Boston, MA: Addison-Wesley.

Bitter, G. B., & Johnston, K. A. (1974). *Facilitating the integration of hearing impaired children into regular public school classes. A technical report.* Salt Lake City: Utah University.

Brackett, D., & Henniges, M. (1976). Communicative interaction of preschool hearing impaired children in an integrated setting. *Volta Review, 78,* 276–285.

Brill, R. G. (1975). Mainstreaming: Format or quality? *American Annals of the Deaf, 120,* 377–381.

Carver, R. L. (1966). A parent speaks out on integration in the schools. *Volta Review, 68,* 580–583.

Clark, M. L. (1985). *Gender, race, and friendship research.* Paper presented at the American Educational Research Association, Chicago.

Dale, D. M. (1984). *Individualized integration: Studies of deaf and partially hearing children and students in ordinary schools and colleges.* Springfield, IL: Charles C. Thomas.

Foster, S. (1988). Life in the mainstream: Reflections of deaf college freshmen on their experiences in the mainstream high school. *Journal of the American Deafness and Rehabilitation Association, 22(2),* 27–35.

——— (1989). Educational programs for deaf students: An inside perspective on policy and practice. In L. Barton (Ed.), *Integration: Myth or Reality?* (pp. 57–82). London: Falmer Press.

Foster, S., & Holcomb, T. (1990). Hearing-impaired students: A student-teacher-class partnership. *Special Educational Needs Review,* Vol. 3. London: Falmer Press.

Furman, A., Rahe, D. F., & Hartup, W. W. (1979). Rehabilitation of socially withdrawn preschool children through mixed-age and same-age socialization. *Child Development, 50,* 915–922.

Garbe, V., & Rodda, M. (1988). Growing in silence: The deaf adolescent. *ACEHI/ ACEDA, 14,*(2), 59–69.

Garretson, M. (1977). The residential school. *The Deaf American, 29,* 19–22.

Greaves, G. (1989). Reverberations. [Special Insert] *The NAD Broadcaster, 11*(2), 2.

Gregory, J. F., Shanahan, T., & Wahlberg, H. L. (1984). Mainstreamed hearing impaired high-school seniors: A re-analysis of a national survey. *American Annals of the Deaf, 129* (1), 11–16.

Grinder, R. E. (1973). *Adolescence.* New York: John Wiley & Sons.

Grotevant, H. D., Thorbecke, W., & Meyer, M. L. (1982). An extension of Marcia's identity status interview into the interpersonal domain. *Journal of Youth and Adolescence, 11*(1), 33–47.

Havighurst, R. J. (1962). *Growing up in River City.* New York: John Wiley & Sons.

Higgins, P. C. (1990). *The challenge of educating together deaf and hearing youth: Making mainstreaming work.* Springfield, IL: Charles C. Thomas.

Holcomb, T. (1990). *Deaf students in the mainstream: A study in social assimilation.* Doctoral dissertation, University of Rochester. (*University Microfilms No. DA0 64793).*

Hunter, F. T. (1985). Adolescents' perception of discussions with parents and friends. *Developmental Psychology, 21*(3), 433–440.

Johnson, D., & Johnson, R. (1980). Integrating handicapped students into the mainstream. *Exceptional Children, 47,* 90–98.

Kaufman, M., Goettlieb, J., Agard, J., & Kukic, M. B. (1975). Mainstreaming: Toward an explication of the construct. In E. L. Meyer, G.A. Vergason, R.J. Whealan (Eds.), *Alternatives for teaching exceptional children* (pp. 40–47). Denver: Love Publishing.

Kindred, E. M. (1980). Mainstream teenagers with care. *American Annals of the Deaf, 123*(9), 1053–1056.

Lane, H. S. (1987). Mainstreaming of deaf children: From bad to worse. *The Deaf American, 38*(1), 15.

Leslie, G. R., Larson, R. F., & Gorman, B. L. (1976). *Introductory sociology.* New York: Oxford University Press.

Lewis, M., & Rosenblum, L. (1975). *Friendship and peer relations.* New York: John Wiley & Sons.

Lippa, M. (1988). *Social distance issues of mainstreamed deaf and hearing impaired in the educational and occupational setting: A research review.* Portland: University of Southern Maine.

Marks, A., & Cohen, M. I. (1978). Developmental processes of adolescence. In A.I. Neyhus & G.F. Austin (Eds.), *Volta Review, 80*(5), 275–285.

Meadow, K. P. (1980). *Deafness and child development.* Berkeley: University of California Press.

Mergendoller, J. R. (1982). *To facilitate or impede? The impact of selected organizational features of secondary schools on adolescent development.* Paper presented at the American Educational Research Association.

Mertens, D. M. (1989). Social experiences of hearing-impaired high school youth. *American Annals of the Deaf, 134*(1), 15–19.

Moores, D. F. (1987). *Educating the deaf: Psychology, principles, and practices.* Boston: Houghton Mifflin.

Mutti, S. F. (1989). Post-demonstration report. *The Deaf Californian,* 8–10.

Northcott, W. (1971). The integration of young deaf children in ordinary educational programs. *Exceptional Children, 38,* 20–32.

Oetting, E. R., & Beauvais, F. (1987). Peer cluster theory, socialization characteristics and adolescent drug use: A path analysis. *Journal of Counseling Psychology, 34*(2), 205–213.

Popenoe, D. (1974). *Sociology.* Englewood Cliffs, NJ: Prentice-Hall.

Reich, C., Hambleton, D., & Houldin, B. K. (1977). The integration of hearing impaired children in regular classrooms. *American Annals of the Deaf, 122,* 534–543.

Rice, R. P. (1978). *The Adolescent.* Boston: Allyn and Bacon.

Roman, A. S., & Tucker, P. E. (1987). Enjoying each other's company: Our model mainstream classroom. *Perspectives, 5*(4), 8–10.

Shettle, A. (1987, May). A call for balance: Mainstreaming vs. institutionalization. *World Around You.*

Siegel, L. (1989, First Quarter). Educational isolation of deaf children. *IMPACT-HI Newsletter.*

Thomas, J. (1989). Why am I transferring to a school for the deaf? *The NAD Broadcaster, 11* (3), 6.

Thomas, R. (1987). How can we better prepare our deaf children and youth for the adult world? In G. B. Anderson & D. Watson (Eds.), *Innovations in the habilitation and rehabilitation of deaf adolescents. Selected proceedings of the national conference on the habilitation and rehabilitation of deaf adolescents.* Little Rock: University of Arkansas Press.

Tripp, A. W., & Turner, B. S. (1986). Hinsdale South High School: A view from the mainstream. *Perspectives, 5*(1), 6–10.

Vernon, M., & Athey, J. (1977). Exceptional children: The Holcomb plan. *Instructor, 86*(5), 136–137.

Weatherford, R. R., & Horrocks, J. E. (1967). Peer acceptance and under and overachievement in school. *Journal of Psychology, 47,* 215–220.

Whitney, J. L. (1989). How to communicate: The continuing controversy. *World Around You.*

Wixtrom, C. (1988). Alone in the crowd. *The Deaf American, 38*(2), 12–15.

PART III

The Deaf Experience: Personal Reflections

CHAPTER THIRTEEN

Growing Up Deaf in Deaf Families: Two Different Experiences

SUSAN C. SEARLS AND DAVID R. JOHNSTON

Translated from the ASL by Susan D. Fischer and the authors

We, David Johnston and Susan C. Searls, have several common bonds: growing up Deaf in Deaf families, having Deaf children, and working at the National Technical Institute for the Deaf (NTID), located in Rochester, New York, the only technical college for the deaf in the world. We considered ourselves as being unique at the workplace because only a few of us have both Deaf parents and children. Even though we both grew up in

This chapter is based on a videotaped ASL conversation between the two authors. The conversational format and ASL were used to facilitate free expression of the author's personal reflections.

Susan C. Searls (M.A., Elementary Education of the Deaf, Gallaudet University), Parent/ Sign Communication/Deaf Studies Coordinator at Rochester School for the Deaf, has seventeen years of professional experience in teaching, curriculum development, networking, and advocacy in the field of the education of deaf people. She is a Deaf native ASL user. Her address is: Rochester School for the Deaf, 1545 St. Paul Blvd., Rochester, NY 14621.

David R. Johnston (A.A.S., Electromechanical Technology, Rochester Institute of Technology), Electromechanical Technician, National Technical Institute for the Deaf, comes from a family of deaf people that has spanned several generations. He is a Deaf native ASL user and is married with three children, ages six, four, and one. He is primarily involved in the Deaf Professional Group Steering Committee at NTID and is serving as a President of the Parent-Teacher Association at the Rochester School for the Deaf. His address is: Industrial Technologies Department, National Technical Institute for the Deaf, Rochester Institute of Technology, 52 Lomb Memorial Drive, Rochester, NY 14623.

Susan D. Fischer (Ph.D., Linguistics, MIT), Professor, National Technical Institute for the Deaf, conducts and publishes research in ASL linguistics. She has coedited with Patricia Siple two volumes of *Theoretical Issues in Sign Language Research* (1991,1992, University of Chicago Press). She holds a Comprehensive Sign Certificate (CSC) from the Registry of Interpreters for the Deaf. Her address is: Department of Applied Language and Cognition Research, National Technical Institute for the Deaf, Rochester Institute of Technology, 52 Lomb Memorial Drive, Rochester, NY 14623.

Deaf families in the 1950s and 1960s our experiences differed quite considerably. In those times, there were no TTYs (the teletypewriter, a device that enables deaf people to communicate through phone lines), no closed-captioned television programs, no legislation mandating increased interpreter services, nor were deaf people viewed as a cultural and linguistic minority. Growing up in two different geographic locations, each of us went to different types of schools: one went to a manual program which used sign language for instruction and the other went to an oral program which used only speech as the mode of instruction. For our college educations, we chose the opposite directions. We shared our experiences and visions in an ASL conversation.

DJ: We'll start with the topic of family experiences. I grew up in a Deaf family. I was the oldest of four children (the other three were sisters); the third child was hearing. My parents had attended residential schools for the Deaf. They attended Gallaudet where they met. They married and had me and my three sisters, settling east of Washington, D.C., in the panhandle area of Maryland. My parents placed me in the Maryland School for the Deaf.

They knew I was deaf because deafness runs in both sides of the family. My mother had a deaf brother. In fact, on my father's side there's a long, unbroken string of deafness. Although the records that would prove this have been lost beyond my paternal grandfather's generation, according to family history, deafness has run in the family for generations.

As I mentioned, my parents placed me in the Maryland School for the Deaf, and I was very happy there. I have vivid memories of my early days at the school when I was around five years old. I remember being all "wired-up" with hearing aids and seeing other deaf kids playing in the schoolyard. I remember eagerly running out to play with them.

SS: Were you a residential student from the time you were five?

DJ: Yes, I was. My parents' home was about fifty miles from the school, about an hour's drive each way. My parents felt lucky to be able to have me at home every weekend, because in their days they had been permitted to go home only for vacations and holidays. So the school was really their first home, where they spent so much time. Whereas in my days, I saw my family every weekend. My mother was very moved because she, in retrospect, could see that I was happier than she had been during her own school experiences.

When I was much older, my mother told me a very touching story about her early days at school. When she was little, there was almost no communication with her parents, who knew little of deaf people or sign language. Her parents heard of a local school for the deaf and sent her there, thinking she would be happy. But my mother, understanding very little because she had no way to communicate with her parents, thought they had put her in prison, and cried her eyes out. At that time, the house parents were very cruel, and spanked children or pulled their hair or hit them on the hands with rulers. My mother remembers being very scared . . .

SS: That's terrible! Why were the house parents so cruel to the children? Was your mother in an oral program?

DJ: During my parents' days, in the 1940s and 1950s, although both of them attended residential schools for the deaf, sign language was forbidden. When someone signed in class, they would be punished; for example, the student would be hit on the wrist with a ruler, or placed in a corner by the teacher. At the same time, house parents, most of whom were hearing, were very mean. Perhaps they were creatures of their times, using old-fashioned means of discipline. My parents lived in fear much of the time while at school growing up, which is why it really hit my mother hard to see how happy l was at the deaf school, and that is why she cried.

Back to my childhood: My parents placed me and my next younger sister at the Maryland School. But the next child in line was a hearing girl.

SS: Oh, yeah? Could you please tell me about your hearing sister?

DJ: When she was born, I was four years old and my next younger sister was two years old. My parents were almost sure that Jody, the new baby, was deaf because she was quiet and slept through our roughhousing. But my father was skeptical, so he decided to try an experiment on Jody. When Jody was eight months old, he waited until she wasn't looking at him. He said "Jody" and she looked right at him. My father knew right then and there, and told my mom that Jody was hearing after all.

SS: How did your parents feel when they found out that Jody was hearing?

DJ: My mother was shocked to find out she was hearing, because Jody hadn't responded to sound until she was eight months old. But my father was thrilled. Although he was deaf, he had never really accepted his deafness. He wanted to be hearing. This was especially true during World War II, as he wanted to emulate his older brother and go to war. When he found out that he couldn't because he was deaf, he was furious! Since he was turned down for military service because he was deaf, he wanted to have hearing children.

ss: Could you explain how your hearing sister felt being the only hearing person in an all-Deaf family?

dj: It's really interesting. Here we had a family where the Deaf people were in the majority, five to one. Being Deaf, we shared the same sorts of experiences, so she often felt left out although she did learn ASL from my younger sister and me. My younger sister and I were so close in age that we constantly played together. All three of us went to the Maryland School for the Deaf, and we would sit in the kitchen telling stories and chatting while Jody sat alone off in another room watching and listening to the TV. My grandmother was hearing, so that's how Jody learned to talk.

Here is an interesting example of a lack of communication within our family. Our family always bought skim milk, and my hearing sister always wished she had a hearing family so she could drink regular milk at home.

ss: But what does the type of milk you buy have to do with being hearing or deaf? I don't understand.

dj: This was the false inference: that she thought that deaf people tended to buy skim milk, while hearing people tended to buy regular milk because her hearing friend drank regular milk at home. Jody, being the only hearing person in our Deaf family, had many interesting views which clearly showed a lack of communication within the family. However, we depended on Jody to serve as an interpreter because at that time there were no decoders and relay services. Please tell me about your family.

ss: As for myself, all of my immediate family members (parents and an older brother) were deaf. My parents were rather disappointed that both of their children were deaf. They felt this way because at that time, deafness was viewed as pathological. My parents were actually pressured by my father's parents (who were themselves deaf) not to bear any more children! My paternal grandmother, who was deaf, became pregnant after having my father. Her family members who were hearing weren't too happy about the possibility of her bearing another deaf child. This influenced her to choose to have an abortion. What made matters worse, she discovered that she had aborted a set of twins!

Nowadays, many Deaf parents *want* deaf children, but in those days it was different. My relatives cautioned my parents not to have more children – they said two was enough. We moved from New Jersey to New York because there were better educational opportunities for us. My parents decided to send me to Lexington School for the Deaf, an oral school for the deaf. I was lucky because just at that time many of the students who went to Lexington School had deaf parents. When I entered, I was immediately accepted because we could identify with other children who had deaf parents.

Now, when I look back, I realize that my personality was formed from the things that I experienced growing up in that school. I didn't have intelligible speech skills. In class, when the teacher didn't understand my speech, I would often feel embarrassed and simply give up and sit back and not bother trying to participate.

DJ: How well could you read lips?

ss: Rather well, but of course, I couldn't get everything from the teachers' lips. With the teachers who understood me well, I participated more. Comparing my experience with nowadays, I now know that my participation in the oral school classes was severely limited. I remember several times when I was punished for signing in class or elsewhere in the school; I was sent to the principal's office and had to write 100 times, "I will not sign in the hallway." Some of my friends were spanked by the principal. Like your mother, I lived in fear of school. In the halls, when we saw the principal coming toward us, stern-faced and cross-looking, we would surreptitiously warn each other, "Cheesit, the C!" – that was our name sign for the principal. We usually felt intimidated.

I had one Deaf teacher and all the rest hearing teachers. This Deaf woman was my role model; I really looked up to her, the one Deaf teacher in an oral school. I think I became a teacher because of her. She had a strong influence on my life. But at the same time, I felt some ambivalence and conflict in regard to her because when I went out of school into the Deaf community, I would see her at Deaf gatherings or events, and there she was: signing! I was disillusioned because of the inconsistencies. Out of school she signed, but in school she didn't. I had similar feelings when my parents who came to visit me at school were prohibited from signing inside the building.

Moreover, I had some humiliating experiences at school. One time I was acting in *Romeo and Juliet*. I played Juliet. I got up in front of a large audience and spoke my lines. The audience didn't understand what I said. What a farce! The next day there was a picture of me with Romeo on the front of one of the sections of the *New York Times*. But I felt that it was really a joke because the audience didn't understand me! The hearing audience didn't understand because the play wasn't voice-interpreted, and the deaf audience didn't understand because the play wasn't produced in sign language or sign-interpreted. Can you imagine the deaf audience having to lip-read us on the stage from their seats!

DJ: How disgusting! Tell me, did you have any friends when you went to school?

SS: Yes, one thing that really helped was that there were so many children at school who also had deaf parents. Home life was pretty lonely, especially after school. My brother had the advantage of being involved in athletics and sports, so he interacted with many of his hearing friends. I, on the other hand, couldn't enjoy playing in my neighborhood with other hearing girls due to my limited speech skills, so I would often play by myself. My deaf friends lived in different places in New York City. I could go over to see my deaf friends, but this required a great deal of effort. There were no TTYs at the time, so we had to depend on hearing people for communicating on the telephone. For example, if I needed to contact a deaf friend, I might go to a neighbor who would in turn call the neighbor of my deaf friend, so four people would be involved in making one simple phone call. All it took was one missing link somewhere along the line to break the chain of communication. It was such a hassle that it was often easier just to go to the friend's house to find out what was going on. Making contact was so difficult! If I finally did get through after involving all those intermediaries, I was delighted. I could go spend the night at the home of one of my deaf friends!

DJ: Your story about speech reminded me of one of my mother's stories. At her school, she had arduous speech training all the way through senior year. The teacher, who had Deaf parents, told the class, "You know, the time is fast approaching when you will graduate. You've had speech training all this time, so when you go out into the real world, you'll be able to speak perfectly on the job and with hearing people." The students looked at each other and thought, "Is this possible?" Then they said to themselves, "No way." They knew only their close friends and some teachers or parents would be able to understand their speech. Anyway, when they graduated, all that speech training went right out the window and they relied exclusively on sign language for communication. What an experience!

ss: Regarding speech, I remember that we were often praised for our good speech. Actually, it was good "deaf speech" but not good enough for the general public to understand. After a speech training session, I would almost always have a headache. We had to do all these same little tedious tasks like blowing on tissues day after day. The monotony was unbearable. Not only was I in an oral school where speech-training was highly focused, I was also sent by my parents to speech therapy every Sunday afternoon. Can you imagine having to go through an entire week of oral school only to have to spend Sunday afternoon in speech therapy? I do understand my parents' good intentions wanting me to develop good speech skills, especially in light of the circumstances they were facing: pressure from family, trends in deaf education, and hopes for my future.

Lexington School and Fanwood were the two well-known schools for the deaf in New York City. Lexington was oral while Fanwood was a manual school and the two were known for their differences. At Lexington School for the Deaf, there were good teachers and a strong educational program. At that time, Lexington School was predominately attended by girls because it was once an all-girl school. The opposite was true for Fanwood, which was attended mostly by boys. As a result, I was placed in Lexington School. I should say that in our Jewish culture, education is of great value and importance. This cultural value, I believe, was also tied to oralism. Additionally, my paternal grandmother , who was deaf, graduated from Lexington School in the early 1900s. She had good speech, so growing up it was expected that I should have good speech too, like the rest of my family.

dj: I remember when I was a little boy, I felt embarrassed to be Deaf, because we were regarded as abnormal, mentally retarded, or crippled. I remember going to a restaurant and asking my mother to keep her hands down so as not to make our signing too conspicuous. Her reaction was, "To hell with that attitude!" She was proud of her own deafness and signing and didn't want to hide either under a bushel basket. But at the same time I was scared! I am working on images and perceptions of deafness. I feel that I am the same as other people in the world, yes I do, but at the same time I am pulled down by my deafness when I least expect it! For example, if I am walking along the street or in the shopping mall, I know hearing people see me and think from my appearance that I'm just like them, but the minute they approach me with a question, I am totally mortified with embarrassment and I have to walk away. My mother encouraged me to revel in my deafness and be proud of it. I am now becoming proud of ASL and Deaf culture.

I've been teaching myself and developing my own internal sense of self-worth. It's been an internal struggle because of the long-held notion of deafness which oppresses deaf people and sign language. In terms of my own Deaf identity, I've had many role models: teachers, supervisors, several administrators, and coaches. They did have a strong influence on me, but I was not aware of how important they were to me. Now I use those memories to develop my sense of self-worth, my Deaf identity, Deaf culture, and my awareness of ASL.

SS: I can see that our parents' values were somewhat different. I have no question that my parents were wonderful. We had love and communication at home, yes, but – when I look at you and compare my experience with yours, I see that in my family oralism was valued, signing in public was frowned upon, and I felt oppressed. Even though I had the advantage of being a day pupil at school and I could go home daily and fully express myself and understand everything at home, I feel somewhat ambivalent about the way I was brought up.

DJ: Do you feel that you expressed yourself fully through your signing?

SS: Oh, yes. I didn't really think about signing. It was just the way I grew up, simply part of my nature. Of course, school was another thing. I had to speak English endlessly.

I should tell you something about my parents and their ASL signing. You know, ASL has its own continuum, which ranges along a scale from a more formal register to an informal register like other spoken languages. My parents took a functional approach to ASL usage; for example, they used greater flexibility in ASL word order as compared to the rhetorical form of ASL. At the same time, my parents emphasized mouth movements for English words. In public places, for example, commuting to school on the subway, I felt I had to suppress my signing. The oral approach and the emphasis on speech therapy made me feel that deaf people were inferior in comparison to hearing people. When comparing the Lexington School to Fanwood, which utilized the "manual" method, my parents emphasized the superiority of Lexington to Fanwood because they felt that the oral approach was better than the manual approach. I internalized the attitude that oralism was best, and that hearing people were superior to deaf people.

My mother's side of the family was hearing. I remember that I always hated visiting my relatives, because I knew my mother would ask me to talk, and my relatives wouldn't understand me well. When they persisted in trying to get me to repeat things so they could understand me, I felt put upon and would resent my mother for forcing me to talk.

DJ: That reminds me of something that happened when I was a little boy and we went out trick-or-treating on Halloween. I went up to one house by myself and a man came to the door. I held out my bag for the candy, but before he would give me any, he prompted me: "What do you say?" He laughed at my efforts, and I was really embarrassed. There was another incident that caused me to finally "turn off" my voice for all time. I had a deaf uncle, and when I was thirteen years old, he took me to a basketball game. We watched the game, and at half-time we wanted to go for refreshments. My uncle didn't communicate well orally, so he usually carried around a pencil and paper for writing notes. Unfortunately, that time he had neglected to bring any paper, so I offered to try to speak for him. The line at the refreshment stand was very long, and I had to wait, but it was finally my turn to order. I held up two fingers and said slowly and I thought clearly, "Two hot dogs." The guy at the counter said "What?" I kept repeating "Hot dogs" over and over. Pretty soon everybody's eyes were on me and people were laughing at me, at my funny voice. I gave up and wrote the counterman a note saying "2 Hot dogs." The response was immediate; I got the hot dogs. That experience had a profound impact on me. I swore never to use my voice again.

SS: I can empathize with you; I went through many situations similar to yours. By the way, did you have any speech classes at school?

DJ: Yes, one hour daily. I was not easy to get along with in speech class. I would try and sweet-talk my way out of it. I didn't really see any need for it. But I remember once I had a confrontation with my speech teacher and I was taken to see the principal, who happened to be deaf. I explained that speech training was unnecessary. The principal replied that nothing could be eliminated from instruction because the state, which provided our funding, had mandated the curriculum. We had to acquiesce and follow what the state required. But I still goofed off and always got a grade of "Unsatisfactory" for speech class on my report card.

Now, my father had ways of interacting with hearing people even though he didn't have good speech. He was a paper-and-pencil man. He kept a number of index cards in his shirt pocket and used one of those pocket protectors. He always said that he felt frustrated without it because he had no ability to communicate if he didn't have access to pencil and paper. He was a terrific writer! He wrote lots of funny things, and had many hearing friends because he believed it was important to take advantage of information gained through reading and writing. He was very assertive in a way that I am not. I'm a little afraid of confronting hearing people, I am basically very shy.

ss: Did you interact with hearing people much when you went to school?

dj: I didn't really interact much with hearing people until my late teens. In my teens, I really enjoyed sports and I played football quite a lot in my deaf school. Once I went home on the weekend and saw the other hearing kids in the neighborhood playing football. They invited me to come over and play with them. I thought it might be too much for me, but they played touch football, with easy tackles. The other kids were really impressed and awestruck by me as a player! One friend was eager to learn signs and fingerspelling – mostly fingerspelling – and so I taught him. He became my mentor and often served as my intermediary between me and other hearing guys. Later when I went home on weekends, those hearing boys would come and knock on the door and invite me to come out and play football with them. I didn't go running after them, they came to me! The guy who was the intermediary between me and the other hearing kids became one of my very best friends and we still have kept in touch although we are in different states.

ss: I see that there is a contrast between our experiences when school was closed for weekends and vacation. Mine was within the Deaf circle while yours extended to the hearing world. For instance, I went to an oral school, but even though it was oral, I had many outlets for associating with the deaf because I had a lot of friends whose parents were deaf. I also associated with them outside of school. We would visit each other, and so on. Also, my parents were involved in a swimming club where many of deaf and hearing children of deaf parents went every Sunday. I took advantage of social opportunities as well as attending a temple for the Deaf where many of my school friends were members. Furthermore, several Deaf parents who were considered to be active leaders in the Deaf community established a Junior NAD chapter in the metropolitan area.[1] Its purpose was to serve students in mainstream and other programs for the deaf who were deprived of a chapter at their own schools. That Metropolitan New York Jr.NAD chapter really helped me to blossom personally. There were two Deaf adults serving as our advisors. They empowered us by giving us opportunities to develop our leadership skills and talents. I would have to say that we had all the communication access we could have.

Tell me, in your school were you tied fast to your desk by the "Y" cords of those earmolds that were attached to the box on the desk?

DJ: Huh?

SS: In our school those painful "Y" cords made us feel stuck like glue to our desks.

DJ: Did you use them voluntarily or were they forced on you?

SS: They were forced on us.

DJ: How did you feel about it? Was it hard to use them?

SS: They were awful! I felt a continual bombardment of sound. Because I was profoundly deaf, they had to have the volume cranked up high, but it had no meaning for me, just a lot of noise. It caused headaches, too.

DJ: I can understand why you would get headaches!

SS: We've talked about family and school. Let's talk about our college experiences.

---

[1] Junior National Association of the Deaf (Jr.NAD) is an organization of, by, and for deaf youths with chapters in residential schools for the deaf and mainstream programs throughout the United States. One of its primary goals is to promote national efforts among adults and educators of the deaf to bring out the best that young deaf people are capable of performing.

DJ: I was intrigued with NTID. It was a new institution with a technological focus. I had always liked working with my hands doing car mechanics and electrical work – handyman kinds of things. I was sort of tired of Gallaudet, because it was in my backyard. I had visited it many times and was, frankly, bored with the idea of the same old social studies and liberal arts curriculum. NTID was brand new and seemed advanced. So I decided to choose NTID.

You know, it had been a family tradition in my parents' families to go to Gallaudet, so when I decided to go to NTID, my family was flabbergasted. I guess they expected me to follow in their footsteps and go to Gallaudet. But my parents understood my desire to go to NTID, and they encouraged me to do so.

When I got to NTID, I was shocked to learn that the predominant culture there was oral, which meant that my small group of ASL users was outnumbered. We felt something was wrong when ASL users were in the minority. Anyway, this gave me the opportunity to examine the situation at NTID and the possible implications. I remember a group discussion class where the teacher brought up the topic of educational options for deaf children. "If you had a deaf child, would you place them in a mainstreamed program or a school for the deaf?" The teacher emphasized the importance of oral skills for future job prospects, as well as the ability to use the telephone. I was absolutely stunned! I expressed my strong support for residential schools for the deaf because of the chances they gave for being involved in sports and organizations, as well as giving opportunities to develop leadership skills and a sense of self-worth and success after graduation. I also said that oral skills were useless and that graduates of oral programs were not leaders but blind followers. We had a really hot and heavy discussion in that class! It was a no-win situation with advocates of learning sign language versus the oralists, the two opposing camps. I strongly supported ASL at that time based on my family experiences.

SS: In a way, my experience was just the opposite of yours. I grew up oral, and signing wasn't allowed in the classroom. That Deaf teacher I told you about planned a field trip to Washington, D.C., to visit places we had learned about in social studies. While we were there, we took the opportunity to visit Gallaudet and saw a theater production. I fell in love with Gallaudet – it was like a utopia for me. Also, my brother had already gone to Gallaudet, and I was somewhat familiar with it, so I decided to go there. Interestingly, Gallaudet is known for having generations of families attending it. Yet in our family, my brother was the first one to attend. My father could have easily qualified for Gallaudet but his own mother who was deaf didn't encourage him to do so. My father instead went to Pennsylvania State, but didn't finish his college education. The notion then was that attending a deaf college was inferior. Naturally, in retrospect my father wished his mother had encouraged him to attend Gallaudet.

When I entered Gallaudet, it was something of a culture shock for me – for I could participate fully in classes and join in ASL conversations. I was "at home" both in classes and outside of class. At first it was wonderful, really – I still think it was the best four years of my life. When I decided to go to graduate school there, it came as a great shock that there were some hearing people in classes in the program! I wondered, "What are they doing here?" I was surprised at my own attitudes, because having grown up oral, I thought I was pretty accepting of hearing people. But I guess my long-suppressed experiences were coming out, because Gallaudet made me a little more defensive, and I questioned the presence of hearing people on campus. I had to struggle with my own feelings. I felt a lot of anger.

DJ: Interesting. Did you feel manipulated by hearing people? What did you dislike about the situation?

SS: I felt that hearing people had no business being at Gallaudet – it was my place, a place for Deaf people, and I didn't want them there. I knew I had to work on my negative feelings toward hearing people and broaden my perceptions of hearing people at the same time. It really struck me when I met a hearing graduate student in my class. We became very good friends – she was a really warm person – and that helped to broaden my outlook.

I became an activist during graduate school, especially when one of my required courses was speech science. I just couldn't relate at all to the course content; as a deaf person, I couldn't understand the technical aspects of tongue movements, etc. With support from my other deaf classmates, we were exempted from this course and given a course specifically designed for us. I think I could do this because I guess I became empowered as a deaf individual.

Someone in graduate school had encouraged me to take speech therapy. They said that nowadays speech therapy is different – they understood what I went through in the past. I ended up having a

truly wonderful speech therapist who could sign and explained everything to me. What a difference from my past experience! That also
broadened my outlook on the profession of speech therapy. Even
though this experience didn't help my speech skills, it helped me
with my attitude and personal needs.

Going back to my school experiences, I remember that after I graduated, people who met me could tell immediately that I had gone to
Lexington School because of my distinctive mouth movements, such
as a protruding tongue for the *l* sound as in "milk." I have learned to
code-switch, so that when interacting with people who went to
schools that used sign language, I don't use that kind of stuff, but
with more oral people I still do.

DJ: I'm curious – when those people identify you immediately as a
Lexington graduate, do they make fun of you?

SS: Not really. I was lucky I was a girl. Lexington was considered to be
the place for girls, whereas Fanwood was for boys.

I'd like to tell something else about myself. I've already discussed
my experiences growing up; I'd like to turn to what my life is like
right now with my family. I'm married, to a deaf man, naturally. We
really wanted to have deaf children. My brother has three deaf children, and I envied him and wanted deaf children of my own, of
course, for selfish reasons – ease of communication, the idea of having children "like us." But when I got pregnant, I had a nightmare in
which the child was born hearing. In the dream, I was in a quandary
over what to do because the child was born hearing. Anyway, when
my son was born, at first we thought he was hearing, and we were
crushed. We went through the same process that hearing parents go
through when they have a deaf child.

DJ: But in reverse!

SS: We were upset. Of course, like other deaf parents, I had him go
through testing – seventeen different evaluations – I'm not exaggerat-
ing! One said he was too young. It just wasn't clear. His ABR (auditory brainstem response) test indicated that his hearing was normal,
but we just didn't feel sure about his ability to hear. We were on an
emotional roller coaster. After going through the stages of grief, we
finally accepted the idea that our son was hearing. But again, the tests
were inconclusive, with highly variable results. Finally, when he was
four, tests showed that he had a progressive hearing loss. We were
rather disappointed about this fact. This time, however, the disap-

pointment was of short duration, and we soon accepted the fact that he was hard of hearing. Finding out that a child is deaf is different from finding out that they have a progressive hearing loss. So we've been fitting him with hearing aids. The deafness in both our children is hereditary like my husband's – they were born with a progressive hearing loss starting with a lot of residual hearing.

My children are both in public schools, for they acquired English naturally and use their residual hearing well and have "hearing" speech. They are doing well, but that may not be the best avenue for most deaf children.

DJ: I'm curious – what kind of communication do you use at home with your children?

SS: When my husband and I discovered that our children were what we then thought hearing, we debated over what communication method to use with them. We sort of shopped around for opinions and advice, asking a lot of other parents. I remember talking with Dennis Cokely, a well-known ASL linguist. Cokely posed the following question: "Suppose research showed that communication works better if you sign left-handed. Would you just go ahead and struggle to sign left-handed if you didn't feel comfortable?" That comment really struck me. You have to use communication methods with your family with which you feel comfortable. If research showed that left-handed signing worked better, I *wouldn't* automatically sign left-handed if I wasn't comfortable with it. So I decided to just sign ASL, because that's my most comfortable language. Matt, my husband, at that time decided to use the simultaneous communication method, that is, spoken English and signs at the same time.

As it happens, my husband had pretty good speech growing up, due to the fact that he started out with a lot of hearing. We agreed that I would use ASL while my husband would use voice with signs. So my children were being brought up bilingual and bicultural. They have heard their father, they listen to TV and have some interactions with hearing people as well. We started the bilingual-bicultural experience from the moment they were born. However, Matt has gradually shifted to his more comfortable communication mode and language, ASL, as our children are growing up. What about your family?

DJ: My wife and I both had strong intuitions that our children would be deaf. Not only did we both have Deaf siblings, but those siblings had Deaf children of their own. I will tell you a funny story. When my wife was six months pregnant with our first baby, I arrived home one afternoon from work to find my wife standing right next to the TV, turning it on and off. I asked her what on earth she was doing, and she explained that she had heard that you could tell if your child is deaf as early as the fifth or sixth month of gestation by seeing if they start kicking when you turn on the sound of TV. She assured me that our baby was deaf because it hadn't responded to the sound. The very day our son was born, my wife was absolutely certain that he was deaf. That day a photographer had come in to take the very first baby picture. She waved a lovely rattle to get the baby's attention, and since there was no response, my wife was sure he was deaf. I was more skeptical because if you recall, I had a hearing sister who hadn't responded to sound until she was eight months old. My wife and I went round and round on the subject of whether our baby was deaf. I preferred to wait until the baby had a hearing test using EEGs when he was three months old. When the test showed that the baby was completely deaf, I knew what to do. I wanted to place him in the Rochester School for the Deaf (RSD) early education program. We used ASL as a first language to communicate with our children.

The reason I was concerned about getting my children right into RSD relates to my own education. When I was about ten years old, my mother was concerned about my reading and writing skills, because I was devoted more to sports than to books. So my mother put aside my allowance of two dollars per week, and sat me down. She said that I would have to go to the library every week, read a book and write about it. Then we would sit down and she would correct my English, and then I would get my allowance. She said, "If you don't have those skills, heaven help you. You may have trouble getting work without adequate English skills and you will be exploited and taken advantage of." I acquiesced because I needed the money. When I went to the library, I was overwhelmed with the size of the place and didn't know where to start. Because I loved sports, we went to the sports section, and almost immediately a book caught my eye. I still remember the title. It was *The Best NFL Linebackers*. I took it down from the shelf, and there snarling at me from the cover was a picture of Dick Butkus of the Chicago Bears. My mom asked, "Did he attend college?" I had to read the words, and I struggled with reading the words. It turned out that Butkus had gone to college. So reading this book really affected me. I wrote about it and with my mother's help, I corrected my writing; when I was done, I got my allowance.

This pattern continued for several years. My mother made me realize that reading and writing skills are of critical importance to deaf people – both are truly necessary for survival.

When I think back to my own experiences and then look at my own children, I wonder what approaches will be successful for them. I've looked into the idea of bilingual-bicultural education, and the idea intrigues me greatly. I like the approach of focusing on ASL to convey information and then teaching English through reading and writing. I'm starting to use that method with my four-year-old son. He watches me with rapt attention when I tell him stories and readings in ASL. Similarly with captioning on TV: I use a lot of tapes such as Walt Disney and Thomas the Tank Engine. These show many facial expression of various sorts. I like to integrate the tape of trains with my signing and occasional trips to town to see real trains, so that he gets the complete concept. He can compare what I sign with what's on the videotape. My two-year-old daughter picks things up really fast. Maybe it's because she's a girl and therefore naturally gifted for language. She has this "Sesame Street" book by Linda Bove with words, signs, and pictures. This book has fifty to a hundred signs and my daughter knows them all, even at age two!

SS: Nowadays, our children get a lot more from media via technological advancements such as TV decoders and captioned programs. When I was young I would watch programs such as "Lassie" and "Popeye" because they had a lot of action and I could understand some of the messages. But of course, it was mostly hit and miss.

How do your parents who raised you compare their upbringing of you and your upbringing of your own children?

DJ: I remember when my son was not quite eighteen months old, and we had a traditional family reunion on Easter weekend. My mother was flabbergasted that he was signing fluently and stringing together three-or-four-word sentences in ASL. My mother said that at that age I was just making my first sign, DRINK – in the wrong location. I was surprised at the disparity, that I had only one sign and my son had so many. I asked my mother how she had dealt with me, whether she had signed a lot to me or just taken care of my physical needs, feeding and changing me but not communicating with me linguistically. She acknowledged that she had been preoccupied with my father's health problems, and hadn't had much time or energy left over to bond with me. It made me wonder. The minute my babies were born,

I started interacting with them, greeting them and signing to them. I believe that even if babies don't see much at first, the more they are able to see, the more they pay attention visually. Their minds are like VCRs. They are ready to absorb so much. My son learned signs in exactly the same way as hearing kids learn spoken language – he got the sign production exactly right the first time without any need for correction. My daughter had more childish pronunciations. For example, she first made the sign FATHER on the back of her head and only gradually got it moved around correctly to the front of her head. Hearing children also make gradual approximations to adult pronunciations, for example, going from "dada" to "daddy." Research has shown that the language development of speech and sign are completely parallel.[2]

SS: I had similar experiences growing up. My parents encouraged me to read, and they also read to me. But I wish I had read more. One thing I remember is that we had an old-fashioned TTY that had a printout. Every time I had a TTY conversation, my parents would tear off the paper and correct my English. I was really grateful to them for that. When I went off on trips, my father would make me write a report about it when I got back, and then corrected my written English. My mother also gave me vocabulary and spelling tests every week! But compared to my children, I did not acquire English skills until much later.

DJ: I was the same way.

SS: Like you, I signed to my children from the beginning, and read them books. We started with picture books. Every time I changed their diapers, I signed to them or told them little stories. I think nowadays we take a more educational approach, emphasizing the importance of reading and communication. I think your children and mine have advantages, and are better off than we were.

DJ: When I think back, I realize it would have been better to emphasize reading and writing earlier rather than later. In my own case, I started reading and writing late.

SS: I'd like to tell you more about my children. At the time we thought our children were hearing, our Deaf friends would ask if the kids

---

[2] See L. Pettito and P. F. Marentette, (1991). "Babbling in the Manual Mode: Evidence for the Ontogeny of Language," *Science, 251,* supplement (March 22, 1991): 1493.

were deaf or hearing. When we replied that they were hearing, they reacted a bit standoffishly. In other words, we would be considered more Deaf (in the cultural sense) if our children were deaf.

DJ: Yes, I can see how that could be a sticky issue. Their reactions would show on their faces.

SS: When we found out that the children were deaf, our Deaf friends were excited and proud for us, but another conflict arose: our Deaf friends immediately assumed that we would send our children to a school for the deaf and were somewhat miffed when we said we would send them instead to public schools.

DJ: That was for educational reasons, right?

SS: We explained that both our children had a lot of residual hearing and speech, but we felt we had to explain and defend our decision. We ended up deciding to refer to our children as deaf, even though when they were small they were really hard of hearing. We had gone back and forth on the issue of how they would feel about their identity, be it hard-of-hearing or deaf, and asked a number of our hard-of-hearing friends for advice. They had also had identity problems growing up, and felt fully accepted neither by the hearing world nor the Deaf world.

DJ: Sort of stuck in the middle.

SS: Yes, marginal to both worlds. I hated that idea. So after further discussion with my husband, we decided to call our children deaf because we knew that they would become progressively deaf like their father and we wanted to ensure that we pass on the Deaf cultural values to them that we hold so dear.

DJ: It's like hot water versus cold water – nobody wants to be thought of as lukewarm.

SS: We called them deaf, but sometimes I would say that they are audiologically deaf but functionally hard of hearing. That clarified it for people. But when we said to our children that they were deaf, they felt some ambiguities because they identified more with their father who spoke better than I, since my speech was not intelligible. This did cause some confusion, because they didn't think of themselves as deaf in the way I am deaf. I explained to them that their deafness was like their father's in that they all have a progressive loss. That helped them to understand. However, my children are becoming more and more culturally and linguistically Deaf with all the experiences we are providing them. I forgot to mention one thing with regard to communicating with my children. When they have their hearing aids on, they communicate with each other via spoken English. But when they have their aids off, they use ASL with each other as they do with us. That shows that they are bilingual.

My children attend our local public school with support services. They have healthy self-esteem and are proud of themselves for who they are. They are truly bilingual and bicultural.

DJ: Tell me about the support services your children receive at school.

SS: They have interpreters and an FM listening system. I was not comfortable with the FM system because it doesn't look natural to have this box dangling on your chest. But I realized that this device has become second nature to them. As for their own hearing aids, they use them all day from the time they get up to the time they go to bed.

DJ: With support services, do you feel that your children are equal to the hearing children in their school?

SS: I would say they are totally integrated and that they interact well with their hearing peers. What really helps is their speaking and listening abilities and the cultural aspect at home. They've never had or needed formal training in speech or auditory training. All they have studied is speechreading and some listening techniques.

One day while I was observing my son's class, I noticed that the speech therapist removed a few children for speech therapy. But what I thought was ironic was that hearing children were receiving speech therapy, not my deaf children!

DJ: I'd like to come back to a point you made earlier that you wanted to have deaf children for selfish reasons. When my wife was pregnant with our son, naturally we both wanted deaf children. I remember when I said that to a Deaf friend, she accused me of being very selfish! The important thing was that the baby be healthy.

But I now think that there is nothing wrong in wanting a deaf baby. We would feel more of a bond. Here is an analogy. If you see a black family with black children, you certainly wouldn't call the parents selfish. Whereas if a black family had a white child, the reaction could be different. That's the kind of perspective I'm talking about. When our son turned out to be deaf, we happily broadcasted the news though we had to be careful and sensitive because some of our friends might be jealous that our baby was deaf. We said the minimum to our friends, merely that he was deaf, that he would learn ASL, and that he would go to a school for the deaf.

ss: I think it's normal for parents to want their children to be like them.

DJ: You want to have something to pass on to them. That's a sensitive issue within the Deaf community. The fact is that there are relatively few deaf children of deaf parents, while there are many hearing children of deaf parents.

What about deaf education? We've discussed our own families but we've said nothing about deaf education in general. Let's talk about that.

ss: All right, I'll start with a concern. I think it is important for deaf children and adults to be bilingual and bicultural. But I think it is important for the two languages and the two cultures to have equal weight. I don't want to see a program where the children are supposed to learn ASL and the English language, but the English language and high educational standards fall by the wayside. I'm worried about the overemphasis on ASL and Deaf culture to the detriment of English and pedagogy. There's a danger of the pendulum swinging far to one side and becoming, de facto, monolingual and monocultural. I met a deaf couple whose deaf daughter attends a school for the deaf. I'm not sure exactly how it happened, but someone asked their daughter a question and she responded, "Get out of here! English isn't my language; ASL is my language." The parents were rather upset about this overemphasis on ASL at the expense of English. It is, of course, normal for people when confronted with something new to gravitate away from the center, but I think it is important to strike a balance between ASL and English.

DJ: I agree with everything you've said. It is important to encourage children to prepare for their future, for both college and the prospects for employment. I have a dream for my children. When they get older, say in junior high school, perhaps they will excel in mathematics or some other subject or course. I want to have the option of sending my children to a mainstream program so that they can continue in that subject as well as learning what that kind of school is like. They will be able to learn more about English and the hearing culture, and will get a taste of that kind of experience. They would still go to a school for the deaf for most of their classes and be involved in student activities and organizations, where they will develop their self-esteem and leadership skills and experience success. So by the time they graduate from college, they will be educated for functioning in the predominantly hearing world and for work. I want to prepare them for that.

ss: I think today we as parents want our children to experience and take advantage of both Deaf and hearing worlds.

dj: When I was growing up, I had many negative feelings toward English and the hearing world. Part of it was because when I was very young I had been excluded from participating in the hearing world by my hearing neighbors, and partly because of all the audiological gizmos. Now things have changed. For example, people have faced up to the linguistic issues, and there is more deaf awareness in the community. I'm really glad about that.

ss: Attitudes have really changed.

dj: True.

ss: Anyway there remains a lot of work to be done.

dj: But I have seen significant changes over time.

ss: I think the future will be even better for our children. Don't you agree?

dj: Yes. I'd like to talk a little about visions for the future related to Deaf culture. I think we feel some anxiety because of advances in technology. I'm concerned that technological developments may outpace Deaf culture. For example, cochlear implants are in their infancy, but perhaps later they will discover better technologies to improve hearing. They may be able to "fix" deaf people and make them into hearing people. I feel that deafness is perfectly normal, so we should just leave it be. Mind you, I can understand the medical perspective, where medical professionals want simply to be able to improve someone's sense of hearing or cure deafness. I can understand the goal of making deaf people just like hearing people, but I am really upset at the fact that we deaf people have been treated like guinea pigs for many years. With sign language we can be normal, and the medical professionals should leave us as we are, just like anyone else.

ss: I agree. Regardless of what happens in the future about using technology in education, I believe that ASL, the language of the Deaf, Deaf culture, and schools for the deaf will survive and must continue indefinitely.

dj: I think that schools for the deaf should work in close cooperation with the professionals in the field of education. For example, suppose hearing parents have a deaf baby and don't know what to do. I feel that the Deaf community bears a responsibility. When a child's deafness is identified, the Deaf community should be informed. Rather than having the professionals do it, the Deaf community should give information and advice to the parents regarding options and what is best for the deaf child.

ss: You are right. The Deaf community needs to become involved and become more politically active. I also think that deaf professionals in the field need to form a close link with the Deaf community and act together in establishing an information network for hearing parents. During the Gallaudet Deaf President Now movement, the deaf people finally got together in complete solidarity.[3]

dj: You've hit the nail on the head. I've had some discussions with friends and family members about why only recently deaf people protested and spoke out successfully. Looking back, I realize that when I used to try to protest in school, I was punished. In the schools, we were controlled and oppressed. I am grateful for the Gallaudet protest for demonstrating that when we express our emotions and strong feelings, we can have an effect.

ss: In fact, it used to be that deaf people themselves considered ASL as inferior. In addition, many hearing people had a patronizing attitude toward deaf people. But now, ASL is recognized as a language of its own. Although it is not spoken, it is nonetheless a language. Increased awareness regarding deafness has helped to change the perspective on deafness from the medical model to a cultural one. A greater number of hearing parents of deaf children need to be exposed to that outlook. That is the key: convincing people that being deaf is OK and that schools for the deaf can constitute the least restrictive environment for deaf children. You are right that we need to educate parents as well as policymakers and hope for a better future for deaf people. I feel that we still have a lot to do.

dj: We could probably talk on and on, but let's pick up this discussion at another time. I'm just thankful for having been born at the right time. We are seeing a lot of growth in deaf education, professionalism, and in the community. In general I feel involved. The ADA is

---

[3] The Deaf President Now movement occurred at Gallaudet University during the week of March 6–13, 1988, when students protested the Gallaudet University Board of Trustees' selection of a hearing person to be the president of the university.

also very good in that it makes me feel more equal with hearing people.[4] I'm thankful for having been born at the right time and also for having been born in America, where opportunities for Deaf people are the best in the world.

ss: Yes, I feel the same. You have said it well.

---

[4] The American's with Disabilities Act (ADA) is the law that gives disabled people the right to equal access to public accommodations.

CHAPTER FOURTEEN

Another New Birth: Reflections of a Deaf Native Signer

PATRICK A. GRAYBILL

In the Deaf community, I am known as an accomplished actor, play director, poet, storyteller, teacher, American Sign Language consultant, and
translator. This chapter will reveal my reflections as a Deaf artist moving
between the written/printed aspect of English and the unwritten system
of American Sign Language. An easy and accurate way of recording ASL
these days is by way of videotape. You may wonder why I have not
mentioned spoken English as one of my territories. That is because I have
not heard a spoken word all my life. In fact, I am proud to be a Deaf man,
am very delighted with the divine gift of ASL, and, indeed, enjoy reading
texts in English, albeit with some struggle.

I was born in a Kansas family of seven children, five of whom are Deaf,
including myself. Because of my joy and talent in using ASL, particularly
in the area of dramatic arts, it is too easily assumed by many people that I
have Deaf parents. However, I am among the estimated 90% of Deaf
children in the United States who have hearing parents. Yet it is a blessing
that I can easily identify myself with the Deaf community whose rich
history and social network have made a significant difference in my life. I

Patrick A. Graybill (M.S., Deaf Education, Gallaudet University), Producer/Director at The
Sign Media Inc., is an accomplished Deaf actor, director, poet, storyteller, and sign language
consultant. He is a former member of the National Theater of the Deaf and has appeared in
many Sign Media Inc. videotapes, including *Four for you* and *Poetry in motion*. He is a sign
master for the Arena Stage and has also served as a sign master for the Genesee Valley
Theater. He is a former faculty member of the Department of Performing Arts at the National
Technical Institute for the Deaf, and now he teaches part-time at Western Maryland College.
His address is: Sign Media Inc., 4020 Blackburn Lane, Burtonsville, MD 20866.

am grateful over and over again that I have hearing parents who have allowed me to be Deaf.

So far, it looks as though I have had a perfect life. But to tell you the truth, I haven't. I do have struggles as a Deaf person. The reason is that I am a member of the Deaf community, which nonmembers tend to label as disabled or handicapped. I am a product of a Deaf culture but I also live in this hearing dominant culture. For this reason, I have often felt like the confused bats in Aesop's fable about a long-lasting war between birds and beasts. The bats had a hard time deciding whether they were birds because they had wings or were beasts because they did not lay eggs. They couldn't decide which group to support, so they stayed out of the war. Over the years, I have slowly learned that it is better to know and stand up for one's values, traditions, language, and community than to assume that other people' s culture is the only way of life. But learning and realizing who I am was not so easy.

As I said, I was born deaf to hearing parents. But fortunately, I have two older Deaf sisters who first went to my alma mater and enriched themselves with the acquisition of ASL and Deaf culture. Very early in our lives, this gift of language and culture was transmitted to me and my younger siblings, including my hearing sister, who eventually became a certified interpreter between Deaf and hearing people. I recall that my family at home sat together around an antique dining table at meal times and used two languages at the same time; my parents and hearing sisters conversed in English and the rest of us in ASL. We Deaf children undoubtedly did not understand fully what the others were saying. Sometimes we asked them what they were discussing. Or vice versa. At other times we simply ignored them. I was frightened at times by the seemingly violent quarrels between my parents. Many years later I mentioned this to my hearing sister who did not remember these quarrels at all. I eventually realized that perhaps my misunderstanding was due to how they looked while discussing a hot topic. I was too afraid to ask Mother; although, not formally trained in ASL, she does have a limited command of ASL and is, indeed, my first facilitator of communication between Deaf people and hearing people. And I could not ask Father, who did not have a command of ASL at all.

When I finally enrolled at the Kansas School for the Deaf at the age of five, I was thrilled. The reason was that during my early childhood, before school started for me, I accompanied my parents frequently to drop off my older Deaf sisters there, and aspired to enter as a student. Residing at a dormitory there was a wise move, for it was the source of Deaf culture in which the subtleties of ASL, the behaviors and manners of Deaf people, and the folklore and arts of Deaf artists were generously and naturally provided. Every morning I went with my schoolmates to the campus school building to experience groans and struggles as students in a Dickensian environment. For the first time in my youth I was not allowed to talk in ASL; signing was forbidden in the classroom. If I did not follow the rule, my hands would be restrained in a pair of white mittens connected by a small string. I was compelled to learn the three R's in spoken and written English, which was not my second language yet. I did not feel as though I could move smoothly between two languages and two cultures as I do now, since I had not had a chance to understand what the second language or culture was about. My early experiences in the classroom were like sailing over rough waters without any proper training. I was an eager survivor who made excellent grades but did not understand why learning was important. It was mostly rote memory for me. It took me nearly four years before the three R's and other courses made any sense to me.

The school focused on training Deaf youngsters to be like hearing people because the world belonged to hearing people, they assumed, and we must learn to adapt to their way of life. The training was unnatural; although we went to schools for Deaf youngsters, we received an impression that we had to have skill to speak like hearing people in order to succeed as citizens of their world.

Now I realize that the world is not really theirs. But at that time we naive students assumed that we had better support the hearing people's way of thinking because who knows, maybe their way of life was really the best. We felt at ease living as Deaf people but we did not support our own Deaf peers who struggled with the hearing people. Whenever we "confused bats" supported the hearing ways and hearing values, I believe we hurt ourselves as well as all Deaf people.

We succumbed to the hearing authorities so much that we developed a false concept that hearing people were right at all times. Instead of criticizing hearing people whom we feared, we verbally attacked our own Deaf peers in order to please the hearing people. For example, Deaf teachers in residential schools for the deaf wanted to be active advocates to educate the public about the lives and rights of Deaf people. Yet they so feared their hearing colleagues and superiors that they learned to restrain their enthusiasm in order to keep their jobs. They sometimes spoke out against active deaf advocates and accused them of being radicals or militants or trouble makers. These attacks and accusations unintentionally made heroes out of those frustrated Deaf teachers in the eyes of their hearing co-workers and administrators and even those Deaf people who did not know their identities and values yet. Another example is that self-appointed Deaf authorities wrote articles for Deaf magazines and news-papers or gave speeches to distort ASL and the Deaf culture. Unfortu-nately this malpractice continues today.

I was fortunate to discover the joy of printed English outside this educa-tional system quite by chance. At that time, at the age of nine or ten, I persuaded my mother to create a new game for me (she had a special talent for thinking up educational games for her children). Because she was busy baking a cake, she asked me to play familiar games such as Tag or Hide and Seek. Being a spoiled brat, I insisted upon a new game. Putting the bowl of cake batter aside, she took me to the living room and gave me a book titled *Beautiful Joe*. The first sentence in the book went something like this: "My name is Beautiful Joe . . . and I am a cur." The word "cur" did not make sense to me, so I asked my mother to define it. Instead of simply telling me the answer, she introduced me to how to use a children's dictionary. Once I realized that the dictionary helped me to find definitions for the words I did not know, I fell in love with reading right there and then. Returning to the kitchen to bake the cake, my mother did not realize that she had introduced me to a wonderful game that I would play constantly and independently. It was like a mystery game to me, and I became a bookworm. The sailing voyage to the world of written and printed English for me became less rough and more enjoyable.

Our real haven was the dormitory where we were allowed to converse in ASL and played, quarreled, and lived like normal youngsters. The older we became, the less and less the spoken system of English at school was emphasized. We were relieved. But we Deaf "bats" were still confused and did not yet know that there was nothing wrong with Deaf culture and ASL, or even with bilingualism. For we still kept the same assumptions that hearing people were right at all times and English was superior to ASL.

When I enrolled at Gallaudet College in 1958, I was awed by my first-year professors, most of whom were Deaf. They were ideal role models for me, and I was inspired to become a teacher like them. In hindsight, they did use a signed system of English. This did not bother me at that time because their command of signed English was clear and fluent in com-parison to that of my teachers back in my alma mater in Kansas except for the few Deaf teachers there. The state policy of Kansas during my training there required no more than 33% of the faculty and staff members to be deaf. It was evident that deaf employees at the Kansas School for the Deaf could not form the majority. We did not fight back because we did not know that we could have power. When I enrolled at Gallaudet College, the pressure of using signed English as a primary mode of communication in the academic environment in order to look intellectual could be too much for us native ASL users. Many of us continued to be the confused "bats" observing struggles between the advocates of ASL and advocates of the artificial systems of signed English who hoped to compel Deaf students to abandon their natural language and use one of those systems in order to learn English. Those advocates of the artificial systems did not truly respect ASL nor the Deaf culture, since they strongly discouraged the use of that language and culture in the academic environment. Therefore, I consider them to be the oppressors of the Deaf culture. Unfortunately, they also included some deaf people who did not want to be members of the Deaf community because they assumed that the artificial systems of signed English would enable Deaf students to learn English. What they did not know is that reading and writing English *in addition* to using a natural language, ASL, is the best way of learning English.

In the area of dramatic arts, I tried my best to transliterate English and American literature texts. By this I mean that I would replace English words with often poorly selected signs which, I thought, were equivalent to them in meaning. My translations were thought to be so excellent that I won many literary prizes and awards. But these translations used signed English more than ASL. It was many years before I realized the flaws in my work. I just glossed English in sign; it was an artificial system of signed English. In those times I was like a bat that did not understand what it was doing.

During the later years of my college education, a few people began to proclaim that ASL is our true language, based on language research done by the chairperson of the Department of English, Dr. William Stokoe. At that time, I majored in English and was bewildered by the proclamation. Honestly speaking, Dr. Stokoe did not use ASL fluently. For this reason, I was not convinced that what he said was true – that ASL was my native language. Because I was very busy with extracurricular activities such as my fraternity, church, and theater, I overlooked this good news that ASL was a legitimate language after all. Although I used ASL in my daily life when conversing with the users of the language, this ignorance continued with me even when I became a teacher of Deaf youngsters and later a member of the internationally acclaimed National Theater of the Deaf. So, like the poor bat, I was going back and forth between the advocates of ASL and their oppressors. For which team should I root? What dugout should I be sitting in? In addition, the waters through which I was sailing were muddied with rapidly developed systems of making English visible. It must be that the creators of those systems reacted negatively to the flourishing use of ASL in academic classes and on the stage and TV, because they thought that ASL caused Deaf people to reject English, which is patently a myth. In hindsight, I used ASL as a way of conversing with the users of the language but I continued to be a bookworm too, in awe of English as my secondary language. It was true of so many Deaf people in the past, and it is still true among us Deaf people today.

People like Ella Mae Lentz, Dennis Cokely, Charlotte Baker-Shenk, Carol Padden, M. J. Bienvenu, and Harlan Lane, to name a few, awakened me to the fact that ASL is legitimate and can be used on the stage. When I left the National Theater of the Deaf, I continued the fallacy of transliterating the printed system of English in the hopes of pleasing everybody. It was a tiresome and useless task. While directing plays or supposedly translating plays for my hearing colleagues at the National Technical Institute for the Deaf, I did not understand what good translation actually meant until one day I met a hearing ally who worked as an interpreter on the campus and had been involved in a staged production there. She challenged me to really translate plays into ASL and forget the lazy and poor idea of replacing English words with signs. The more I translated literary pieces, the freer I felt. I felt more and more like myself as a Deaf person. The more I learned about ASL and Deaf culture from the people named above and others, the better I felt as a Deaf person and the freer I felt to be an actor on the stage. For example, when as an actor I used the artificial system of signed English on the stage, I was not completely able to use the grammar of ASL, including proper markers, to express what actual meaning the playwright wanted to convey to the audience. The experience of using the signed English on the stage was like writing a text in stilted English. Although people commented on how clearly I signed on the stage, I felt like a wooden soldier. After feeling proud of using ASL on the stage, I was able to be a real live actor who could allow his feelings to flow out and add the meaning to the language used on the stage.

Now this was a new thing for me and I really appreciated the very free sensation, and I felt less and less like a bat. The more I want to be with the advocates of ASL, the more willing I am to face my oppressors. My days as a bat are over. And I have experienced a new birth.

Carol Padden and Tom Humphries's book, *Deaf in America: Voices from a Culture* (1988, Harvard University Press) has a wonderful chapter, the third, about two centers – two ways of thinking. We Deaf people have our own center, whereas hearing people have theirs; therefore, conflicts have arisen. For instance, our idea of silence and theirs are not alike at all. They think that silence means a lack of sounds. As for us Deaf people, silence is feeling lost in a room full of hearing people who chat with their mouths and do not use ASL. This is a very interesting way to look at each other in terms of sound and silence and other differences. So I look at these two views as a member of the Deaf community and realize more and more that people's attitudes toward Deaf people actually depend on which viewpoint they have of the Deaf community. Sometimes, the viewpoint is sickening and biased perhaps because they are afraid of who we Deaf people are and how different we are from them. Besides, it is possible that they are scared of losing their power over us. I am currently a proud member of the Deaf community. And I enjoy being with the advocates of ASL. It creates positive feelings for me as a Deaf actor, poet, storyteller, and translator. However, I have compassion for those deaf "bats" who remain behind, for example, deaf people coming from schools where they have not been given an ASL language base and who do not yet have a clear sense of self-identity. My answer for them is: Go get a good education. I believe that their education has to be based on a very solidly developed bilingual, bicultural curriculum which reflects the use of ASL as the primary language in an academic environment and English as the secondary language. Then students can have the three R's and have a history, science, language, and arts curriculum that reflects Deaf culture so that they can help formulate their self-identity and develop a sense of dignity. Once they understand the Deaf culture better, then they will understand and enjoy their first language, ASL, as well as their secondary language, English. I know what it will be like, for it is my story too!

CHAPTER FIFTEEN

Raising Deaf Children in Hearing Society: Struggles and Challenges for Deaf Native ASL Signers

GARY E. MOWL

In 1893 Bell wrote his *Memoir upon the Formation of a deaf Variety of the Human Race*. In it, he asserted that "evidence shows a tendency to the formation of a deaf variety of the human race in America." While he could not alter the inheritability of deafness, he could address the issue of intermarriage among deaf people. He suggested two types of measures – preventive and repressive. Among the preventive measures were an end to the segregation of deaf children in special schools, an end to the employment of deaf teachers for deaf students, and an end to the use of sign language. (Van Cleve, 1987, Vol. 1, p. 139)

So, you may say, "Well, A. G. Bell is history." I am warning you, history does repeat itself, if we do not learn from it. I predict there will be a "neo-Bell" movement in this country (just like there is a Neo-Nazi movement alive in the world today). When the movement comes it will be called "Neo-Bellism." (Bahan, 1989, p. 87)

Impulses such as Bell's to eliminate deafness from the face of the earth are very much alive and real. My wife Brenda and I are witnessing a very

Gary E. Mowl (M.S., Deaf Education, University of Tennessee at Knoxville), a former Assistant Professor at the National Technical Institute for the Deaf, has been primarily involved in developing and implementing interpreter training programs. He holds a Reverse Skills Certificate (RSC) from the Registry of Interpreters for the Deaf. Mr. Mowl, who is a native user of ASL, has a hearing loss and comes from a family of Deaf and hard-of-hearing people that has spanned four generations. His address is: 517 West Fleming Drive, Morganton, NC 28655.

powerful movement through government funding and support from influential organizations and individuals for eliminating deafness. The goal, for many, is the extinction of deafness. We have noted that serious investments have been made in genetic engineering and cochlear implants. We believe that the ideals promoted by Alexander Graham Bell are still very much alive and prevalent throughout the world.

> Disability organizations usually react positively to new medical and technical findings that help to restore physical functions. It is therefore unusual that organizations of the deaf react negatively to cochlear implants and find themselves advocating against these operations on deaf children. It is often difficult for hearing people to understand this viewpoint, with the result that Deaf people are regarded as ungrateful and without insight into medical matters. (Soderfeldt, 1991, p. 141)

We believe that the move toward extinction is very real. Brenda and I have been asked numerous times by colleagues who work with Deaf people and friends if we would consider having our children, Amy, Anthony, and Jon, who have a range of hearing loss from moderate to severe, receive cochlear implants if they were considered eligible candidates. In the course of our deliberations, we tried to be as honest and open as possible because, like parents everywhere, we want the best for our children. Being honest and open to the possibility of cochlear implants meant temporarily forgetting about the rich tradition of having Deaf people in the family that now spans four generations. Being honest and open meant setting aside our egos, as we are very proud of being Deaf.

Being honest and open also meant taking a good look at the world and the future, and how we can provide the necessary ingredients to enhance the development of the mind and character for our children. What would it take to foster an environment that will lead to happiness and encourage our children to become productive members of our society? The decision became rather simple, perhaps too simplistic for some but very real from our perspective. We decided to have world history inform our thinking and to rely on our faith. We found that the existence of deaf people has been recognized in scriptures.

Our deliberations regarding genetic engineering and cochlear implants no longer focused on the issue of deafness but rather on the world's attempt to create a perfect race which, if history is correct, is not possible. We believe that there are powers beyond our control, beyond anyone's control, and that Deaf people are in this world for mysterious and unknown reasons. Brenda and I, therefore, have adopted the position that we cannot and will not support the genetic engineering research and development that will lead to a perfect race nor will we use the option of cochlear implants for our children.

> Granville Seymour Redmond, who became a successful landscape artist was born on March 9, 1871 in Philadelphia. Guilbert Braddock states that Redmond was totally deaf from infancy. . . . Tall, sturdily built, with a shock of thick wavy hair, and round-rimmed wire glasses, Redmond was a good friend of Charlie Chaplin, the star of silent films. . . . Albert Ballin gives Redmond credit for influencing Chaplin's acting. Chaplin did not move his lips in his silent films. He used gestures and expressions resembling those used by deaf persons. (Gannon, 1981, p. 136)

However small or large the deaf population may be, there must be significant reasons for the existence of Deaf people, and there is a legitimate place for Deaf people in this world. The history of Deaf people is fascinating and their contribution to society in general has been and still is marvelous. Books such as the *Deaf Heritage* (1981) and the *Gallaudet Encyclopedia of Deaf People and Deafness* (1987) provide many examples supporting my point. One has to ask, if Deaf people make meaningful contributions, why are there some people trying to make this group extinct? Are Deaf people that worthless? What more must Deaf people do?

Brenda and I wanted and were pleased to have Deaf and healthy children. However, given the tremendous challenges of surviving and functioning in a very competitive and demanding society, especially the challenges of raising children to the best of our ability, we never expected or dreamed that their being Deaf would pose additional issues for us as parents that would consume time and energy. But we found that the external forces of the society are so powerful that we must constantly address the issue of their being Deaf, which to us is a nonissue. In Crammatte's (1987) survey of issues related to employment and performance on the job, the Deaf respondents felt that being Deaf did pose significant issues.

> My present supervisor . . . said he is real satisfied with me except for communication. I asked him during my work evaluation about how to improve communication. He advised me to "read, write and hear like hearing workers in your office." (Crammatte, 1987, p. 89)

> Yesterday I talked to my supervisor and learned the real reason why I was almost not hired. My inability to hear and speak was the reason – and the

others who were offered the job turned down the offer. I was the last person, therefore I was offered the job. (Crammatte, 1987, p. 89)

Very powerful messages have been and still are being sent to Deaf people throughout the world. Deaf people must hear. Deaf people must speak. This is the real world. One escalating and controversial debate is whether American Sign Language should be accepted as the language to be learned, studied, and used by Deaf people, especially starting with infants. In this debate, the term "the real world" has been used in a variety of contexts in discussing why ASL may hinder the functioning of Deaf persons as members of our society. When establishing educational expectations for our children, great value has been placed on preparing them for "the real world."

We have often wondered: What is this "real world"? Whose world is it? By whose standards? Who should define "real world" if such a definition is needed? Apparently, a real world has been defined for our children. For the education of our children, the real world is defined by our school district led by a team of special educators who shape educational plans for our children. For example, Brenda and I regularly participate in school district meetings where individualized education plans are designed for our children. In earlier years of educational planning, I recall that fifteen minutes were devoted to forming an educational plan, including school placement and support, for each child. This implied to me that these special educators, with no experience of growing up Deaf, think they understand the education of deaf children and are able to assess our children to figure what the future holds for them in this world. They also believe that they can develop an effective individualized education plan for the whole school year in a mere fifteen minutes! Our discussions have always lasted past fifteen minutes because Brenda and I are stubborn. We had a meeting once that lasted four hours. We have a reputation of being difficult. We have had and still do have conflict with the team on issues of how educational plans are to be devised to help our children prepare for the real world, how we as parents perceive the real world, and how we have set our goals for the education of our children to function successfully in that real world. We do not see eye to eye on many issues but they do not seem to be bothered by that.

For example, in the most recent meeting of our committee on special education, the issue on the table was the use of an FM system in the public school classroom for Amy and Anthony. Even though Brenda and I knew as parents that they were not using them, the director of the committee on special education was surprised to hear from other committee members that the FM system was not being used as prescribed by the individualized educational plans that had been established in prior years. We added that both Amy and Anthony have told us that the FM system had not been helpful and that even the classroom teachers had given up using it.

To our surprise, in the course of our discussion, the team members suggested that the system was not being used because of our children's fears of stigmatization. This may be true since, we noticed that Jon, enrolled in a school for the deaf, uses the FM system regularly. We explained that there are other children in Jon's class who use the system as well. We tried to point out that it is important to have children be with other children like themselves and this must be realized. We wondered out loud if the school for the deaf might really be the best option. But we were reminded that the school for the deaf is not an option because Amy and Anthony do not have 80-decibel losses in their better ears, a state education department requirement for admission to a school for the deaf.

Furthermore, we were disappointed to see that very little recognition was given to the fact that our children have had more experience with what "works" than any person at the table, except perhaps us as Deaf parents. In fact, no one at the table has had any experience at all of being a person with a hearing loss, not even our parent representative. Further, we have observed that all of our children really understand how best to use hearing aids and have learned very well when or when not to use them. They know and they are going to decide for themselves how best to use what residual hearing they have. Perhaps our children do not use the FM system because of the fear of stigmatization, but the committee could at least listen to what our children had to say about what works and what is helpful, and respect their account.

Ever since the diagnosis confirmed our belief that our children did have hearing losses, Brenda and I have been confronted with many experts who claimed that they understood Deaf people and deafness. Decisions were made for us. In addition, advice on how to raise our children was freely given, whether asked for or not. Advice from hearing experts. Advice from Deaf experts. Advice even from our next-door neighbors. In fact, Brenda told me one afternoon that a woman whom we had never met before was driving by our house and noticed that our children were signing while playing in the yard without their hearing aids on. This person stopped, got out of the car, entered our property, identified herself as a teacher of the deaf and told Brenda that our children should have their hearing aids on at all times – a complete stranger, a teacher of the deaf of all people, having the nerve to tell us what to do. We have become immune to unwanted advice and to complete strangers telling us how to raise our children. But, perhaps more important, if kids cannot be kids while they are kids, when can they be kids? Why in the world, we wondered, is being Deaf more important than being a kid playing in the yard?

> Lest this be off-putting, may I add that I am one who had used sign language for 38 years, and thus – blush – I am something of an expert at being deaf. The other day, a pencil and the back of an envelope helped me to calculate that I've had direct, first-hand, continuous and uninterrupted experience at being profoundly deaf for 24 hours a day, 7 days a week, 12 months a year, over the amazing period of 44 years. . . . In thinking more about those 376,000 clock hours "behind the wheels" of deafness, it struck me that these were roughly equal time periods spent not in abstract theorizing or writing but in actually living as a deaf person and trying to communicate with hearing folks as well as deaf folks day in, day out. (Stewart, 1990, p. 117)

Brenda and I have met our share of so-called experts. For example, a meeting was held with the principal of the middle school where Amy was going to enroll as a sixth grader. The principal made clear to us in a rather arrogant way that he had experience with deaf children and experience with educational interpreters as well. I get exasperated with such claims mainly because I often find them not to be justified.

Later, an orientation was scheduled one week before the start of school, led by this very principal who is an expert, for new students and their parents. Arrangements were made for an interpreter to be at the orientation. When the event began, Brenda and Amy sitting in the audience wondered where the interpreter was, and the interpreter sitting in the main office wondered where they were. The "expert" principal just thought that somehow they would find each other. His original thought was that we would just know the interpreter and she would know us. First of all, we were not even given the interpreter's name. Secondly, we live in a county where there are over 200 interpreters and it is pretty naive on his part to think we know all of them. Finally, what person who is experienced with handling interpreting services would have the interpreter sitting in the main office waiting while the event is being held in the auditorium for 1,500 people? And this principal calls himself an expert?

To make matters worse, the day before the orientation, we had a meeting of the committee on special education. We had specifically requested that sensitivity training and orientation be provided to school personnel.

The committee wanted clarification on this request. The example just given proves this very point. If this so-called "expert" principal cannot even realize that since the event is in the auditorium, children and parents will naturally go there and not to the main office, then what is this "expert" going to do if the school is on fire and does not have a fire alarm system? We were told that the school has a buddy system and that "buddies" will help our children out. We say, if this is our experience with this "expert" principal, how can we trust the system?

On the other hand, we have often been viewed by many parents as experts because our children are acquiring and developing fluency in ASL and in English. Because Deaf people are prevalent in Brenda's family and in my family, our children are native users of ASL. We are very proud of this fact and we do discuss the grammatical aspects of ASL as our children ask questions about the language. They enjoy the language immensely and often play with the language. And while we watch them enjoying their language, we have to read the so-called experts.

> This obsession against signing has scared parents of Deaf children away from Deaf adults who use sign language. Many parents have been told that those who use signs become clannish when they grow up and that many live in "Deaf ghettos." (Gannon, 1981, p. 360)

Brenda and I have frequently been told and have read that deafness is an invisible handicap. I am not so sure that it is that invisible, as ASL is indeed a visual language. For example, our family used to live in a small town of approximately 10,000 people. Once, a Deaf couple who wanted to visit us could not find our house and stopped a person on the street about two miles from us to ask for directions. That person did not recognize the street name but inquired if they were visiting "the death [sic] family," which was us. The couple said yes and that person gave excellent directions which led them right to our very doorstep. The couple, upon arrival, described what had happened and we had a good laugh at the concept of invisibleness.

I have observed that Deaf children with excellent use of ASL, especially if they are native users of the language, are extremely visible. I believe that this holds true for hearing parents who have Deaf children or Deaf parents who have hearing children as they desire and seek opportunities to further enhance ASL acquisition and development for their children. We have had parents asking us if our children could play with their Deaf children because our children are excellent role models and their children could benefit from such play with our children by acquiring and further developing ASL. In addition, hearing parents have said that they themselves need practice in ASL and would benefit by talking with us as Deaf adults.

Initially, Brenda and I were somewhat resistant as we felt that our children were being exploited. The approach the hearing people used in asking for such experiences for their children led us to feel this way. For example: "Can my child come over to your house to play with your children so that my child can learn more ASL?" This kind of question made us feel that goals are being established by parents without regard to the need for children just to play. We want our children to have friends and to play with other children. Again, why is being Deaf more important than playing a game of checkers or playing in the sandbox?

During the course of our deliberations, Brenda and I concluded that perhaps our children were not really being "used." Perhaps we were being approached because ASL is disregarded by the educational institutions in this country and parents and children have become hungry for communication, a basic human need. It became apparent to us that there are hearing parents who want to be "adopted" by Deaf people and that those parents realize that their children have linguistic, social, and emotional needs that have to be met to further development and growth.

Moreover, Brenda and I no longer feel that our children are being exploited, as they do enjoy playing with other people who are like themselves. The need for a sense of belonging and comfort is very real. No matter how hard society pushes inclusion, especially in educational opportunities, people's acceptance of each other without regard to race, sex, or disability is a formidable task and this society has been trying to address it for years and years. The name change from mainstreaming to inclusion is like "old wine in a new bottle." The underlying issues remain unresolved. Inclusion does not guarantee acceptance.

For example, even nowadays, the view that Deaf people are dumb is very much alive. One day, Amy and Anthony came home upset, saying that Mom had been called a "DAD." Brenda and I did not understand what "DAD" meant. They said that it meant *Deaf And Dumb*. They explained that children on the school bus had been calling them DAD for some time, but both had become quite upset when our next-door neighbor's son called Brenda a DAD. This family is black. Anthony, very angry, went ahead and told him that his mother was a "nigger." That child reacted by hitting my child in the head with a shovel and kicking him in the stomach.

We felt that this episode called for a conversation with the boy's parents. The father said that no one is allowed to call his wife a "nigger." I said that our children feel exactly the same way, as no one is allowed to call their mother a "DAD." He said that they are not niggers but we are in fact deaf and dumb, and that his son had spoken the truth. We were so shocked! This family is an educated middle-class family and we had no idea that they held such a prejudice against us! To make matters worse, other children in the neighborhood banded together in support of the neighbor's son, claiming that Anthony had started the whole thing. These kids knew exactly what had happened on the bus. We were left helpless, but we learned from the episode that it is crucial for our children to interact with other children like themselves to nurture their self-esteem and family pride. We have now concluded that hearing parents who want to give their Deaf children more exposure to ASL by befriending our children are not really "using" our children. It was more a matter of children needing other children like themselves to play, to argue, to talk, to laugh, to cry, to fight, to love. . . . We must continue in our efforts to teach all children to accept each other. But meanwhile, we must allow Deaf children to establish their own group where they can form healthy self-identity.

All of our children entered a school for the deaf when they were three years old. When Amy was beginning third grade and Anthony first grade, state regulations dictated that both children could not be considered for ongoing placement at the school because they did not have an 80-decibel loss or greater in the better ear. This was against our wishes, because after visiting all options for our children, we had determined that this school provided the best educational opportunities and, also, had the best oral education program in a bilingual setting. But apparently, there were people who knew more than we did and had decided that it was in the best interest of our children that they move to a program that was "more appropriate." Appropriate for whom, we wondered! Given limited choices, we elected to enroll both children in a public school in our home district and in "regular" classes with interpreting and notetaking services provided. Speech instruction was also included.

We were very anxious the day when Amy's and Anthony's report cards, their very first in a public school, came home. We saw that one got a "D" in English. We wondered why, since we knew that all of our children could speak, read, and write English well. We had read to them, they to us, and they to each other since they were born. Their English education at the school for the deaf was excellent. We finally learned that this child was pulled out of English class so that speech instruction could be provided.

We objected and changes were made. When the second report card came home, the grade for English improved, but this child got a "D" in arithmetic and for the very same reason. We objected once again. A meeting was called to hear us out. We were asked which subject was the least important. We said no subject was unimportant because if anything was offered by the school, it had to be important; otherwise it would not be offered. The school asked about physical education. We said not even that because we believed that physical education was good for the mind and built character.

We asked about the possibility of having speech instruction provided before or after school hours. All kinds of excuses were given as to why this was not possible. One excuse was bus transportation difficulties. The loudest objection was from the speech teacher, who said that she only worked during school hours.

But the cost to Deaf people of ineffective formal instruction has grown much greater of late. We are living in an increasingly technological world. Nearly three-fourths of all jobs now require technical training beyond a high school diploma. Projections for the year 2000 – just ten years from now – show that new jobs will require a workforce with an average education of 13½ years. That means that the workers who fill these jobs must have some college training. Not to be the boss, mind you, just bring home a paycheck. (Lane, 1991, p. 83)

Speech instruction, of course, is important. But at what cost? Speech or English? Speech or math? Speech or science? Speech or physical education? Our choice was quite simple. The goal of education for our children, in our opinion, should be to maximize their intellectual abilities, to develop their character, and to give them an appreciation of the society at large.

The Congress of Milan was a momentous event. In September, 1880, a group of educators from several European countries and the United States met in Milan, Italy, and declared that sign language had no legitimate place in the education or the lives of Deaf people. Deaf persons should speak and lipread in their national oral language, the congress stated, for oral skills would rescue them from their ignorance and brutish ways; their communication problems, isolation, and clannishness would disappear; and they would be restored to society. (Van Cleve, 1987, Vol. 2, p. 63)

Brenda and I wondered out loud how the school for the deaf we had wanted could provide for all of the educational goals established and still be able to promote the learning of speech and speechreading. We also wondered why the school would not be flexible about the speech instructors' working hours. Why couldn't our desire to provide speech instruction before or after school hours be accommodated? This wondering out loud has been to no avail and we are still struggling and fighting. Believe it or not, Brenda and I were told by a school principal to "let our children go," "let the school take care of our children," and that we should "seek therapy to deal with our past so that we can better cope with our deafness." This came from the expert principal mentioned earlier. These were his responses to one of our requests that he consider the possibility of enriching sign language and cultural experiences of the children in the middle school so that children's experiences and relationships among deaf and hearing peers could be enhanced. We had only suggested something like a small sign language club and the purchase of a few sign language books for the library, suggestions that were met with disapproval.

> A new race of pharaohs that knew not Joseph are taking over the land and many of our American schools. They do not understand signs, for they cannot sign. They proclaim that signs are worthless and of no help to the Deaf. Enemies of the sign language, they are enemies of the true welfare of the Deaf. (George Veditz in Padden & Humphries, 1988, p. 36)

Given the experiences we have had thus far, it has become very clear that "hearingizing" our children is the first step toward successful education. This step has left us feeling that there is complete disregard of ASL. Further, if the belief exists that deafness is an illness and must be cured, then ASL will not be accepted because if there were no Deaf people, there would not be a need for ASL. If this is the case, we have wondered why in the world are our children attending a public school and why in the world is the public school putting up with Deaf children? I say this because ASL is our children's native language and I believe that it must be recognized and used as a bridge to learning English. But instead, our children's background and experiences are totally ignored. The schools that we have dealt with just do not want to accommodate such experiences. Brenda and I asked another principal in an elementary school if he wanted to have Deaf children in his school. His response was no. Then we asked why he is having Amy and Anthony there. His response was that he has no choice as he has to have them there. It is the law. We thought, "Oh, great!" Frederick Schreiber (Garretson, 1991, p. 96) once said, "As far as deaf people are concerned, our civil rights are violated daily."

It is critical to accept and recognize that Deaf people understand very well the importance of ASL and English.

> The members of these language minorities are usually realistic about language and power; they recognize that their child needs to know the majority language to get ahead. They generally favor an education for their child in his or her primary language, but an education that will make the child bilingual. (Lane, 1990, p. 79)

The Deaf persons that I have interacted with in the United States, ever since I was a little boy, and still to this very day, use ASL and English daily. It is impossible to avoid English. I smile when I read of a "Deaf ghetto" consisting of Deaf persons who cannot speak. If there is such a ghetto, then English must be very much alive in it. So is ASL. While degree of fluency and use of ASL and English may vary among individuals, both languages are without question critical and important to the lives of Deaf people; Deaf people have said this over and over again.

> Most countries in the world are multilingual. The number of independent countries is less than 200, while the number of languages spoken in the world is between 4,000 and 5,000. There are more multilinguals than monolinguals in the world but power lies mostly in the hands of monolinguals. (Lane, 1990, p. 79)

Anyone who claims that people who study and use ASL have disregard of English, from my perspective, should refrain from making such a statement. We live in a country where English is in fact a majority language and I believe that Deaf people are realistic about this fact. I believe the problem lies in defining what role English has in the lives of Deaf people.

Brenda observed a presentation to parents of children with hearing losses made once by an oral educator. The presenter explained that deaf children must learn to speak so that they can "talk" with their parents and other family members. In her presentation she alluded to the importance of being able, through speech, to order food in a restaurant. She used pronouncing "french fries" as an example. I chuckled when Brenda told me of this presentation because establishing educational goals in order to be able to get french fries in a restaurant is rather strange.

I believe that the time has come for people like Brenda and myself to provide a more solid description of how English is actually used in the lives of Deaf people. For us, reading and writing English and signing ASL is a way of life, especially in our home and at work. Let's look at our home.

The television programs we watch, through closed-captioning, are in English. The telephone calls, through using the TTY, are in English. All of the computer software is in English. All of the correspondence we get or send is in English. All of the magazines, newspapers, and books we read are in English. All of the recipes and cooking instructions in the kitchen are in English. All of the annuity, insurance, banking, and other personal financial needs are dealt with in English. Need I elaborate more when I state that English has a role in the lives of Deaf people?

Furthermore, Brenda and I have seen numerous programs on television and have read numerous articles over the years describing illiteracy as America's number one education problem. There is so much emphasis now placed on literacy, meaning reading and writing. We have seen many hearing people on television, for example, giving testimonies on being illiterate. This "live" demonstration sends to us as parents a valuable message. That message is we must not make improving the speech and hearing skills of our children a major goal of their education. For us, English literacy means reading and writing. Therefore, we do not consider the oral approach as English language education. Furthermore, we must make sure that education for our children is conducted in a way in which information is readily understood. For our children, it must not be education through speech and speechreading. Perhaps speech training has its value as a subject to study, but to expect our children to acquire education through spoken English is wrong, very wrong!

In conclusion, it was not my intent in this chapter to be cynical or to express negativism. The goal was simply to share our experiences in dealing with educators and our own thinking and the insights that developed as we deliberated on what it would take to successfully raise our children. Obviously, politics and attitudes on both sides have had a major impact on our decisions. Deaf people, whether there are efforts to "hearingize" them or not, will always be Deaf. Acquisition and development of fluency in ASL, at least from our experiences as Deaf persons and from our observations as parents, has done nothing but wonders. Acquisition and development of fluency in English, in its printed and written form, is important to success and is an enormous challenge. Acquisition and development of fluency in speech and speechreading may have a role but it is not *the* priority, as it has been in deaf education historically. I close with this marvelous statement made by George Veditz in 1913 on film:

> As long as we have Deaf people on earth, we will have signs. . . . It is my
> hope that we all will love and guard our beautiful sign language as the

noblest gift God has given to Deaf people. (Quoted in Padden and Humphries, 1988, p. 36)

Acknowledgments

I wish to acknowledge Brenda L. Tress-Mowl for her support in writing this chapter; her help in validating the accuracy of the descriptions of our experiences was invaluable. I also wish to acknowledge our three lovely children, Amy, Anthony, and Jon. I sincerely hope that as they get older they will understand and appreciate the need for me to share stories so candidly about our experiences as parents.

References

Bahan, B. (1989). What if . . . Alexander Graham Bell had gotten his way? In S. Wilcox (Ed.), *American deaf culture: An anthology* (pp. 83–87). Burtonsville, MD: Linstock Press.

Baker-Schenk, C. (1985). Characteristics of oppressed and oppressor peoples: Their effect on the interpreting context. In M. McIntire (Ed.), *Proceedings of the 1985 RID Convention*. Silver Spring, MD: RID Publications.

Crammatte, A. (1987). *Meeting the challenge*. Washington, DC: Gallaudet University Press.

Gannon, J. (1981). *Deaf heritage: A narrative history of deaf America*. Silver Spring, MD: National Association of the Deaf.

Garretson, M. D. (Ed). (1991). *Perspectives on deafness: A Deaf American monograph*. Silver Spring, MD: National Association of the Deaf.

Lane, H. (1990). Bilingual education for ASL-using children. In M. D. Garretson (Ed.), *Communication issues among deaf people: A Deaf American monograph* (pp. 79–85). Silver Spring, MD: National Association for the Deaf.

(1991). Perceptions of deaf people in a nation on the threshold of educating deaf children. In M. D. Garretson (Ed.), *Perspectives on deafness: A Deaf American monograph*. Silver Spring, MD: National Association of the Deaf.

Padden, C., & Humphries, T. (1988). *Deaf in America: Voices from a culture*. Cambridge, MA: Harvard University Press.

Soderfeldt, B. (1991). Cochlear implants and the deaf community. In M. D. Garretson (Ed.), *Perspectives on deafness: A deaf American monograph*. Silver Spring, MD: National Association of the Deaf.

Stewart, L. (1990). Sign language: Some thoughts of a Deaf American. In M. D. Garretson (Ed.), *Communication issues among deaf people: A deaf American monograph*. Silver Spring, MD: National Association for the Deaf.

Van Cleve, J. (Ed). (1987). *Gallaudet encyclopedia of deaf people and deafness*. New York: McGraw-Hill.

CHAPTER SIXTEEN

In Search of Self: Experiences of a Postlingually Deaf African-American

DIANNE K. BROOKS

For the first twelve years of my life, I was one of five normally hearing siblings in my family. My existence revolved around my African-American family residing in the nation's capital at a time that I often characterize as a kind of twilight in the African-American experience. I came of age in the post-1954 school desegregation era, when the law had been declared, but when the realities of one's life as an African-American fell into a timeless zone between what had been mandated by the law and what was yet to be. And for African-Americans in the years immediately following *Brown v. Board of Education*, "that which was yet to be" had not dissolved the invisible but still discernible physical and geographical boundaries that shaped my life and experiences from early childhood to early adulthood. In this "post-desegregation" era, I lived in neighborhoods and attended schools populated only by other African-Americans.

Like my siblings and my mother, I was born in Washington, D.C., and the early years of my life, as I knew it, were beautiful, rich, and thoroughly rewarding. My life was centered around a close-knit nuclear family. It was also dominated by many extended family members, including a maternal grandmother whose story-telling and reminiscing provided wonderfully engaging volumes of folklore that instilled in me a sense of ethnic and

Dianne K. Brooks (M.S., Counseling, Gallaudet University), Associate Director, Recruitment and Admissions, National Technical Institute for the Deaf, has been involved in the field of education and counseling of the deaf for twenty-two years and has published many articles on those topics. Her address is: Department of Recruitment and Admissions, the National Technical Institute for the Deaf, Rochester Institute of Technology, 52 Lomb Memorial Drive, Rochester, NY 14623.

personal pride that remains even today a fundamental core of my self-identity. My grandmother described her own youth and the prejudice she encountered growing up as the child of a Native American mother and an African-American father. She related vivid accounts of the Great Depression and of the family's unsuccessful venture as operators of a moving and hauling business. In spite of these obstacles and hardships, my grandmother's dialogues always concluded with a portrait of my family as survivors whose sense of pride and tenacity could not be defeated.

Those first twelve years were filled with many joyful events: Saturday afternoons at the local theater matinee; roller-skating races around the immediate neighborhood; family gatherings at Thanksgiving, Christmas, and Easter; a school field trip to New York's Hayden Planetarium; summer days at the local playground/recreation center; learning to gyrate with a hula hoop around my waist; watching American Bandstand after school each afternoon. There were the inevitable sibling free-for-all encounters and grudgingly completed household chores. There were the birthday celebrations and school plays. And there was, finally, the last joyous sound of music I was ever to hear: a class trip to Constitution Hall to hear the Washington Philharmonic Orchestra.

Thus, I spent my early years in this family milieu, in a neighborhood of other families like mine, all members of a proud, albeit struggling African-American working class. While my family's struggle for economic survival dominated our lives, a strong sense of determination and personal pride provided the mainstay of my life. Then, at the age of twelve and in the ten ensuing years, my world went into a tailspin, and the strength of my personal convictions and my sense of self were put to the test. My journey into deafness began on a warm sunny spring day a few months before summer vacation.

The First Day of the Rest of My Life

The morning began pretty much like any other: heading off to school with enthusiasm and getting to the bus stop on time. I actually loved school then. I was always meticulous about homework and thorough to the point of challenging a teacher if I thought facts had been misstated or misrepresented. Perhaps the best way to describe my enthusiasm is to say I actually loved learning. From the earliest days I loved to read. At the age of seven, I came across a huge old volume of Grimm's Fairy Tales, and later I "graduated" to more hefty fare in the works of James Fenimore Cooper,

Greek mythology, Thomas Hardy, Langston Hughes, Richard Wright, and a wide array of other literary works which I obtained both at home and at school. I enjoyed the new vistas that school and learning opened up to me.

The elementary school where I had been enrolled since kindergarten was not very large. The average class size was approximately twenty students. Teachers remembered and greeted former students in the hallways, even years later. The school environment was, in essence, an extended family, and I embraced its sometimes rigid and always rigorous demands in much the same way that one would ultimately come to accept and embrace both the discipline and love of one's family.

By mid-morning on this spring day, the class was deep into a social studies lesson, and, as expected, our textbooks were open as we followed the teacher's narration of a specific paragraph, poised for the questioning we all knew would follow. Within the span of a few minutes, I became perturbed by what I thought to be the teacher's sudden mumbling and diminished voice. When I looked up at her with growing irritation, she seemed unfazed, as did the rest of the class. And when her voice faded altogether in mid-sentence, my irritation grew to anger. In the next instant, I felt I was watching a freeze-frame in a movie where everything seemed to fade into the background, motionless, except for the teacher standing in the center of the room, soundlessly mouthing her words. In that brief, inexplicable time, I left behind the safe, familiar world I had known as a hearing child, and entered an unknown realm of deafness.

The family home was situated on a long, winding street in what is still known as the Upper Northwest part of Washington. Ours was one of a network of one-way streets interconnecting so that automobile traffic was limited primarily to residents and visitors. The neighborhood was sandwiched between two main avenues connecting the Upper Northwest with Downtown. Though we were within walking distance of these thoroughfares, the neighborhood was far enough away to be an oasis of attached rowhouses, each with a small, well-kept lawn shaded by large old trees lining the streets. On warm spring and summer nights, with windows open to capture a breeze, one could hear the familiar hum of night insects, punctuated only by the occasional screech of a cat or the bark of one of many neighborhood dogs that spent the night inside the tiny fenced-in backyards.

On this night, having just lost my hearing that morning, I eased into bed still numb from the shock and trauma of the day. I went through all the usual rituals: I ate dinner; I watched TV; I played with the family's German shepherd; I prepared for bed. And yet I was unable to think, feel, or comprehend.

And this night, as I turned out the light and the room became entrenched in darkness, a sudden, profound awareness descended on me: gone was the sound of the night creatures; gone was the occasional barking dog; gone was the murmur of the TV my family was watching downstairs; gone were the familiar sounds as my brothers and sisters prepared for bed; gone was the ticking of my large old bedside clock. Gone was every sound that characterized the world as I had known it: the constant flow of dialogue among family members, and the late-night conversations in the dark with my sister who shared the room. That night, I truly came to understand the phrase, "silence can be deafening." This profound silence, so new to me and exacerbated by the profound darkness, was more than I could tolerate. I reached for the bedside lamp, turned it on, and in that instant established a new ritual that would eventually replace what I had lost: reliance on my vision in place of my lost hearing. To this day, some kind of nighttime illumination, whether from an opened window blind or a shaded lamp, continues to be an unrelinquished reminder of my entry into the deaf world.

Journey into Deafness

On my first day back in my old classroom, after more than a week of inconclusive medical tests, I knew as I entered the room that everyone had been told that something "awful" had happened to me. Instead of old friends crowding around to ask what had happened, I was met with long stares and curious glances. During the day, people walked up behind me and screamed in my ear to "test" my hearing loss. Right before my face, classmates whispered together and stared at me boldly. I sat in my old familiar seat all that day hearing nothing, understanding little, and anticipating the end of the day when I could retreat to the safety of my home.

Within a few weeks, these experiences drained from me the last positive feelings about school that I was to recall. I withdrew from participation in the school play scheduled for the end of the year; I withdrew from planned participation in the May Day program; I retreated from working on the school newspaper; and I never attended another student council meeting.

I looked forward to the summer as a relief from all the anxiety and disillusionment I had come to feel, and I hoped that in those ensuing months, through some miracle or happenstance, I would regain my hearing.

For the remainder of the school year, activities and events that had once been of little or no consequence became major challenges, major struggles. One such event was the weekly spelling test, which was once a source of pleasure for me. I excelled in the competitiveness and enjoyed a solid record of success, as language, literature, and vocabulary were my academic strong points. On the first Friday after my hearing loss, I quickly wrote my name and the date on my test paper, and numbered the sheet for the twenty-five words the teacher would call out. The first word was recited, followed by a brief definition and a repetition of the word. As the other students wrote, I sat immobile, pen hovering over the paper as I wracked my mind trying to recall a portion of what she had said, or a phrase or clue of any kind. And on it went to the end of the test when papers were collected. I had only a few words on my list, and while they were all spelled correctly, they were not all the words that she had called out. My teacher was as perplexed as I was, then decided I should be given a special "individual administration" of the test by one of my classmates. This proved to be unsuccessful, and eventually I was "excused" from taking the test altogether.

In short succession, I was excused from group discussions and all oral quizzes. I was also excused from my role as class spokesperson at the closing graduation ceremonies. Each such exemption seemed only to reinforce my gradual retreat to introspection and social isolation.

In the summer, the visits to doctors and clinicians continued sporadically, and after each visit I rallied myself with the expectation that in the fall, I would enter junior high school with my hearing once more intact. But as the summer waned, the hope became desperation. I also sensed that my mother shared this desperation. Late that summer, on the advice of a family friend, she agreed to send me to an evangelical faith healer.

While I look back on this occasion with a measure of humor, it signifies to me the only time my mother's own quiet, determined struggle with my hearing loss became clearly evident.

And so my mother, her friend, and I entered the huge circuslike tent on a hot summer evening, the last day of a four-day tour of the Oral Roberts evangelical campaign. I took my place in a long line of people with all sorts of ailments and disabling conditions, and I walked along a narrow metal catwalk that reverberated with the sounds coming from a large band on stage. I received a blessing and a healing touch from the evangelist. The whole event was highly emotional and totally captivating, but it did not restore my hearing. I left as I had arrived: still profoundly deaf.

The Diagnostic Odyssey

I sat in the large swivel chair, much like a dentist's chair, and watched as the doctor assembled an assortment of strange and formidable-looking metal instruments. I recall the shock of cold steel as he inserted one – first in one ear and then in the other – and peered for some time into the depths of my ear. I also remember the pain of the tongue depressor and how extraordinarily rough his examination of my throat seemed. Next came the sharp pain and suctionlike sensation when he inserted a long, thin, tubelike instrument with a small, ball-shaped rubber tip deep into my ear canal.

Through it all, I sat in a kind of trance, fearful and deeply perplexed as the doctor talked to my mother, who sat off to one side. The sight of these two people whose lips moved rapidly but silently, the abject sense of terror, and the speed with which these incomprehensible events where happening left me numb. I could do little more than watch. And watch I did. I watched every move the doctor made. But most of all, I watched my mother's face, particularly her eyes. I looked for a sign of reassurance, for a sign of explanation, but most of all, I think, for a sign of hope. My mother's gaze frequently locked on mine as she sat alternately watching me and the doctor. Even as I flinched with pain, her gaze never faltered.

Some days later, I sat in yet another strange chair in yet another aseptic office. This one, however, looked like a classroom with its brightly colored chairs and desks. I sat at a table on which were laid out numerous wires with tiny disks attached to each. These wires and disks were taped at intervals along my arms and around my head, extending to just behind my ears. I sat facing a tinted mirror, and after the wires had been attached, I was left alone in the room. Again, bewilderment set in. This time my mother was not in the room, so there was no comforting or familiar face to turn to. There was only the sudden jolt of a slight electrical shock, and then another, and another, each one gradually intensifying until the last one practically lifted me out of my chair.

The electrodes, as I later learned they were called, were removed, and I was left alone again for several minutes until my mother appeared and silently we left for home.

A few days later my mother and I made our way up the walkway to yet another strange place, a huge old hospital situated on a hill overlooking the city, and directly across the street from the high school I would eventually enter. This time, with the help of a notepad, it was explained to me that I would be having my tonsils removed. The surgery was not due to any illness, but to explore the possibility that perhaps there might be a connection, an explanation, a causal relationship between my tonsils and the sudden onset of deafness.

Following the surgery, my continued sense of terror was relieved temporarily by the glow of attention from family and friends. As the get-well cards and gifts poured in, so my sense of self-importance increased. Out of the trauma and bewilderment of those days, my most vivid, pleasant memory remains the large shiny blue gift book entitled *Birds of the World*, which I devoured during the days of recuperation.

My tonsils were successfully removed, but the recovery of my hearing (which I had hopefully expected) did not occur.

From this point, I remember a blur of clinics, doctors, gadgets, tests, and appointments. They gradually decreased in frequency until I was fitted with a large, shiny, body-type Zenith hearing aid, and sent off twice weekly after school to the local hearing and speech center for lip-reading classes.

The search for a meaning to these medical visits, the effort to return to normal, had finally ended, almost a year later. The diagnosis: My hearing loss – a profound, sensorineural hearing loss – was irreversible. There would be no return to normality as I had known it.

My "Hearing Problem"

The first day in junior high school – a new and much larger school, new faces, a new regimen, and a new phase in my journey into the world of deafness.

On this day all new students assembled in the auditorium, where class assignments were announced, teachers were introduced, and everyone eventually trooped off to their new classrooms. I was the only kid whose mother was present in the auditorium. When my name was called, she accompanied me to where my new teacher stood assembling the class, and in as few words as possible tried to explain my predicament to the teacher. As I watched my mother walk up the aisle and out of the auditorium, I realized that I was truly alone with this phenomenon called deafness, and that as I faced this new world of junior high school, my mother couldn't be there with me every hour of every day. It was a profound realization that left me yearning for the old and familiar, and genuinely terrified of the new and unknown.

A few days later, I sat at a table in the school cafeteria, alone, as usual. I glanced over at another table where five or six girls I recognized from algebra class were seated. The scene is frozen in my memory: They were all watching me while one of their group was apparently mimicking me. Her eyes were wide open, her neck was extended, and she was frantically looking about her. I didn't know how I looked that day, but I knew that was exactly how I felt. These classmates later became good friends whose friendship remained into adulthood. Years later, when I recounted this scene, my friend apologized to me, but on this day her behavior actually pushed me out of a personal quagmire of fear and self-abasement. It forced me to hold up my head. It planted the first seed of anger, and gave rebirth to the sense of pride (and sometimes aloofness) that my family had long instilled in me and my siblings. In essence, I gained the pride to withstand peer rejection. I gained the fortitude to withstand an eighth grade foreign language teacher who chastised me before an entire class because I couldn't hear her when she called on me, and couldn't keep up with the class because of my "hearing problem."

In the ensuing years I alternated between defensiveness and aggressiveness in dealing with teachers and peers regarding my "hearing problem." Inwardly, I remained in turmoil fighting a sense of rejection, sensitive about my "difference," and fearful of the future. The only real solace I found was in the unwavering support of my family, who out of their own sense of denial about my hearing loss actually provided a foundation for my personal and psychological survival.

To my family, as to me, deafness was an unheard-of appellation. And so to family and friends, I became the child who "doesn't hear very well anymore." And rather than face the inevitable and unknown consequences of my hearing impairment, family members chose to ignore it. This became a positive rather than negative influence on me. It allowed me to maintain a semblance of normalcy and minimized the trauma of additional changes in my life. And so my family's love and support provided a valuable refuge, a much-needed "balance" to the turmoil and pain I faced in school and in dealing with peers.

In essence, my home life remained the same. I retained my "status" as the eldest daughter, and I continued to share chores and responsibilities with my siblings. I remained a fully participating member of the family, and my loss of hearing never became a focal point, at least not in this comfortable, protective cocoon.

From the age of twelve to about eighteen, I lived in a state of marginality. I continued to be the family member who "doesn't hear very well anymore." And I continued the inward struggle with myself in search of a sense of self-definition and insight into, and understanding of, what the future might hold for me as a person who could no longer hear.

The Deaf World

I was introduced into the world of deaf people at the age of eighteen, and for the next two years my curiosity and fascination were insatiable. For the first time I discovered that there were others in the world like myself. I discovered the language of signs, which minimized the untold hassles of relying only on lip-reading. It was almost too good to be true. I immersed myself in this new world order and made an honest and determined attempt to accept its cultural requisites. I learned sign language. I learned for the first time that I was deaf. I joined social organizations; I attended social and cultural events for deaf people. At last, I seemed to have found my niche in life.

But the glow and attraction did not prevail. I began to feel stifled in this new-found mecca called the Deaf community. The more I immersed myself into Deaf culture, the more I began to feel suffocated by what appeared to be a social anomaly that was too exclusive, too separated or isolated from the world at large. I began to feel that in my search for an identity, I was further distancing myself from all vestiges of the familiar. My goal had been to find a means by which I could re-create and reaffirm myself. Instead, I discovered that the tightly interwoven social system of the Deaf world did not allow or encourage any such re-creation. I also discovered that my having a hearing loss did not automatically ensure membership or social acceptance.

In the early days, my motivation, fascination, and determination to learn sign language remained high. But a number of sobering experiences dampened my enthusiasm, and I found myself once again on the margin socially. One incident in particular served as a reminder of my marginal social status. I had a young deaf roommate during a special summer orientation program for college-bound high school seniors. Some of the participants were engaged in math and English remedials. A very few, like myself, were immersed in hours and hours of sign instruction as we struggled to master the language.

My roommate, a "native" signer, extremely fluent in the language, made it clear she had neither interest in nor patience with "my kind." On one occasion, she stood with her face just a few inches from mine, vehemently telling me what a fake I was because I thought and acted like a hearing person. This eventually became a familiar refrain, and subtle, pervasive lines of demarcation between "manual" and "oral" began to appear. While others were not quite so vehement in their rejection of me, I began to realize that "bonding" with Deaf culture would not be achieved quickly or easily.

Once again I was at odds with myself and with my circumstances. I felt like I was straddling the proverbial fence, with one foot in the world of the Deaf and the other in the world of the hearing, but I couldn't or wouldn't get off the fence. I did not belong completely on either side. The issue was not a question of race, but a question of identity: deaf versus hearing; Deaf world versus hearing world; old versus new; familiar versus unfamiliar. I was searching for a way to define for myself a sense of self, a level of self-acceptance, that would lessen the impact of my hearing loss and the frequency with which it dominated my every thought and behavior.

Two years later, at age twenty, unable to find the answer, I made yet another retreat. This time I shunned all the vestiges of the Deaf world. I refused to use sign language; I withdrew from social interaction with other deaf people; and I made my way back to the only place I felt I truly belonged. I enrolled in a hearing university. It seemed my journey had come full circle.

However, my short time immersed in the Deaf world was more than a memory. It was an experience from which there was no escape. There was no denying that it had a profound and lasting effect on me. My journey back to the hearing world was an odyssey born of desperation. It was not that I felt I belonged there; rather, it was a refuge where I could at least reclaim part of my identity. For the next several years, I continued this marginal existence as a formerly hearing person trying to find a peaceful way of living with myself.

Reconciliation

Many years have passed since I lost my hearing. Today, I am comfortable in the knowledge of who I am. My deafness no longer occupies center stage in my life. Instead, I feel a sense of enrichment for having survived this unexpected, traumatic event. Although the lessons learned were not easy, I believe that the determination and fortitude which I used to reconcile my inner conflicts about my deafness are strongly rooted in my ethnic background. As a child growing up in the nation's capital, I had learned quickly that there were certain areas of the city and suburbs which were off limits to African-Americans. In the post-1954 era, there were no visible signs pointing to these lines of demarcation, but all of us young children knew the lines existed, and that we were unwelcome in certain areas, in certain theaters, certain shopping malls, certain schools, and certain residential enclaves. Yet our elders did not share this knowledge with me or my siblings by chastising us. I recall that the tone of these lessons was never self-defeating, but rather served much like a rallying call for us youngsters not to let these circumstances cause us to waver in our sense of pride. We were encouraged not to forget the price so many Black Americans had paid to pave the way for the present, and that each of us by pursuing our goals would contribute to paving the way for the future. There was never a feeling of self-abasement. Rather, the occasions were more like an opportunity to uplift the spirit, to reaffirm pride and perseverance, and most of all, to remain undaunted by whatever barriers or challenges might be placed before us.

I cannot recall the day, but at some point I came to construe my sudden loss of hearing as just another hurdle that I had to overcome, just like the many hurdles that my forefathers endured. And true to my family's teachings, I would not give up, I would not be defeated. I would hold up my head, and I would show the fortitude that was part of my racial and ethnic legacy. Essentially, I would never let race, or for that matter deafness, dilute my spirit.

Today, my perception of the world around me is no longer conditioned by terms like "the hearing world" and "the Deaf world." There is no proverbial fence on which I am straddled. Instead, my life is a mosaic of people who are not defined by race, ethnicity, mode of communication, or the status of their hearing.

Homecoming

A few years ago during a break in a conference I was attending in Washington, I ventured back to the old neighborhood. I had been back only once before, shortly after my mother's death in 1974.

The red brick rowhouse with beige trim and small yard was still there. The same hedges bordered the yard, and the large matured shade trees now formed an interlocking canopy over the street. The street itself was still one-way, and it remained a small, relatively quiet enclave bordered on two sides by the large avenues that are still the main links to Downtown, Upper Northwest, and suburban Maryland. The end-of-the-line bus terminal remains a short two blocks away. As I approached the house on foot, I was struck by the fact that the nostalgia and emotion I felt had little or nothing to do with my sudden, still inexplicable loss of hearing. I had spent the first twelve years of my life as a normally hearing youngster in this neighborhood, and although more than thirty years had passed since the day I returned home from school profoundly deaf, I realized that the pain or trauma of the experience could never weaken the bond I had formed with my family and with the neighborhood and surrounding community. I thought not so much about what I had lost in the way of my hearing, but what I had gained, learned, inherited, from all the lives that had earlier intertwined with my own. In essence, the home, the street, all the familiar landmarks of my childhood, epitomized a part of me that no degree of hearing loss could displace or take away. I wasn't recalling the silence of deafness, but rather the richness of my life. The emotions I felt this day were derived from a sense of the passage of time, the inevitability of change. I am heartened by the fact that my sense of self and the values instilled in me have served me well. I am first and foremost an African-American. And I happen to be deaf.

Acknowledgments

This chapter is dedicated to my mother, Ann Elizabeth Brooks, to my grandmother Kate Virginia Sheppard, and to my daughter, Tisha Marlene Smith. I am grateful for the fortitude, sustenance, and unconditional love they provided to me. This chapter is a compilation of journal entries and reflections I have written down intermittently since I lost my hearing at the age of twelve. I have attempted to highlight some of the events that I believe have had the most profound effect on my eventual adjustment to deafness.

CHAPTER SEVENTEEN

Living in a Bilingual-Bicultural Family

LYNN FINTON

Thirteen years ago when I married my husband, Ken, I believed the biggest difference between us was that I was Catholic and he was Lutheran. The fact that he was Deaf and I was hearing seemed inconsequential. The idea that we were entering into a bilingual and bicultural marriage and its potential impact on our relationship and future family did not enter our consciousness. Thirteen years and two children later, I have come to appreciate the significance of living in a bilingual-bicultural family.

Only recently have I reflected upon and analyzed bilingualism. When the editor of this book invited me to reflect upon the experience of living in a bilingual-bicultural family and write about it, I hesitated. I felt uncomfortable proclaiming myself a "bilingual." I believed a true bilingual was someone raised from birth with two languages or someone who moved from country to country and developed fluency in two or more languages. I also hesitated to proclaim myself a bilingual since I didn't start learning American Sign Language (ASL) until age eighteen. Although I was fluent in two languages, I didn't fit what I believed to be the definition of bilingualism. In addition, in my field of sign language interpreting, making a claim of bilingualism seemed to belong solely to children of Deaf parents.

Lynn Finton (M.S., Instructional Technology, Rochester Institute of Technology), Assistant Professor at The National Technical Institute for the Deaf, is in the field of interpreter education. She holds a Comprehensive Skills Certificate (CSC) from the Registry of Interpreters for the Deaf. She has served on local, state, and national boards and has presented numerous workshops in the field of interpreting. Her address is: Center for Sign Language and Interpreting Education, National Technical Institute for the Deaf, Rochester Institute of Technology, 52 Lomb Memorial Drive, Rochester, NY 14623.

The challenge to write about my bilingualism led me to a literature search and a real awakening. In the book *Life with Two Languages: An Introduction to Bilingualism*, François Grosjean (1982) defines bilingualism as "the regular use or two or more languages" (p. 1). That definition allowed me to see myself as a bilingual. I am fluent in two languages and use them on a daily basis both at work and at home. In addition, this book explained for me some of the puzzling experiences my husband and I have had as our daughters developed their two languages. As I read Grosjean's book, I came to realize that these experiences are common aspects of childhood bilingualism. Most importantly, I realized that the experiences of an English/ASL bilingual child are quite similar to the experiences of a Spanish/English or German/French bilingual child. It had never occurred to me to look at the bilingual literature as a source for understanding some of the phenomena that emerged as my daughters developed their languages. It was a wonderful and reassuring revelation to know that what was happening in our family was not unique, that the stages of language development my daughters were going through were typical of bilingual children.

Grosjean's book has also had a significant impact on how I think about Deaf/hearing issues. The terms "Deaf" and "hearing" are on opposite ends of the continuum; they are polar opposites. When Deaf/hearing issues are discussed, it is often in a negative context. Polar opposites and negativity were not, however, the appropriate words that described our Deaf/hearing marriage. The terms "bilingual" and "bicultural" and the positive connotations they carry are much better suited to describe who we are: a bilingual-bicultural couple. With this realization, I gladly accepted the editor's invitation to reflect on living in a bilingual-bicultural family.

This chapter will provide a glimpse of my family and our backgrounds, a look at how our bilingualism-biculturalism is manifest in everyday life as well as at some of the interesting phenomena of raising one's children bilingual-bicultural.

My Background

I am a hearing, native English user. All members of my family are hearing. My initial interest in sign language came about through watching a young Deaf boy communicate in sign language with his family at my church. I was so fascinated! As a result, my best friend and I learned fingerspelling during elementary school so that we could have secret "talks" at church or school. This interest eventually led to my career path in deaf education.

I began learning sign language at age eighteen through a community continuing education course while I was attending college. Having no opportunity to use the language outside of the classroom, I developed minimal fluency. During my junior year I transferred to a college in Sioux Falls, South Dakota, a city with a very active Deaf community. Here I met and began socializing with some Deaf men around my age and only then did I really begin to use the language enough to develop fluency. I remain forever grateful to the Sioux Falls Deaf community for their encouragement and their tolerance of my many cultural faux pas and language errors inevitable in the process of learning a second language. I am particularly indebted to one of those young Deaf men who led me on this journey toward bilingualism-biculturalism – my husband, Ken.

Ken's Background

Ken, who is profoundly Deaf, comes from a predominantly hearing family. He has hearing parents, two hearing siblings and a Deaf sister. Ken was not diagnosed as being deaf until he attended kindergarten in a public school. After this diagnosis, he attended a residential school for the deaf. His younger sister was diagnosed as deaf at approximately the same time and also attended the South Dakota School for the Deaf. Upon learning of the deafness of her two eldest children, Ken's mother began a correspondence course with the John Tracy Clinic, a well-known program for promoting oral education. Through this program, Ken's parents stressed the use of speech and speechreading at home. The program discouraged his parents from learning sign language, even though their children quickly learned sign language while attending the school for the deaf. The family did learn to use fingerspelling, but they only used it when speechreading failed. Ken and his sister lived in the dorms at the school for the deaf. At home, they relied primarily on speech and speechreading to communicate with hearing family members. As a result, Ken and his sister often felt left out of family conversations. Despite their parents' efforts, speech and speechreading failed to provide full access to communication within the family.

Ken transferred from the residential school for the deaf to a public school for his junior high and high school years. Although this decision was not supported by Ken's parents or himself, the residential school promoted it as the best way to challenge Ken academically. He spent these years in school using his residual hearing, speech, and speechreading to communicate. He did not have the benefit of interpreting or note taking services except for the last semester of his senior year. Socially, Ken had little contact with his hearing peers since communication was difficult and thus tended to be superficial. He continued to socialize after school with his friends from the school for the deaf since he felt more comfortable using sign language and interacting with those who shared that language.

Our Mixed Marriage

I attribute our lack of concern in entering a "mixed" marriage to naiveté. Deaf people were only beginning to be recognized as a linguistic and cultural minority back in the late 1970s. I had taken a course or two in American Sign Language, and I did appreciate it as a language separate and distinct from English. I was a fluent signer, not from the course work I took but from frequent interaction with the Sioux Falls Deaf community. Having interacted regularly with Deaf people for several years prior to my marriage, I had an appreciation for the fact that Deaf people were different from hearing people, that they saw things in a different way at times, that their rules of behavior weren't always the same as mine. Beyond that, I gave it little thought.

Over the years Ken and I came to understand these differences and attribute them to our different cultural experiences. It was easy for me to get used to the artifacts of Deaf culture: the TTY, the flashing lights, the caption decoder. It was not that difficult to get used to the typical behaviors Deaf people exhibit: tapping a person to get attention, the importance of eye contact, the lengthy leavetaking. What was most difficult to understand was the different world view that Deaf people have. On one occasion, early in our relationship, the topic of cochlear implants arose. A late-deafened acquaintance of ours had a cochlear implant. It was a relatively new procedure at the time, and she was thrilled with the results, limited as they were. I asked Ken, if he could magically become hearing whether he would do so. His response was an emphatic "No!" He explained that he was Deaf, that he identified with others like him and had no desire to be hearing. Knowing some of the obstacles, discrimination, and occasional frustrations he faced as a Deaf person, I couldn't understand what I perceived as his stubbornness in not wanting to become hearing. It wasn't that I wanted him to become hearing, I just felt that he was displaying a false sense of pride in not being willing to admit that it would be easier to be hearing. I can now greatly appreciate that Ken's identity is tied to his deafness – his language and his culture. Rare is the person who is willing to give up a crucial part of their identity just to have life a little more convenient for them. I realize that there might be certain advantages if I were a male, but I sure have no interest in being one.

Another conflict we faced early on, which was influenced by culture, was the relative importance placed on family versus friends. I come from a very close-knit family with a value system that places family above all else. Ken lived in the dorms at the residential school for the deaf. As is often the case with Deaf people, a familial bonding between peers occurs in this setting. Such was the case with Ken, and although I could intellectually appreciate the concept, at an emotional level I couldn't grasp how friends could be more important than family. I have now come to understand that the Deaf community is very close-knit, and living 1,200 miles from my own family, we now have a group of Deaf friends who truly are our second family.

Another issue we faced was the commonly held belief in the Deaf community that Deaf/hearing marriages don't work. Although common in South Dakota, mixed marriages were rare in Kansas, where we lived during our first year of marriage. I have seen no research data that support or deny the allegation that Deaf/hearing marriages don't work. What I do know is that our marriage is successful. Are there tensions? Sometimes. Are they caused by the fact that Ken is Deaf and I am hearing? No, I don't believe so. Mostly the tensions are because we are both stubborn, we disagree on when and how to spend our money, we have different ideas of child rearing, and so on. Is it difficult to be married to a Deaf person? Sure. He calls to me when I am in the basement and expects me to walk up to see what he wants. It takes him a long time to leave a social gathering. He doesn't want to go to the symphony. Is it difficult for Ken to be married to a hearing person? Sure. I walk all over the house when I talk on the phone. I sing along with the radio, and he thinks he married a nut case because it looks like I'm talking to myself. Are these marriage-shattering issues? Hardly.

Do I interpret for Ken? Sometimes I do, with neighbors, with family members, for the insurance agent and the car salesman. With the availability of captioning and telephone relay services, I interpret much less now than in the beginning of our marriage. Does it bother me when I have to interpret? No. Do I feel as though I am making sacrifices to make this bicultural marriage work? No, I don't! All marriages are a matter of give and take. When conflicts occur, we are not quick to place blame on our hearing status as the cause, but rather we look beyond to the root of the issue. Rarely does the cause lie in the fact that he is Deaf and I am hearing. We have come to accept, appreciate, and respect our cultural differences and perhaps that is the key to our success.

Our Family

Ken and I have two hearing daughters. Erin is seven years old and Kaylee is three. Our family uses American Sign Language and spoken English at home. We socialize with both Deaf and hearing people. We attend a church for the deaf. Ken and I both work at the National Technical Institute for the Deaf, where many people are English/ASL bilinguals. Erin attends a monolingual English school, and Kaylee is presently in a monolingual English home care environment.

Before the children, life in our household was uncomplicated. We used sign language exclusively in our home. Our friends were ASL/English bilinguals, both Deaf and hearing. The birth of our hearing daughters added a new dimension to this existence. We now encounter and interact with many more hearing people who are English monolinguals. Moving into a family-oriented neighborhood brought with it interactions with monolingual English-speaking neighbors. Our daughters found hearing playmates from the neighborhood and school, which brought many hearing monolingual English speakers into the household. Interactions with child-care providers and school personnel, along with our daughters' involvement in extracurricular activities, increased our contacts with hearing monolinguals. We didn't foresee the dramatic increase in the amount of contact with monolinguals before the birth of our children or its impact on our somewhat insular life with English/ASL bilinguals. These changes have resulted in my doing more interpreting for Ken. He has also had to start using his speech and speechreading skills with more frequency.

Language Use in the Home

Because I am married to a Deaf man, people frequently ask what language is used in our home. Until I began reading about bilingualism that question was difficult to answer; language choice is an unconscious process, so I really had to stop and think. My response would be "ASL," qualified with "most of the time." This qualifier refers to all of the influences of language choice and code-switching that goes on with bilinguals.

Because Ken can't hear spoken English, it isn't a fully accessible or comfortable communication option for him. We always sign with him.

Whether I speak or sign to my daughters is often dependent on who else is in the environment and the purpose of the communication. For example, when I am with my daughters in public, we often sign. I have not fully determined the reason for this, but my sense is that ASL is the language of privacy for us. After so many years of signing in public without having anyone eavesdrop, it now seems very awkward to talk in public when we can sign and keep our conversation private. I often sign to my daughters in the presence of hearing people to ensure privacy in conversation. It is interesting, though, that I do not feel comfortable speaking with my daughters in front of Deaf people to ensure privacy. Deaf people have been left out of conversations all of their lives because most hearing people can't sign. Because I am bilingual, to deliberately speak in front of a Deaf person without signing seems disrespectful and potentially oppressive.

Ken signs primarily, but at times uses spoken English when reading books, when his hands are otherwise occupied, or sometimes when disciplining. Kaylee signs to Ken and talks to me. Erin signs to me more frequently than ever before, again depending on the environment and the purpose of communication. Erin realizes she has control of two languages and can use them to her advantage. During Erin's kindergarten orientation she didn't say a word to anyone but signed to me throughout. She recognized that no one knew sign language except the two of us and she could communicate her thoughts freely without anyone "overhearing."

Only when it's called to my attention do I realize the amount of language switching and code-switching done in our family. After watching our family interact for about five minutes, a friend once remarked, "Your children must be very confused. They never know what language will be coming at them." I would always feel bad after hearing this kind of remark. Although the girls never appeared confused and always answered appropriately, I would feel that maybe we needed to establish a clear communication policy. But that seemed to impose artificial rules on what was happening naturally within our family. After reading about bilingualism, I am comforted to know that we are not just a family with hodgepodge communication. Now my response to these remarks is, "No, they are not confused, they are bilinguals!"

Language Development in our Children

Ken was adamant that his children be fluent in sign language. While superficial communication was acceptable for acquaintances, it was not acceptable within the intimate confines of the family. So early in our marriage we agreed that our children would be fluent in ASL. Although it would seem natural that a child would become fluent in sign language just by growing up in an environment where sign language is used, unfortunately this is not always the case. We have often seen Deaf parents use sign language with each other but use spoken English with their hearing children. In return, these children speak to their parents. This situation results in children who can comprehend some sign language but gain little mastery in using it themselves. We wanted to make sure that our children had adequate exposure to ASL. Because English is the majority language in American society, we felt assured our children would develop fluency in spoken English. Although the goal of making our children fluent in both English and ASL was clear, the process of achieving it was an unconscious one. We assumed that exposing them to both languages from the cradle would be effective.

It has been fascinating to watch our daughters' language development. I learned ASL as my second language, so I was interested to see how language learning would be different when learning English and ASL simultaneously. As a teacher in an interpreter education program, I frequently see the difficulty that adults endure when attempting to learn ASL as a second language. I was very curious to see how the learning process would be different for my daughters, who were learning two languages in a natural setting, our home.

Both of our daughters seemed to follow a similar pattern of language development. Their first signs were different from their first spoken words. Erin's first signs were MORE, DOG, and AIRPLANE, all appearing around nine to ten months of age. Her first spoken words were "Mommmy" and "Daddy," occurring around age one. Both communicated primarily through sign language, with approximately a fifteen-sign vocabulary but only one or two spoken words, at twelve months. While they could comprehend spoken English, they expressed their needs in sign language. It happened that our child-care arrangements changed when each girl was about one year old. We became concerned about putting them in a new monolingual English environment where their ability to express themselves in sign language wouldn't be understood. In order to prevent frustration, we taught our child-care providers the signs necessary to comprehend our daughters' communications. This seemed to be an effective strategy for the girls until they became more expressively fluent in English.

By eighteen months the girls primarily signed for communication purposes, although they were talking at this time as well. The girls could communicate some things in both languages and some things in just one of the languages. At age two they could communicate fairly equally in the two languages. From age two to three, their use of spoken English increased dramatically and they could communicate more in English than in ASL. As with language development in general, their comprehension of ASL far exceeded their ability to express themselves in that language at this age.

Age two presented some new challenges for us. Nursery rhymes and music became an important part of the girls' childhood. This sound-based entertainment was not part of Ken's cultural experience and is often impossible to translate effectively into sign language. He knew few fairy tales and even fewer nursery rhymes. An unspoken rule that has developed in our house is that I do not interpret between Ken and the girls. They always communicate directly with him. However, for this phase of their childhood it was necessary for me to interpret certain things in order for Ken to appreciate their burgeoning command of English and their recitation of nursery rhymes and songs.

Kaylee, at present, is in a phase in which her ability to express herself in English exceeds her ability to express herself in sign language. This phase can be frustrating for both Ken and Kaylee. She signs to her dad and sometimes just mouths words without voice when she doesn't know a sign for a particular word or concept. She can communicate her basic needs effectively but can't always communicate everything she wants to with him. Speechreading, guesswork, and some interpreting help to alleviate this problem.

When Erin went through this phase, we worried whether she would reach the point where she could express herself equally in both languages. Now, having experienced this phase once before, we are reassured to know that Kaylee will grow out of it, too.

At age three, friends would marvel at the facility with which Erin could switch between ASL and English in a mixed group. She never confused the languages and never used the wrong language with anyone. She could, with total ease and very unconsciously, talk to a hearing person, turn around and sign to a deaf person, and switch right back to English to speak to the hearing person again, never missing a beat!

Erin is now seven. She can communicate equally well in both languages. I believe that her exceptional reading and spelling abilities are, in part, due to her bilingualism. Additionally, her continual exposure to closed-captioning and her interest in using the TTY may have been motivating factors in her wanting to learn to read and spell.

To date, our daughters' experiences as bilinguals have been positive.

They have gotten a lot of attention and positive reinforcement for what is perceived as a unique ability. Complete strangers comment frequently and ask such questions as, "When did you start teaching them to sign?" My response is often, "The day they were born!" I go on to explain how children acquire sign language in the same way they acquire any spoken language. Our daughters are good ambassadors for the recognition of ASL as a language. We have educated countless curious people in malls, restaurants, and libraries.

The Use of Fingerspelling

The use of fingerspelling has been one fascinating part of our daughters' acquisition of ASL. It is often believed that fingerspelling is a way to represent English by spelling out words using the manual alphabet. As such, it would appear that fingerspelling would not be appropriate for children until they reach school age. This has not been our experience.

Erin and Kaylee began to comprehend fingerspelling at a very early age. At twelve months, they recognized fingerspelled words such as B-I-B and C-H-E-E-R-I-O-S and would respond appropriately to commands or questions using these fingerspelled words. It appears that children comprehend fingerspelling through the shape or configuration of the letters in combination, not by seeing each individual letter, much the same way a child begins to recognize words in written English.

Ken and I used fingerspelling as a way to communicate privately and prevent our daughters from comprehending. This strategy began to fail us when the girls were around age two. When Kaylee was two I signed to Ken, "AFTER THE KIDS GO TO BED, DO YOU WANT A C-O-K-E?" Kaylee, who had been watching, responded, "Yeah! I want Coke!"

Kaylee now recognizes many fingerspelled words. She can fingerspell words such as P-I-Z-Z-A and Z-O-O. She is unable to spell the words "pizza" and "zoo" out loud because she recognizes them as signs, not as individual letters of the alphabet. She can, however, spell all the names of her immediate family, including those of her maternal grandparents. She recognizes that the fingerspelling of names corresponds with the letters of the alphabet and can spell these names out loud when asked to do so. The concept of spelling was introduced very early to my daughters through the role fingerspelling plays in sign language. Erin and Kaylee could spell their names at age two, an unusual feat among their monolingual hearing friends.

If Kaylee doesn't know a sign for something she wants to communicate, she often does what I call "fingerbabble." She moves her fingers as if she is fingerspelling a word but no distinct letters are evident. To the nonsigner, it may appear as though she is communicating quite effectively. She gets frustrated when Ken can't understand these finger movements. Of course, Ken becomes frustrated too. Erin currently uses a lot of fingerspelling in her use of sign language. It may be that Kaylee sees this and is attempting to emulate that behavior.

Erin began using fingerspelling with much more frequency around age four. Some friends were visiting around Christmas of that year. Erin told us the story of the three wise men. She fingerspelled the words B-E-T-H-L-E-H-E-M and M-A-N-G-E-R. This seemed to us to be an impressive feat for a four-year-old. The spelling was not completely accurate but close enough for the Deaf observers to understand the message. After noting this incident, we began to watch for additional use of fingerspelling. It fascinated us that Erin was fingerspelling these complex words. In addition, the fluency of her fingerspelling made it clear she was not sounding out the words in her head prior to fingerspelling them. We thought perhaps she was fingerspelling words that she had freequently seen fingerspelled and that explained her unique ability. Then we observed her fingerspelling words that she probably had never seen fingerspelled before. When we asked her to spell on paper a word that she had just fingerspelled with amazing accuracy, her response would be, "I dunno how to spell *that!*"

Erin began using fingerspelling with much more frequency in her signing around age five and continues to do this, even at age seven. Even though she knows the correct sign usage, she often chooses to fingerspell words rather than sign them. We have no explanation for this, but the answer may lie in the parallel between her reading development and increased use of fingerspelling.

Person–Language Bond

An interesting phenomenon started to occur with both of my daughters at age two. With my first daughter, Erin, whenever I signed to her rather than spoke, her response would be an emphatic, "Mommy! *talk* to me!" With no explanation for this odd behavior, we were left to guess at the reasons for her rejecting my use of sign language. What I discovered after reading about bilingualism was that a perfectly logical explanation exists for this common phenomenon in bilingual children. The bilingual literature (Grosjean, 1982) identifies it as the person–language bond, where the child associates a particular language with a particular person and expects that person to use that language only. I am the English speaker, Ken is the ASL signer. It was interesting to see how firmly entrenched this was in Erin's mind and her reaction when the person–language bond was broken. Her response was not to answer me unless I used the appropriate language for me – English.

This phenomenon became evident with Kaylee at age two as well. The first time we recognized it, we were sitting at the kitchen table and she wanted my attention. She said "Mommy!" I looked right at her and used the facial expression appropriate in sign language to indicate I was attending. She continued repeating "Mommy" until I said "What?" Even though she responds to Ken in sign language when he uses this facial expression to indicate he is attending, she wanted appropriate spoken English from me. Now, at age three, when I sign, she says, "Mommy, I can't *hear* you."

The person–language bond continued to be strong for Erin at age three. At the dinner table, she would tell me something in English, then repeat the same idea to Ken in sign language. She was repeating everything twice, once in English, once in ASL. Even though I repeatedly reminded her that she could just sign something once and we both would understand her, she continually communicated things in two languages. She would even go so far as to tell me in English what Ken signed to her, as if I didn't understand him!

At age five, the person–language bond was less strong but still quite evident. Sometimes Erin would want to tell me something, and she would start talking to me in the presence of Ken. Upon my reminding her to sign rather than talk so that her father could comprehend, she would do so, but then she would look at Ken as she signed rather than look at me.

Sometimes her response to our request to sign would be, "But I want to tell Mommy!" This translates into: "If I'm telling Mommy something I'll use *Her* language. If I want to tell Daddy, I'll use *His* language." At this age she seemed to have developed more confidence in my ability to comprehend sign language, because the number of times that she communicated everything twice had diminished considerably.

Now at age seven, the person–language bond is much less evident. Erin now signs to me frequently and responds to me in either spoken English or ASL. She can effectively communicate in either language.

Our Children's Biculturalism

Grosjean (1982) defines biculturalism as "the coexistence and/or combination of two distinct cultures" (p. 157). Living in a bicultural environment is the norm for us as a family. It is not something we discuss, it just is. Kaylee knows that in order to communicate with her dad, she has to get his attention by tapping him or banging on the table, something she has been doing since she could crawl. No one told her she had to do this, she just observed these behaviors and copied them. I don't believe she connects these behaviors with the fact that her dad can't hear. The first time Kaylee actually figured out that her dad can't hear was at age two. She was yelling "Daddy, Daddy" while she was in one room and Ken was in another. After getting no response she said to me in yet another room, "Mommy, Daddy can't listen to me!" She now understands that Ken can't hear and takes it upon herself to interpret noises in the house such as the stove timer or the doorbell.

Although we don't talk about what it means to be Deaf, it is always interesting to get a glimpse into our daughters' thinking by verbal comments and behaviors they exhibit. We don't talk about who among our friends is Deaf and who is hearing, but the girls have always figured it out and used the appropriate language. Even when Kaylee plays "telephone," if she is calling a friend who is Deaf, she puts the telephone receiver on the TTY.

One evening at the supper table, when Kaylee was approximately three months old, Erin asked very seriously, "Do you think Kaylee is deaf or hearing?" It was quite evident to me that she was hearing, so I chuckled and replied that of course she was hearing. Erin again replied very seriously, "I don't think so. She doesn't talk." In her world , if you didn't talk, it only meant one thing: you were Deaf.

I recently posed a hypothetical question to Erin to get a feel for her perception of what it means to be Deaf. Because deafness can be viewed from a pathological or cultural perspective and because we never discuss the issue, I was curious about what she had to say. I told her a Martian had just landed on earth and had never encountered a Deaf person before. I asked her how she would describe to this Martian what it means to be Deaf. Her response was enlightening. Erin said, "They sign. They can't talk . . . well . . . they can talk but they don't unless they are at home or with people they know well. They go to church with other Deaf people with a priest who signs like them. They *Can* drive [with sarcasm], they watch TV, all that stuff and they use captioning. That's it!"

I was amazed and thrilled with her response. She describes the cultural definition of Deaf people, the view Deaf people have of themselves. Erin begins her description with the most important and unifying feature of the culture, which is their language. She includes the concept of community when she suggests Deaf people go to a church for Deaf people. Erin goes on to say, "They *Can* drive, they watch TV." She is responding to a common myth about Deaf people that she has been exposed to at some point, that Deaf people can't drive. She is also identifying Deaf people as "normal" people who do "normal" things. Most importantly, she never mentions the fact that Deaf people can't hear. Living in a bilingual-bicultural environment, she realizes that Deaf people can't hear but that the essence of being Deaf isn't the lack of hearing.

Conclusion

I have come to embrace the terms "bilingual" and "bicultural" in describing my family. I am very grateful for having had the opportunity in this chapter to delve into the issues of a deaf/hearing marriage and raising children with two languages. Grosjean's book and the thinking I have done have given me a new way to articulate my perspective on these issues. The positive connotations of the terms "bilingual" and "bicultural" much better describe the positive experience we have had in living in a home with two languages and cultures. Being bilingual and bicultural is an integral part of our family and adds a unique dimension to our lives. My initial perception about the biggest difference between Ken and me is also resolved. He is now Catholic!

Acknowledgments

I would like to thank my family for their encouragement in sharing our story and to thank the many friends and colleagues who read the manuscript and provided feedback.

Reference

Grosjean, F. (1982). *Life with two languages: An introduction to bilingualism.* Cambridge, MA: Harvard University Press.

CHAPTER EIGHTEEN

On Being Both Hearing and Deaf: My Bicultural-Bilingual Experience

PATRICIA MUDGETT-DECARO

Jim's family. My husband, Jim, and I hopped into the car for the long ride to his parent's house – our first visit to his Italian-American family. I wanted to be as polite as it was possible to be! When all seven of us sat down around the dinner table, I was immediately bombarded with questions from all sides, all at once. Turning my head frantically from side to side, I tried to look at everyone as they spoke to me. My Deaf and Hearing worlds were clashing again.[1] My parents, who

Patricia Mudgett-DeCaro (M.S., Minority Counseling, State University of New York at Brockport) publishes ethnographic research on deaf and hearing interactions and teaches at the National Technical Institute for the Deaf. Ms. Mudgett-DeCaro, herself hearing, is a native user of both ASL and English. She grew up in a small town, close to the school for the deaf where her parents taught. She is currently completing a Ph.D. at the University of Rochester in the sociology of deaf education while teaching part-time at NTID. Her address is: Department of Education and Career Research, National Technical Institute for the Deaf, Rochester Institute of Technology, 52 Lomb Memorial Drive, Rochester, NY 14623.

[1] Within the deaf community, there has always been a distinction between deaf people at the core of the culture and those outside it. Recently, this has been codified into the written forms "Deaf" and "deaf." Currently the form "Deaf" is often reserved for those deaf people who share the use of ASL and the Deaf identity, while "Deaf" is used to refer to deaf or hearing people who may share the group identity but not the language, or to the audiological condition of deafness. However, in its emphasis upon the use of ASL, this has created a narrower definition of "Deaf" than existed in the past and thereby, ironically, appears to exclude many people who used to be unquestionably at the "core" of Deaf culture.

In the past, ASL was not recognized as a language, and most educated deaf people counted it as a mark of status and success to be skilled in English usage even though most knew ASL (today many deaf people use ASL with pride). Therefore, many older deaf people whose entire education, social life, and professional careers revolved around the Deaf community and residential schools for the deaf used signed English fluently and *were Deaf, always taught me that it was polite to look directly at the person with whom I was talking, but here it was impossible! After dinner Jim's younger sister pulled him aside and said, "I like Pat a lot, she is really nice. But is there something wrong with her that she jerks her head so much? Is it something physical or is she a little odd?"*

My life has always flowed between my two worlds – Deaf and Hearing. Recently I lost both of my parents. My parents were Deaf. I am hearing. It has been a time for reflection upon my life in these two worlds, and a time to reexamine my own sense of identity.

I agree with Padden & Humphries (1988) notion that there are two different perspectives, one Deaf, one Hearing, through which the world can be understood and judged; two lenses through which the world can be viewed. I regard myself as a bilingual-bicultural person who sees through both lenses, and whose everyday life is influenced by both, although the relative weight of each sometimes shifts. My early life consisted of an unconscious understanding and acceptance of both Deaf and Hearing ways of being. I neither saw nor felt any conflict between them, nor did I think they were identical. Rather, I kept the two worlds relatively separate, in a kind of parallel, "separate but equal" status, and jumped back and forth between them. As I became older I began to become consciously aware of the differences between the two cultures and that society perceived my parents to be different. Not until much later did I realize that many of my social "mistakes" (in the Deaf and Hearing worlds) were a consequence of applying the rules of one culture to a situation in the other – "two cultures in conflict." As an adult I have struggled with issues of inclusion and exclusion in the Deaf and Hearing worlds, a synthesis of the two, and the ways in which my status as a hearing person affects my relationships with people who are deaf. In this chapter, I will chart the course of the journey of this bicultural identity.[2]

---

preferentially, even those who had deaf parents. These people do not fit easily within today's definitions of "Deaf," yet they were clearly at the core of the Deaf culture. Therefore, I use uppercase "Deaf" in referring to cultural identity or perspective, but lowercase "deaf" when referring to the broader deaf community which may include others who are not at the cultural core. I use uppercase "Hearing" only to emphasize a cultural difference.

[2] This chapter is written for many audiences: for my children that they may understand me better; for hearing audiences who may find it easier to believe that there is a Deaf culture when the news comes from a hearing person; and for Deaf audiences, many of whom have hearing children of their own. Certainly not all hearing children of Deaf parents share the same journey, but many aspects of our lives surely overlap, and therefore my experience may serve as a beginning point.

Childhood: Separate and Equal Worlds

I was an only child in a very close, extended family of predominantly Deaf members: Mom and Dad, my aunt and uncle, my grandparents and great-grandparents, and many of Mom's cousins and uncles.

Joshua Davis at the kitchen table. I held my body very still, no movements to visually distract, no thumping to cause distracting vibrations. My eyes followed Mom, my aunt, and my great-uncle filling the air over the kitchen table with family stories in sign language, their faces a constant play of animated expression . . . During the Civil War, eighteen-year-old Joshua Davis (the first known deaf person in our family) was squirrel hunting on the family plantation in Georgia, when a group of Union soldiers under General Sherman came upon him. Through gestures he tried to tell them that he was deaf, but they didn't believe him, nor did they believe his parents who talked to the soldiers. Just as they were readying a rope to hang him as a spy, their captain rode up. When he heard the story, the captain immediately fingerspelled to Joshua, "Are you deaf?" and "Where did you go to school?" Joshua answered, in fingerspelling and signs, "The School for the Deaf in Cave Spring," thus proving that he really was deaf. The captain not only spared his life but also left soldiers behind to protect the plantation although he took some horses and mules. It turned out that the captain had a deaf brother back in Illinois.

I loved this kitchen-table "oral" history in American Sign Language (ASL). These were not just family stories, but also metaphors for the more general Deaf experience, and they would be easily recognized by many deaf people. A version of this story is published in Gannon's (1981) book, *Deaf Heritage*, and Padden & Humphries (1988) have used it as an example of an American Deaf folktale. In this case, sign language is shown to have the power to save a deaf person's life.

In contrast, I knew very little about my father's hearing family. Either he did not know or did not choose to share much information outside of his personal experiences and the family genealogy which he had read. He was close to only one brother who learned fingerspelling. Otherwise, he said, he did not have much communication within the family. However, at the residential school for the deaf, surrounded by Deaf students and sign language, he became a part of the Deaf community. Learning the stories of the national Deaf community, he became himself a great storyteller.

Every culture has its center, a set of characteristics or experiences that are very important to the shared identity. Being part of a Deaf family, attending and teaching at residential schools and Gallaudet College, using sign language, and participating in the social life of the Deaf community, all made my family a solid part of this center. Due in part to their educational attainments, they were also leaders within this community. From the Deaf adults in this community, I learned the ways of participation in the Deaf world. Jim says that when I am in a group of people who are culturally Deaf, I automatically "push the Deaf button," meaning that I change my facial and body motions, my language, and my social behaviors to fit the Deaf norms. Like many other children of deaf parents I attended and played at the community gatherings like potluck suppers and business meetings, where any deaf adult in the community had the right to discipline us, as in a large extended family of aunts and uncles. Their judgments, positive or negative, carried tremendous weight. The works of significant and famous deaf educators, actors, artists, businessmen, and athletes, filled our house: "Dummy Hoy" the deaf baseball player, the self-portrait by Cadwallader Washburn, the Texas landscapes of Kelly Stevens, the bear sculpture by John L. Clarke, and so on. These people and others were important in our house, although they are largely unknown to hearing people. *I grew up knowing, and knowing about, very successful and competent deaf people in every walk of life*, including many within my own family.

Thus, I felt very much a part of this Deaf world, but I was simultaneously very much a part of the Hearing world. My "ears worked." The entire society around me was hearing, and unlike my family, I had unlimited access to it. I had music that filled my life, and like other hearing children, I chattered with my hearing friends over the telephone, but I also taught them signs. Unlike some other children of deaf parents, I don't ever recall being teased about my family's deafness. When hearing people did not know that I came from a deaf family, they automatically assumed that I fit into the norm in every way, and indeed I did for the most part. In fact my life didn't seem much different from other hearing children's, except for the inconveniences of not being able to call home, and often having to make phone calls for Mom and Dad.

As for language, both English and ASL were my native languages. According to Mom, I learned both simultaneously. The world around me used English, school was in English, and Mom and Dad were fluent in English as well as ASL. Dad wrote poetry in English, in fact his letters were more poetry than prose, and mom, while she spoke only a very few words, made sure that I spelled every English word correctly.

Switching between Worlds

Like most bilingual-bicultural children I didn't give much thought to multiple sets of norms or languages or meanings, they were simply rules for different settings, people, or situations, to follow accordingly. I switched between one and the other linguistically and culturally, as needed.

> *Language hopping. When I was three, there was a gathering which included my parents, some hearing people who signed well, and some who did not sign. An elderly hearing woman recalls that as I circled around the room, I consistently altered the structure and mode of my language to fit each person: sign only with Mom, sign and voice with Dad and fluent hearing signers, and speech only for others.*

This was a practical set of choices. In a mixed group (deaf/hearing), when I am signing and speaking at the same time, I automatically switch back and forth between languages to match the language preference of the individual I am looking at; the other language is unconsciously subordinated to the language appropriate to the moment.

A single word or phrase must sometimes be accompanied by a very different behavior in the Deaf and Hearing cultures, like "be quiet."

> *Be quiet! I learned how to "walk lightly" so I could sneak down to the refrigerator at 2 a.m. without making vibrations that "ran up the bedpost and down Mom's spine," thus waking her up. When I told my hearing friends to "be quiet" they obliged by shutting their mouths, but still walked heavily and woke Mom up!*

For my deaf parents "be quiet" meant either to use less space when signing, or to stop making vibrations. From a hearing person I knew it meant to stop talking or making other auditory sounds.

> *The child interpreter. Like most well-educated deaf people, my parents made all their own decisions, expecting me only to interpret literally what was said. One time my dad was very angry with a salesperson and shouted (in sign), "You are a damn liar!" I nearly died, I was so embarrassed. How could my dad say such a thing, and how could I say that over the phone to an adult? I turned my back so Dad couldn't lip-read and said politely, "My dad doesn't think that you are quite telling him the whole story."*

One of the most common family roles for a hearing child of deaf parents is that of interpreter. In this case, I altered the message because I didn't feel comfortable with it. At other times (especially as an early teenager), I "improved" the English in translation, to protect my parents from a negative image, but mostly to protect myself from embarrassment. I'm sorry to recall that I was quite mischievous too.

> *But I thought you wanted the dog! The dog and I often shared my bedroom space. When Mom called my name for me to come downstairs I gleefully postponed*

the inevitable by letting the dog eagerly scamper off for a treat. I knew it was me she wanted, but her voice sounded nearly the same when she called me or the dog and the dog couldn't tell the difference.

Of course I knew better, but what kid can resist the temptation to pretend that they "didn't know" (with large innocent eyes).

Within the Deaf community there are behavioral norms defining appropriate and inappropriate behaviors. Many of these are the same as the Hearing norms, while others are different, or are expressed differently.

I refused to look! When I was eighteen I committed an unpardonable sin. I deliberately looked away from my mother as she signed to me – I refused to see! In an instant my father leaped up, and I saw his hand already begun on the arc down to my bottom. I had never been spanked before, but then again, I had never done anything so rude. I never did that to a deaf person again! To this day I become extremely angry if my own hearing children do not look at me when I speak to them – even though they don't need to in order to understand me.

Some hearing people have told me that when they first meet deaf people they feel very uncomfortable with this eye contact, wondering why the deaf person is staring at them! Hearing people may think that I look directly at them when they talk because I am sincerely interested, or forthright, or even bold. While these assumptions may be true, it is also true that not looking at them, to me, would be worse than holding my hands over my ears while someone talked to me. Looking away during a conversation has very different meanings in the Hearing and Deaf worlds, and is therefore an area of frequent misunderstanding between the two groups.

Growing Up: Cultures in Conflict

As I grew older, I began to feel tremors in this otherwise normal life, and began to recognize that in the Hearing world, hearing is "normal" while deafness is a "tragedy," and that deaf people are seen as "lacking" in many ways compared to hearing people.

Self-introductions. When I introduced myself to strangers, I often added that my family was deaf, because it was important to me as a part of my identity. However, I also dreaded the look of pity that often came over hearing people's faces, the pause, and the three inevitable responses (in a variety of forms): "Do they speak or hear at all?" (as if that were the most important issue), "How did you learn to speak?" (as if the whole world wasn't speaking around me), and "It must have been difficult for you growing up." After I explained my parents' education and work, there was usually a comment about how incredible they must be (the usual "if they are competent it must be a miracle" perception)!

After all my experiences, the idea that people who are deaf should be pitied or helped was ridiculous, yet I encountered that attitude constantly. Over time I began to see the conflicts not only between my experiences and others' perceptions, but also between the two sets of norms and assumptions, Deaf and Hearing.

Understanding the differences between my two worlds often came as a result of conflicts which caused enough distress to force me to be aware of and to analyze the interactions between the two cultures. In my younger years, I was sometimes puzzled and distressed by the occasional lack of communication and understanding between myself and someone else. I often thought that it was some problem of my own. However, over time, I began to appreciate the influence of culture and early learning. Then I began analyzing conflicts with the question, is it possible that this problem is a conflict between my Deaf and Hearing cultures rather than an idiosyncratic problem?

Overlapping Worlds

Telephone talk. When we're in a hurry and I am on the phone, my family starts making faces and motions at me to get off the phone quickly, but I can't, it would seem too rude. However, when we need to give directions to someone, I am called to the phone. I give wonderfully elaborate directions.

Within the Deaf culture, proper telephone etiquette usually dictates getting quickly to the business, then having a long, social good-bye. It is generally the reverse in the Hearing culture. A Deaf friend recently told me that he believes Deaf and Hearing people think differently. He said that it is hard for a Deaf person to understand what the topic is because hearing people "start so general." In these areas I tend to follow the Deaf norms and state the topic or my business first.

I think the detail in directions results in part from my attempts to put very graphic visual, signed directions into linear English form. Since ASL sets up the scene in space visually, drawing it in the air with both hands, much more detail is simultaneously available to the receiver. In fact, I am often mentally signing and placing these items in space as I speak. My spoken directions are essentially a translation of what I "see" in front of me. Some laugh at the detail, but few people get lost with my directions!

Leave-taking rituals. For many years, whenever my husband, children, and I went as a family to any affair with many people who were deaf, there was tension. Everything went fine until it was time to leave. Jim and the kids just hopped up and left after some quick good-byes. When I was along they knew it would take an hour. By the time I was finally in the car Jim's teeth were clenched with annoyance, and the kids were grouchy. The ride home was usually made in angry silence.

Lengthy leave-taking has often led to frustration and impatience among my hearing friends or family members, and sometimes their anger at my "inability" to leave quickly. At the same time I was angry and embarrassed at leaving *too* quickly. As with telephone etiquette, it takes longer to politely leave a gathering in the Deaf world. However, we have since learned to allow for this polite leave-taking by beginning to leave, earlier than we really intend to leave and Jim has come to accept longer and "more polite" good-byes himself. I also learned that it was OK to leave hearing people more quickly.

Like many other bilingual-bicultural people, I sometimes use my languages differently.

Double-talk. Once when I was very angry, someone asked me (in English) what I felt. I answered with very rational, controlled words, but Jim noticed that under the table I was signing "hate, hate." I was entirely unaware that I was giving two messages simultaneously.

I often find that if I am upset, only ASL expresses the emotion to my satisfaction. Sometimes I use English to control the emotion, as in the example just given.

How do I say "I love you"? Early in our relationship, Jim and I were uncertain about the other's feelings. Eventually we realized that for Jim, the speaking of "I love you" had great emotional meaning, while for me it had very little meaning. Conversely the sign, facial expressions, and touching had more emotional meaning for me. For a while neither of us was convinced that the other one really meant what was expressed. He wondered why I never said it, and I wondered why he never showed it!

I find ASL more expressive of deep emotion than English, and the opposite is true for Jim. ASL is my personal, emotional, social, and entirely comfortable language, whereas English is my intellectual language much of the time, although like Dad, I use English to express thoughts in poetry.

Beware the shrug. Once I asked Jim a simple, noncontroversial question. He didn't know the answer and simply shrugged. I became furious! Without knowing it, he had linguistically informed me that not only did he not know but he really "didn't give a damn." Once I calmed down enough to think about it, we realized that he had shrugged with a mouth shape in which the corners were turned down, eyes partly hooded, eyebrows down, and a sideways jerk of his head – a very clear expression of rudeness in ASL. If he had shrugged with the corners of his mouth turned up and the middle down, eyebrows high, eyes wide open, and a small shake of the head, I would have understood what he really meant, that he just didn't know.

This misunderstanding between Jim and me occurred as a result of a lack of understanding on his part that the simple shrug has two meanings in ASL, depending upon the associated facial expression. Had the two forms of shrug not carried very different emotional messages for me, I might not have noticed. Had we not been close, I might have been furious in silence and have gone away with the impression that he was a very rude person.

Nonlinear storytelling. When I'm teaching, I've sometimes had hearing students complain that I seem to wander all over the map – one point leading to another related issue, but not in linear fashion. Yet Deaf students in the same class have understood clearly. I struggle to stay on some linear course, but what I see in my mind is a visual map of thoughts on which it is easy to see at a glance the connection between an idea over here in "California" and a related idea in "New York."

I find it quite natural to think and talk as if I am telling a story. Storytelling in ASL often involves departure from the main point to explain or elaborate, and then return to the main stream of thought. When signing, this is accomplished by using one hand to physically "hold" the original thought, and the other hand to elaborate. In addition, the main thought can be held in a certain space while side comments are given in a different physical space. Finally, you can "stack" details on top of one another. The receiver can "see" the relationship between side and main comments. Signing allows for this simultaneous form of thought, while speech, being linear, has to lay thoughts out in a string. I find that with spoken side comments, not only do I confuse students, but I am also more likely to become confused myself and forget my main point.

Graduate school notetaking. In graduate school there is a clear expectation that students should be sophisticated enough to think and participate during class. It was made very clear that to take extensive notes is considered too passive (high school behavior). Nonetheless I took verbatim notes for years, while wondering what was wrong with me. I tried to hide the fact that I was taking notes by doing it on my lap under the table and just looking occasionally to see if I was still on the paper, but the fact is that I just couldn't remember anything if I didn't write it all down!

Only later did I begin to recognize that I took such extensive notes because I think and remember better when my hands are involved in some way. Hearing professors often make the assumption that a person cannot write and think simultaneously. However, perhaps because I have translated sound into sign language all my life with little conscious thought involved, for me writing and thinking rarely interfere with each other. I have also noticed that when I can't remember the spelling of a word I need to fingerspell it in the air to see if it looks right. Jim recalls that I have more than once asked him to help me think of a word using the size or shape of the fingerspelled letters as the clue. For example, once I asked, "What's a word that is small in the beginning and big at the end and has to do with sticking things to walls?" The word turned out to be "tack" (although the letter *t* is a tall letter in writing, it is small in fingerspelling). I often felt inadequate until I realized that it was just the particular way that I remember things, perhaps in part because I grew up signing.

Many of the stories in this section have demonstrated conflicts that I have encountered because I was approaching the issue from the Deaf perspective. I am aware of these because I have found in Jim a hearing friend willing to confront and discuss the instances in which I seemed to be rude to hearing people or in which he appeared to be rude to deaf people. In contrast, I am not as aware of the mistakes that I have made in the Deaf world. I believe that I do make just as many mistakes when I am "thinking Hearing," but I have only one Deaf friend close enough to really confront me with them.[3]

Adulthood: Forging a New Relationship

After I left home for college in 1963, only family visits and occasional interpreting kept me in touch with the Deaf community. In 1970, I returned to the Deaf world, this time at the National Technical Institute for the Deaf (NTID). There, though I had daily contact with deaf people, I wasn't a part of the Deaf community. I had deaf friends, but there were relatively few deaf faculty at NTID at that time and most were from my parent's generation. My daily contact was primarily with deaf students, not with peers who were deaf. I made my close friends among hearing people. My hus-

---

[3] This issue suggests two concerns that I have had in the writing of this chapter. One is that I have inadvertently broken some taboo within the Deaf community regarding things that should not be told to outsiders; the other is that I might have made a mistake that hearing people make frequently, that is, assuming a greater knowledge and understanding of the Deaf world than I actually possess.

band and children are hearing. But as my parents aged, I realized that my *personal* connection to Deaf people was still "wired" through my parents and relatives. It shocked and alarmed me to realize that their deaths might mean the end of any close relationship with people who were Deaf, and the closing of the door to the Deaf community. Understanding at last that I had taken my acceptance into the Deaf community for granted, as a birthright like inherited wealth, I began a few years ago to build friendships with my Deaf peers. I had forgotten that friendship and acceptance have to be earned. I also realize that it is a *new* kind of connection to the Deaf community that I am building, that of a hearing adult with close ties to the Deaf community.

Marginality

"Marginality" means being on the margins. We often think of that only in the negative sense, that of someone on the outside wanting to get in, but it is also true that the margins give access to the far side as well as the near side, and can lead to inclusion as well as exclusion. Bilingual-bicultural people are often on the margins, both deaf and hearing bilingual-bicultural people. I find myself a part of a rather large group of deaf and hearing people who move between two worlds. A part of building a new relationship with the Deaf community involves understanding, accepting, and exploring this marginality.

The first thing that I had to understand was that even though I had grown up in the Deaf community, I could not simply "rejoin" the community as an adult. In fact, I had to understand that I was marginal.

You're hearing! Once I remember trying to tell Mom about how I sometimes made mistakes in the Hearing world when I was momentarily "thinking Deaf." She looked at me in disbelief and said, "How can that be, you're hearing!" It felt like a door slammed in my face; I can still feel the hurt and confusion.

Mom didn't mean to hurt me, she just didn't understand how there could be any "Deaf" in me. She hadn't thought about how I first saw the world largely through Deaf eyes and had automatically internalized Deaf culture. It struck me as ironic that Mom's assumption seemed to be the reverse of hearing people wondering how I learned to talk (as if the world around me weren't speaking). I don't recall ever thinking that I was deaf, or pretending that I was deaf, but I did think that I was fully a part of both

Deaf and Hearing communities.[4] Therefore it was hard to discover that when I grew up I could not be a full member of the Deaf community – like Peter Pan's Never Never Land.

Willard Madson wrote a beautiful poem entitled "You Have to Be Deaf to Understand" (Gannon, 1981, p. 380) in which he eloquently described the experiences of being deaf in a Hearing world. Because many of these shared experiences are not about signing or the culture alone, but also about difficulties encountered and overcome, there is much truth to the title. Yet sometimes I get very, very angry. Once a woman who was deaf, but had only recently learned signs and was just learning about Deaf culture, told me that no hearing person could ever understand deafness. In my thoughts I shouted, "I'm more Deaf than you are. I'm the native signer. I'm the one who grew up in the Deaf community!" Even so, I do *not* experience the barriers and disadvantages of being deaf in a Hearing world. I do not experience directly the frustration or struggles for access and communication. It is this part of being deaf that I know only through observations or through the stories in the community. I may be Deaf in many ways, but I am not deaf.

Yet, because I'm on the margins, these are the barriers I saw my family encounter. I lived in a world where these barriers were real, the consequences were real, and anger, sadness, and frustration were real. A child cannot see her parents hurt and yet feel nothing; a child cannot ignore a slight or insult to those he loves. Perhaps it is not too farfetched to say that in the end, an insult to deaf people is also an insult to me – the Deaf part of me.

> *If only they asked! There were no other deaf members of a local golf club, and Dad loved to play golf. Most of the time he and I played together, but other times he would show up by himself and look for others to play with him. With no phone communication, it was difficult for him to arrange a group ahead. If he asked hearing people to join him they often would, talking among themselves most of the time, excluding Dad. However, never in all those years did any hearing person ever ask Dad to join a group.*

Dad never complained, and it may seem presumptuous for me to say that I felt the rejection in any way, but I boiled inside for many years, and even to this day I hold it against country club people. I don't recall hearing any of them say anything other than good about Dad, but their actions told me

---

[4] Whether as a child I was considered a member by the Deaf community, I cannot say. Certainly I felt myself to be fully a part of the community.

that they didn't really accept him as their equal. No one really went out of their way to make him feel like one of them.

ASL isn't a language: Internalizing inequality. Around 1985 I recall coming home and excitedly telling Mom what I was learning about the structure of ASL. She looked far into the distance for a long time, then said, "I always insisted on English, English, English. I thought ASL was just bad English. It is hard to believe that it is a language. I don't use it." There was nothing to say.

Indeed, Mom was fluent in English, but she knew ASL perfectly too. Even though she insisted she did not use ASL, she used ASL when she was telling stories over the kitchen table, and when I studied the structure of ASL, I recognized ASL fingerprints all over her everyday conversation too! However, English and ASL are not considered *by society* to be of equal status. English is the standard for "correct" behavior and language and she had internalized this norm. In any case, when she was growing up ASL was not recognized as a language.

Some of the saddest stories I ever heard from Dad regarded his education and work.

Limits: No Ph.D. His Master's advisors at the University of Illinois in the 1950s encouraged Dad to study for a doctorate. But he said sadly, "No, I'll never be able to have any job other than teacher regardless of my degree; I'm deaf."

Dad was brilliant, but in those days deaf people had very few choices and he seemed to resign himself to it. Dad was a few years early. In another decade deaf people began getting doctorates; my uncle Dick was the second Gallaudet graduate to do so, in 1969. Even then the move to positions of authority has been painfully slow.

These examples, and the many smaller incidents, like waitresses asking me what "they" want, or giving the change from the ten dollar bill to me instead of to Dad, were demeaning to the people I loved and respected. On the other hand, I would say that my family wasted very little time fretting over these incidents. Most often what I saw was their busy and productive involvement in their work and in the community, like Mom's and Dad's teaching, their excitement directing plays at the School for the Deaf, Mom's visits to deaf patients, and Dad's work for deaf people at the state level. There wasn't a lot of time for sadness amid the travel, painting, teaching, gardening, and social affairs! My impression was certainly not that being deaf was a tragedy, just that it was sometimes very annoying that the rest of the world was hearing and largely ignorant with regard to deafness.

My marginality in the Hearing world is not so obvious, since I do hear. I am not excluded in any way. My social errors are usually ignored or put down to eccentricity. Yet I often feel restrained in the Hearing world, as if it would not quite be proper to let my hair down and say what I really think. When I feel like an outsider it is usually because I have been criticized for doing something the "wrong" way and realize it is the "Deaf" way, or when I feel lonely because I cannot seem to share or explain my thoughts or feelings to a hearing person, or in English.

My dad, who became deaf at age seven, once said to me, "Sometimes, Pat, I think you are the only person who truly understands what I say and mean." At that moment we shared overlapping bilingual-bicultural space. I, on the hearing side of the fence, experience very few obstacles in the Hearing world, but I must leave some of my Deaf world unexplored and undeveloped. For Dad on the other side, it was the opposite. This is OK.

Working Out a New Relationship

Padden & Humphries (1988) say, "Hearing children of Deaf parents represent an ongoing contradiction in the culture: they display the knowledge of their parents – skill in the language and social conduct – but the culture finds subtle ways to give them an unusual and separate status" (p. 3).

While I haven't tried to "pass" as deaf, I have sometimes caused consternation among deaf people in situations where I am mistakenly thought to be Deaf.

> *Passing for deaf. When I was first introduced to Tom, I noticed that he was using ASL and I immediately and very comfortably followed suit. Much later, when we were friends, he told me that he had originally thought I was Deaf and then became very angry when he found out that I was hearing. He felt betrayed and made a fool of, even though he realized that it had not been intentional. Who knows what he might have said about hearing people that could have been embarrassing to both of us!*

Since then I have always tried to indicate early in an ASL conversation that I am hearing, although sometimes there is no natural way to do it quickly. This is one of the few times when a deaf person has explained clearly to me the mistake I've made and I appreciated it deeply.

I sometimes don't want to tell deaf people that I am hearing, because of the "closing" that often occurs as soon as I do so. Immediately the conversation becomes more guarded, the language more English, and I feel like an outsider. Yet with my close friends who are Deaf I can feel completely relaxed and at home, free to express thoughts and emotions, in sign language with full facial and body expression. It is the Deaf person who signals our relationship by making the choice of language for us to use. At the same time, when I am introduced to a Deaf person as having Deaf parents and as a fluent signer, there is very often a lifting of the eyebrows, tilt of the head, nod, and a smile. It is their recognition that I can understand, and that puts me in a different category of hearing people. It is the same sort of reaction that I encounter in Denmark when I speak Danish. There they do not expect that any American will be able to speak Danish.

From the margins I often see problems that others are having that I realize may be the result of the two worlds overlapping.

> *Meanings of touch.* One Deaf student in our class complained that hearing people always seem to be so authoritative and demanding when they want his attention. They firmly tap on his shoulder or arm with one pointed finger. I cringed. I knew that this usually signifies an emergency or a demand, and that a more respectful way of getting a deaf person's attention is to gently lay an open palm on the person's shoulder for a short time to indicate "I'm here, but not in a hurry for your attention." On the other hand I also knew that this would be too intimate for most hearing people. Knowing both, I was able to explain the cultural difference to the class.

For many hearing people, minimal physical contact with others is the rule. For these people a one-fingered tap would be the most polite. Thus they are astonished to see annoyance on a Deaf person's face.

> *How to pass a signed conversation.* A hearing faculty member complained to me once that deaf students were often so inconsiderate that they would never "let her through" when they were conversing. She explained that deaf students often stood on opposite sides of a hallway, leaning up against the walls and signing. When she came along they just kept signing, ignoring her. She just didn't want to walk between them and interrupt their conversation! All they had to do, she said, was to either both be on the same side of the hallway, take one step into the middle to let her pass, or stop talking for a second to let her by. At that moment the enormity of the gulf between Deaf and Hearing cultures struck me. Despite working for years with deaf students, and being a sensitive person, she didn't know that it was she who was rude in forcing the conversation to stop so that she could pass, instead of just quickly walking straight through!

All of her suggestions struck me as unworkable, unnatural strategies that Deaf people would not use, nor expect others to use. For example, lining up along one wall would have resulted in elbows bumping into the wall during the signing process. Signing needs a lot of elbow room! Once again, knowing both norms allowed me to help her to understand the differences. It is a privilege to be a friend and partner with both Deaf and Hearing people, in the quest to bridge the cultures.

Synthesis: More than the Sum of the Parts

A friend from Rwanda once said, "A man who speaks only one language, sees with only one eye" (F. Utazirubanda, personal communication, 1988). Having two languages and two cultures allows a new perspective. Insights and feelings that would not be possible from only one perspective assume a multidimensional form in binocular vision.

I find a special excitement in exploring this bicultural-bilingual margin, a place neither Deaf nor Hearing, yet both. It is charting a new course, and like all new courses, involves some risk, some pain, and some fear, but also all the joy and excitement of the discoveries. For example, in the last few years I have found great pleasure in writing poetry that uses and requires both ASL and English – Deaf and Hearing cultures. After all the years of wondering about which parts of me were Deaf or Hearing, it has been very exciting to realize that I just can't be divided that way. Thus I am still on a journey. Yet I am certainly not alone in these waters. There are so many other bilingual-bicultural people out there with whom I enjoy many hours of sharing. As I look back at my life's choices of marriage, career, child raising, and friends, it is clear that in every choice I've made, it has been important to involve both the Deaf and Hearing worlds. As I navigate, I must, and do, continually adjust my sails to the Deaf and Hearing worlds.

Acknowledgments

I wish foremost to acknowledge my parents, David and Grace Mudgett, who lived lives so interesting that I could scarcely have had a richer environment within which to grow. I would also like to thank my husband, Jim DeCaro, for the many hours spent discussing differences in our lives, for validating the accuracy of my memories of our experiences together, and for his unfailing support. Many thanks to Alan and Vicki Hurwitz for their support and advice through some tough spots in the writing of this chapter, and finally to Ila Parasnis for her continual and cheerful encouragement and prodding to complete and improve the chapter.

References

Gannon, J. R. (1981). *Deaf heritage: A narrative history of deaf America*. Silver Spring, MD: National Association of the Deaf.

Padden, C., & Humphries, T. (1988). *Deaf in America: Voices from a culture*. Cambridge, MA: Harvard University Press.

Name Index

Subject Index